Principles of Quality Costs

Also available from ASQ Quality Press

Linking Quality to Profits: Quality-Based Cost Management
Hawley Atkinson, John Hamburg, and Christopher Ittner

Quality Costs: Ideas and Applications, Volume 1, Second Edition
ASQ Quality Costs Committee; Andrew F. Grimm, editor

Quality Costs: Ideas and Applications, Volume 2
ASQ Quality Costs Committee; Jack Campanella, editor

101 Good Ideas: How to Improve Just About Any Process
Karen Bemowski and Brad Stratton, editors

Success Through Quality: Support Guide for the Journey to Continuous Improvement
Timothy J. Clark

Principles and Practices of Organizational Performance Excellence
Thomas Cartin

To request a complimentary catalog of publications, call 800-248-1946.

Principles of Quality Costs

Principles, Implementation, and Use

Third Edition

Jack Campanella

Sponsored by the American Society for Quality
Quality Costs Committee of the Quality
Management Division

ASQ Quality Press
Milwaukee, Wisconsin

Principles of Quality Costs
Jack Campanella

Campanella, Jack, 1934–
Principles of quality costs : principles, implementation and use /
Jack Campanella. -- 3rd ed.
p. cm.
"Sponsored by the American Society for Quality, Quality Costs Committee of the Quality Management Division."
Includes bibliographical references and index.
ISBN 0-87389-443-X (alk. paper)
1. Quality control--Costs--Case studies. 2. Service industries--Quality control--Costs--Case studies. 3. Manufactures--Quality control--Costs--Case studies. I. American Society for Quality. Quality Costs Committee. II. Title.

TS156.C344 1999

658.5'--dc21 98-46411
CIP

10 9 8 7 6 5

ISBN 0-87389-443-x

Acquisitions Editor: Ken Zielske

Project Editor: Annemieke Koudstaal

Production Coordinator: Shawn Dohogne

ASQ Mission: The American Society for Quality advances individual and organizational performance excellence worldwide by providing opportunities for learning, quality improvement, and knowledge exchange.

Attention: Bookstores, Wholesalers, Schools and Corporations:
ASQ Quality Press books, videotapes, audiotapes, and software are available at quantity discounts with bulk purchases for business, educational, or instructional use. For information, please contact ASQ Quality Press at 800-248-1946, or write to ASQ Quality Press, P.O. Box 3005, Milwaukee, WI 53201-3005.

To place orders or to request a free copy of the ASQ Quality Press Publications Catalog, including ASQ membership information, call 800-248-1946. Visit our web site at http://www.asq.org.

Printed in the United States of America

Printed on acid-free paper

Quality Press
611 East Wisconsin Avenue
Milwaukee, Wisconsin 53202
Call toll free 800-248-1946
www.asq.org
http://qualitypress.asq.org
http://standardsgroup.asq.org
http://e-standards.asq.org
E-mail: authors@asq.org

Dedicated to my father,
Frank Campanella,
who was always a "quality" man.

Contents

List of Figures

Foreword

The year is 1949. I made my first quality cost studies in several plants of General Electric. Now, a half century later, we can identify some useful lessons learned:

1. The language of money is essential. For a successful quality effort, the single most important element is leadership by upper management. To gain that leadership, we can propose some concepts or tools. That is the wrong approach. Instead, we should first convince management that a problem exists that requires their attention and action, i.e., excessive costs due to poor quality. A quality cost study, particularly when coupled with a successful pilot quality improvement project, is a solid way to gain management support for a broad quality improvement effort. (Excessive cost is one quality-related hot button for management; loss of sales revenue is the other hot button.)
2. Quality cost measurement and publication do not solve quality problems. We must also identify improvement projects, establish clear responsibilities, provide resources to diagnose and remove causes of problems, and take other essential steps. New organization machinery is needed to attack and reduce the high costs of poor quality.
3. The scope of traditional quality costs should be expanded. Traditionally, quality costs have emphasized the cost of nonconformances. Important as this cost is, we also need to estimate the cost of inefficient processes. This includes variation of product characteristics

(even on conforming products), redundant operations, sorting inspections, and other forms of nonvalue-added activities. Another area is the cost of lost opportunities for sales revenue.

4. Traditional categories of quality costs have had a remarkable longevity. About 1945, some pioneers proposed that quality costs be assigned categories of failures, appraisal, and prevention. Many practitioners (including myself) found the categories useful and even devised ingenious ways to adapt the categories beyond manufacturing (such as in engineering design) and to the service sector (such as in financial services and health care).

This latest edition of *Principles* recognizes these lessons learned. The additional material on ISO 9000 and QS-9000, Activity-Based Costing, small businesses, team-based problem solving, software quality costs, impact on sales revenue, as well as the case studies on banking, education, and software development, have brought us a long way from the old days of quality cost in manufacturing. We are moving toward a broader view of quality cost elements and their application to manufacturing and service industries in both the profit and nonprofit sectors: powerful stuff in 1949, powerful stuff today.

Frank M. Gryna
Distinguished University
Professor of Management
The University of Tampa

Preface

How does management currently view the impact of quality on the results of their enterprise? In general, they are aware that quality has some impact on customer satisfaction, but, unless they know that unhappy customers are causing lower sales, some may not be directly concerned. Many realize that quality has an impact on profits, but this understanding may be well focused only when rising costs are due to major quality problems. Management, in general, may not directly translate quality or lack of quality into its true impact on their enterprise, yet understanding this impact can easily spell survival in today's marketplace. Fortunately, due to the efforts of many, management's understanding is improving at an accelerated pace.

A basic commitment of management should be to continuously pursue quality improvement. To achieve the most effective improvement efforts, management should ensure that the organization has ingrained in its operating principles the understanding that quality and cost are complementary and not conflicting objectives. Traditionally, recommendations were made to management that a choice had to be made between quality and cost, the so-called trade-off decision, because better quality would somehow cost more and make production difficult. Experience throughout the world has shown, and management is beginning to see, that this is not true. Good quality leads to increased productivity, and reduced quality costs, and eventually to increased sales, market penetration, and profits.

The purpose of quality cost techniques is to provide a tool to management for facilitating quality program and quality improvement activities. Quality cost reports can be used to point out the strengths and weaknesses of a quality system. Improvement teams can use them to describe the monetary benefits and ramifications of proposed changes. Return on investment (ROI) models and other financial analyses can be constructed directly from quality cost data to justify proposals to management. Improvement team members can use this information to rank problems in order of priority. In practice, quality costs can define activities of quality program and quality improvement efforts in a language that management can understand and act on—dollars. Any reduction in quality costs will have a direct impact on gross profit margins and can be counted on immediately as pretax profit.

The purpose of this book is to furnish a basic understanding of the principles of quality costs. It should provide readers, from both the manufacturing and service sectors, with sufficient understanding to develop and implement a quality cost system suitable to their organization's unique needs. It is not intended to directly affect the cost accounting system of an enterprise, but its use may suggest ideas that can enhance the effectiveness of overall financial management.

Acknowledgments

As a product of the Quality Costs Committee of ASQ's Quality Management Division, this book was truly a team effort, containing inputs and articles submitted and reviewed by the experts that make up its membership, both past and present. The editor would like to thank the following individuals for their contributions to this work.

FOR NEW MATERIAL:

Joan Alliger—for her input on QS-9000 and as Quality Costs Committee chair, her continuous support and nudging (in a nice way, of course)

Chuck Aubrey—for his case study on quality costs in banking

Dennis Beecroft—for his case studies on quality costs in education and, as Committee chair-elect, for volunteering to take on many of the necessary tasks involved

Frank M. Gryna—for his section on quality costs in small business, for his paper on Activity-Based Costing, and for the foreword of this book

Dan Houston, J. Bert Keats, and Herb Krasner—for their extensive chapter and case study on software quality costs

April King and Nick Shepherd—for their assistance in making this edition more service industry oriented

William Ortwein—for his section on quality costs in the defense industry

Jim Robison—for his material on team-based problem solving

John Schottmiller—for his sections on ISO 9000 and Activity-Based Costing

William O. Winchell—for his material on customer satisfaction

FOR PREVIOUS MATERIAL:

In addition to new material, this third edition relies heavily on information from four of the Quality Costs Committee's previous publications on the subject. The books and the editors for each of these publications are listed below. Individual contributions are included within each of the publications themselves and, although not repeated here, are no less appreciated. These contributors, as well as the editors, are acknowledged and sincerely appreciated.

- *Principles of Quality Costs* (first edition)—*John T. Hagan*
- *Principles of Quality Costs* (second edition)—*Jack Campanella*
- *Guide for Reducing Quality Costs*—*W. N. Moore*
- *Guide for Managing Supplier Quality Costs*—*William O. Winchell*

A SPECIAL THANK YOU FOR CONTRIBUTIONS WELL ABOVE AND BEYOND THE CALL:

Frank Alessi—for his continuous support providing words of wisdom, advice, and counsel, countless reviews of and comments on the material, and for his many missed golf outings so that we could meet to discuss what we called THE BOOK (and all the extra pounds he gained at all those working lunches)

Frank M. Gryna—who, in addition to supplying the material acknowledged above, was the first reviewer of completed material and provided timely review of each and every section after my editing. His comments and advice, enhanced by his wealth of experience, were invaluable to this effort

Herb Krasner—who, as software quality costs subject-matter expert for the Quality Costs Committee's Principles Task Group, coordinated the effort (besides writing much of the material) on software quality costs

John Schottmiller—without whose editing assistance, reviews, and advice this project would have been infinitely more difficult. John never turned down a request for help, and there were many. I depended on John and he always came through for me

LAST, BUT DEFINITELY NOT LEAST, A PERSONAL THANK YOU TO:

My wife, Camille—whose patience, understanding, and support, once again enabled the sacrifice of weekends and evenings so THE BOOK could be completed

My grandchildren, Vincent, Eric, Billy, John, Jacquelyn, Matthew, and Ryan—who would have liked to be able to spend more time with their "pa-pa". The feeling was mutual . . . I'll make it up to you!

Principles of Quality Costs

Principles, Implementation, and Use

Third Edition

Chapter 1
Quality Cost Concepts

HISTORY OF QUALITY COST DEVELOPMENT

One of the earliest writings pertaining to the general concept of quality costs can be found in Dr. J. M. Juran's first *Quality Control Handbook* (McGraw-Hill, 1951). Chapter I, "The Economics of Quality," contained Dr. Juran's famous analogy of "gold in the mine." Most other papers and articles of that time dealt with more narrow economic applications. Among the earliest articles on quality cost systems as we know them today are W. J. Masser's 1957 article, "The Quality Manager and Quality Costs," Harold Freeman's 1960 paper, "How to Put Quality Costs to Use," and Chapter 5 of Dr. A. V. Feigenbaum's classic book, *Total Quality Control* (McGraw-Hill, 1961). These writings were among the first to classify quality costs into today's familiar categories of prevention, appraisal, and failure.

In December 1963, the U.S. Department of Defense issued MIL-Q-9858A, Quality Program Requirements, making "Costs Related to Quality" a requirement for many government contractors and subcontractors (see page 38, *Quality Costs in Defense Contracts*). This document helped to focus attention on the importance of quality cost measurements but provided only a general approach to their implementation and use. It did, however, elevate interest in the subject of quality costs.

More recently, with the international popularity of the ISO 9000 and QS-9000 standards (see pages 21–29 and 29–30), quality costs continues to take its rightful place as a quality improvement tool and a measure of quality management.

The ASQ Quality Costs Committee was formed in 1961 to dramatize the magnitude and importance of product quality to the well-being of a manufacturing business through measurements of the cost of quality. In 1967, the committee published *Quality Costs—What and How* to detail what should be contained in a quality cost program and to provide definitions for categories and elements of quality costs. This popular document became the largest seller of any ASQ publication until its successors, *Principles of Quality Costs, 1st and 2nd Editions,* were published and sold even more.

The ASQ Quality Costs Committee progressed from these initial efforts to become the ASQ's recognized authority for the promotion and use of quality cost systems. In addition to sponsoring professional training programs and annual presentations on the subject, this committee has also published *Guide for Reducing Quality Costs, Guide for Managing Supplier Quality Costs,* and *Quality Costs: Ideas and Applications,* Volumes 1 and 2.

In 1983, the Quality Costs Committee joined the ASQ's Quality Management Division (then named the Administrative Applications Division) to become one of the division's most active and productive committees.

Today, more and more contracts, both government and commercial, are spelling out quality cost requirements—from the collection of scrap and rework costs to the most sophisticated quality cost program. Almost all quality management consultants have quality cost programs as an integral part of their repertoire. Service industries are undergoing more in-depth scrutiny by consumer and regulatory groups questioning the validity of price or rate hikes. In these times, a clear understanding of the economics of quality and the use of a quality cost system in support of quality improvement efforts and the management of quality may make the difference between maintaining the status quo and beating out the competition.

THE ECONOMICS OF QUALITY—A MANAGEMENT PHILOSOPHY

As an expression, "the economics of quality" has contributed to some confusion surrounding the true business and economic value of quality management. There are those who believe there is no "economics of quality"—that is, it is never economical to ignore quality. At the other extreme are those managers who believe it is uneconomical to have 100 percent quality. These managers feel free to make arbitrary decisions about the needed quality of a product or service, usually expressed by the term "that's good enough." While it might appear that either of these attitudes could create a problem for management, the real dilemma occurs when many managers, supposedly working together, operate with varying degrees of these divergent views on quality. This situation will guarantee that quality never achieves its optimum role in the accomplishment of business objectives.

Because of its direct relationship to the economics of quality, regardless of how one views it, the "cost of quality" is another term that has inadvertently created confusion. Among the key points emerging from the National Conference for Quality (1982) was the idea that the, phrase "cost of quality" should never be used, since quality is profitable, not costly.[1] Some individuals, including H. J. Harrington[2] and Frank M. Gryna,[3] label it as "poor quality cost," or the "cost of poor quality." The Department of Defense has referred to it as "costs related to quality."[4] This text will continue to refer to it as "quality costs" or the "cost of quality," since they remain the most familiar and widely used terms. Whatever it is called, it must be remembered that the cost of quality includes more than just the cost of the quality organization.

To set the record straight from the beginning, let's state the facts about quality management and the cost of quality. The real value of a quality program is determined by its ability to contribute to customer satisfaction and to profits. The cost of quality techniques are a tool for management in its pursuit of quality improvement and profit contributions.

To develop the concept of quality costs, it is necessary to establish a clear picture of the difference between quality costs and the cost of the quality organization. It is important that we don't view quality costs as the expenses of the quality function. Fundamentally, every time work is redone, the cost of quality increases. Obvious examples are the reworking of a manufactured item, the retesting of an assembly, the rebuilding of a tool, or the correction of a bank statement. Other examples may be less obvious, such as the repurchasing of defective material, response to customer complaints, or the redesign of a faulty component. In service organizations, obvious examples include the reworking of a service, such as the reprocessing of a loan operation, and the replacement of a food order in a restaurant. In short, any cost that would not have been expended if quality were perfect contributes to the cost of quality.

Almost any company function can be responsible for mistakes of omission or commission that cause the redoing of work already accomplished. This is the essence of the failure costs of quality.

Scrap and *rework* are common terms in manufacturing companies. They are even expected in many companies. While not referred to in similar terms, the same phenomenon occurs in the service sector of American industry. For example, insurance policies are rewritten, garments are exchanged or repaired, meals are returned to the kitchen, baggage is lost, hotel rooms are not ready. In other words, a failure equivalent exists for service companies—that portion of operating costs caused by nonconformance to performance standards.

Formal quality management for service companies is a direct result of the realization that quality is the major factor in maintaining and increasing the all-important customer base. A comprehensive quality management program starts with management's understanding and support. Whether for a manufacturing or a service company, the program includes establishment of performance standards in each area of the operation, monitoring of actual performance, corrective action as required, and continuous quality improvement.

Whether for manufacturing or service, a quality cost program will lend credence to the business value of the quality management program and provide cost justification for the corrective actions demanded. Quality cost measurements provide guidance to the quality management program, much as the cost accounting system does for general management. It defines and quantifies those costs that are directly affected, both positively and negatively, by the quality management program, thus allowing quality to be managed more effectively.

Simply stated, quality costs are a measure of the costs specifically associated with the achievement or nonachievement of product or service quality—including all product or service requirements established by the company and its contracts with customers and society. Requirements include marketing specifications, end-product and process specifications, purchase orders, engineering drawings, company procedures, operating instructions, professional *or* industry standards, government regulations, and any other document or customer needs that can affect the definition of product or service. More specifically, *quality costs* are the total of the cost incurred by (a) investing in the *prevention of* nonconformances to requirements, (b) *appraising* a product or service for conformance to requirements, and (c) *failing* to meet requirements (Figure 1.1). **Quality Costs represent the difference between the actual cost of a product or service and what the reduced cost would be if there were no possibility of substandard service, failure of products, or defects in their manufacture.**

Prevention Costs
The costs of all activities specifically designed to prevent poor quality in products or services. Examples are the costs of new product review, quality planning, supplier capability surveys, process capability evaluations, quality improvement team meetings, quality improvement projects, quality education and training.

Appraisal Costs
The costs associated with measuring, evaluating or auditing products or services to assure conformance to quality standards and performance requirements. These include the costs of incoming and source inspection/test of purchased material; in-process and final inspection/test; product, process, or service audits; calibration of measuring and test equipment; and the costs of associated supplies and materials.

Failure Costs
The costs resulting from products or services not conforming to requirements or customer/user needs. Failure costs are divided into internal and external failure cost categories.

Internal Failure Costs
Failure costs occurring prior to delivery or shipment of the product, or the furnishing of a service, to the customer. Examples are the costs of scrap, rework, reinspection, retesting, material review, and down grading.

External Failure Costs
Failure costs occurring after delivery or shipment of the product, and during or after furnishing of a service, to the customer. Examples are the costs of processing customer complaints, customer returns, warranty claims, and product recalls.

Total Quality Costs
The sum of the above costs. It represents the difference between the actual cost of a product or service and what the reduced cost would be if there were no possibility of substandard service, failure of products, or defects in their manufacture.

Figure 1.1. Quality costs—general description.

Although it is rare that a company would go so far as to identify quality costs down to the level of a secretary correcting a letter containing a mistake, every company lives with significant elements of costs that fit this description. Unfortunately, significant chunks of quality cost are normally overlooked or unrecognized simply because most accounting systems are not designed to identify them. As this is generally the case, it is not too difficult to understand why most company top managements are more sensitive to overall cost and schedule than to quality. The interrelationship of quality, schedule, and cost without attention to the contrary is likely to be unbalanced in favor of schedule and cost—and often unwittingly at the expense of quality. This imbalance will continue to exist as long as the real cost of quality remains hidden among total costs. In fact, such a condition can easily set the stage for a still greater imbalance whenever the rising, but hidden, true cost of quality grows to a magnitude that can significantly affect a company's competitive position.

When the cost of quality rises without constraint, or is tolerated at too high a level, failure to expose the condition will ultimately become a sign of ineffective management, yet it is entirely possible for this condition to exist without top management's awareness. A quality cost program can provide specific warning against oncoming, dangerous, quality-related, financial situations. An argument for needed quality improvement is always weak when it must deal in generalities and opinions, but it will become unmistakably clear when a company suddenly finds itself in serious, costly quality trouble.

In the 1980s, competition from abroad, particularly Japan, became so fierce that many U.S. companies found it increasingly difficult to stay in business. Quality played an important role in this competition. If all the facts were known, it is highly probable the companies that failed had excessive, but well-hidden, quality costs. Companies that measure quality costs for the first time are usually shocked at what they find.

To prevent being passed over by strong quality and price competition or, in a positive sense, to constantly improve your quality and cost position, quality must be managed in all aspects of company operations. To enhance the ability to manage quality, implement a quality cost system. Quality cost systems were created for this purpose.

On the premise that any dollar expenditure that could have been avoided will have a direct but negative effect on profits, the value of clearly identifying the cost of quality should be obvious. Achieving this clarity of identification, however, is more easily said than done. A real danger lies in finding and collecting only a small portion of the costs involved and having it represented as the total. There are as many ways of hiding costs in industry as there are people with imagination. This is an all too natural phenomenon in organizations that are never fully charged with all inefficiencies—because some inefficiencies are hidden and not measured—and thus are able to maintain an illusion of effective management. In this kind of industrial organization, departments that cause inefficiencies in areas besides their own frequently get off scot-free because the problems they create, and their responsibility for them, are never properly identified. The costs of handling such problems are buried in the same way that other real quality costs are buried—as an accepted cost of doing business. If top management had all the facts, it would demand the measurement and control of significant quality costs.

Each identified quality performance problem carries with it a tangible recovery cost, which can be assigned a value. This is the essence of quality cost measurement. In a certain percentage of cases, however, the value of the intangible costs entailed may transcend the pure economics of the situation. For example, what is the cost of missing an important milestone in a schedule? Quality problems are more often at fault here than other problems. But the most important of all intangible quality costs is the impact of quality problems and schedule delays on the company's performance image in the eyes of its customers, with all of its implications for the profit picture and the company's future.

The effect of intangible quality costs, often called "hidden quality costs," is difficult, if not impossible, to place a dollar value on. (See pp. 12–15 for a discussion of Taguchi's Quality Loss Function for approximation of hidden losses.) Some companies, however, have found a "multiplier effect" between measured failure costs and "true failure costs. Westinghouse Electric Corporation, for example, reported that its "experience indicates that a multiplier effect of at least three or four is directly related to such hidden effects of quality failure."[5] Figure 1.2 compares true failure costs to an iceberg with the more commonly measured failure costs as just the "tip of the iceberg." The bulk of failure costs are "hidden" below the surface and are usually responsible for "sinking the ship."

The negative effect on profits, resulting from product or service of less than acceptable quality or from ineffective quality management, is almost always dynamic. Once started, it continues to mushroom until ultimately

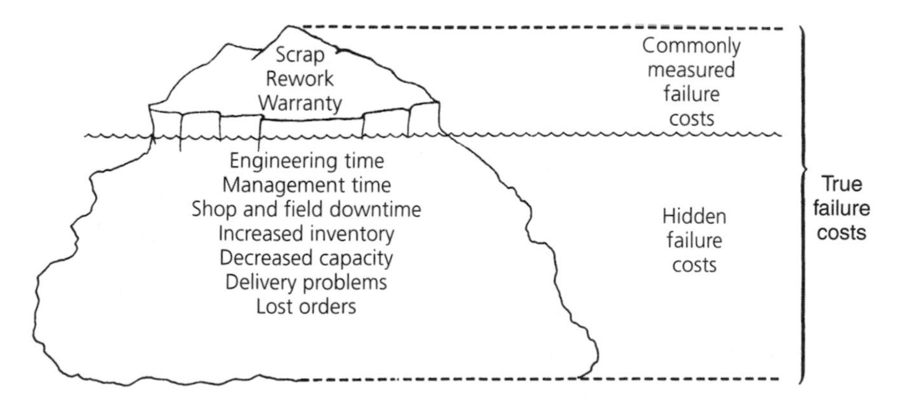

Figure 1.2. Hidden costs of quality and the multiplier effect.

the company finds itself in serious financial difficulties due to the two-pronged impact of an unheeded increase in quality costs coupled with a declining performance image. Management that clearly understands this, understands the economics of quality. Fortunately, a ready-made prescription awaits its decision—effective use of a forceful quality management and improvement program, fully supported by a quality cost system.

GOAL OF A QUALITY COST SYSTEM

As illustrated in Figure 1.3, the most costly condition occurs when a customer finds defects. Had the manufacturer or service organization found the defects, through much inspection, testing, and checking, a less costly condition would have resulted. If the manufacturing or service organization's quality program had been geared toward defect prevention and continuous quality improvement, defects and their resulting costs would have been minimized—obviously, the most desirable condition.

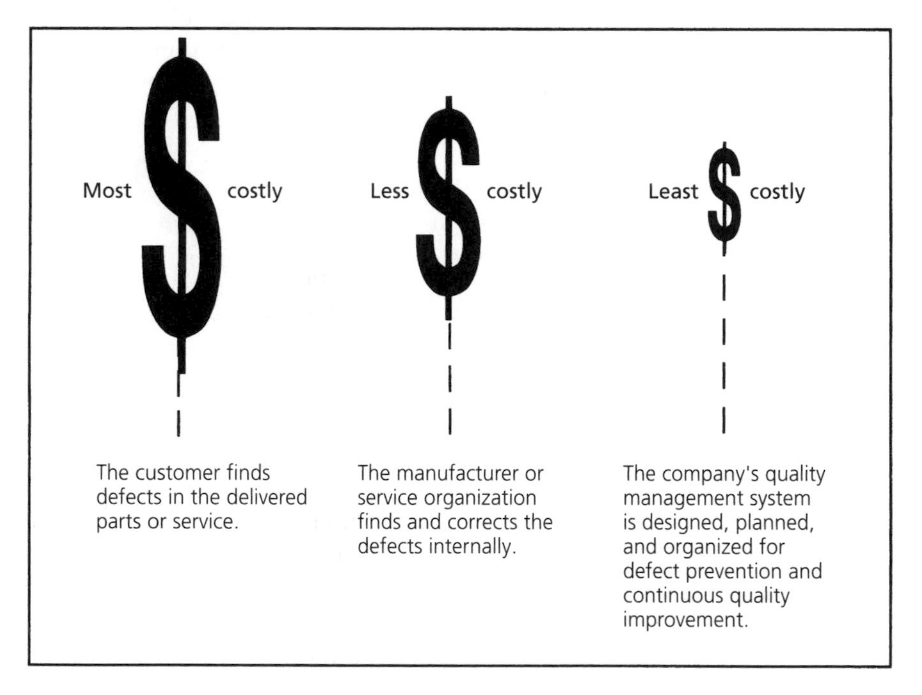

Figure 1.3. Comparative cost of quality.

Adapted from "Principles of Quality Costs" by Jack Campanella and Frank J. Corcoran. In Annual Quality Congress Transactions. Milwaukee: American Society for Quality Control, 1982.

Recent successes have resulted in revisions to the classic model of optimum quality costs. Previously, prevention and appraisal costs were portrayed as rising asymptotically as defect-free levels were achieved (Figure 1.4). There is increasing evidence that the processes of improvement and new loss prevention are in themselves subject to increasing cost effectiveness.[6] New technology has reduced inherent failure rates of materials and products, while robotics and other forms of automation have reduced human error during production, and automated inspection and testing have reduced the human error of appraisal. These developments have resulted in an ability to achieve perfection at finite costs[3] (Figure 1.5).

The goal of any quality cost system, therefore, is to facilitate quality improvement efforts that will lead to operating cost reduction opportunities. The strategy for using quality costs is quite simple: (1) take direct attack on failure costs in an attempt to drive them to zero; (2) invest in the "right" prevention activities to bring about improvement; (3) reduce appraisal costs according to results achieved; and (4) continuously evaluate and redirect prevention efforts to gain further improvement.

This strategy is based on the premise that

- For each failure there is a *root cause.*
- Causes are *preventable.*
- Prevention is always *cheaper.*

In a practical sense, real quality costs can be measured and then reduced through the proper analysis of cause and effect. As failures are revealed through appraisal actions or customer complaints, they are examined for root causes and eliminated through corrective action. Elimination of root causes means permanent removal. The further along in the operating process that a failure is discovered—that is, the nearer to product or service use by the customer—the more expensive it is to correct. Figure 1.6 is an illustration of this concept taken from manufacturing. The concept applies to service as well. Usually, as failure costs are reduced, appraisal efforts can also be reduced in a statistically sound manner. The knowledge gained from this improvement can then be applied, through prevention activities or disciplines, to all new work.

As straightforward as this approach may appear, it cannot work unless there is first a basic quality measurement system that clearly identifies the correctable elements of performance failures which represent the best potential for cost improvement. Such a system is designed to use the data from inspections, tests, process control measurements or evaluations,

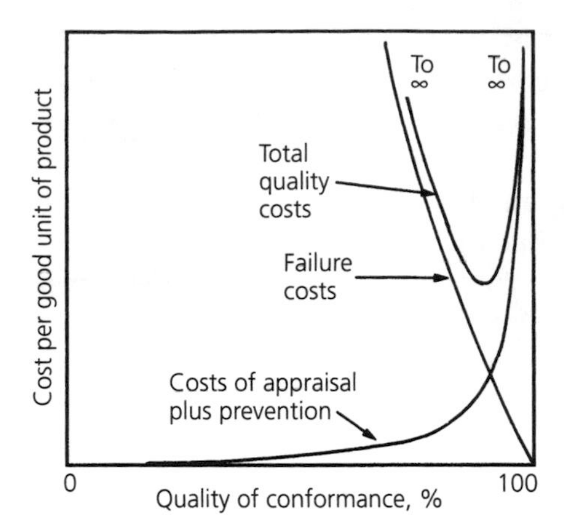

Figure 1.4. Classic model of optimum quality costs.

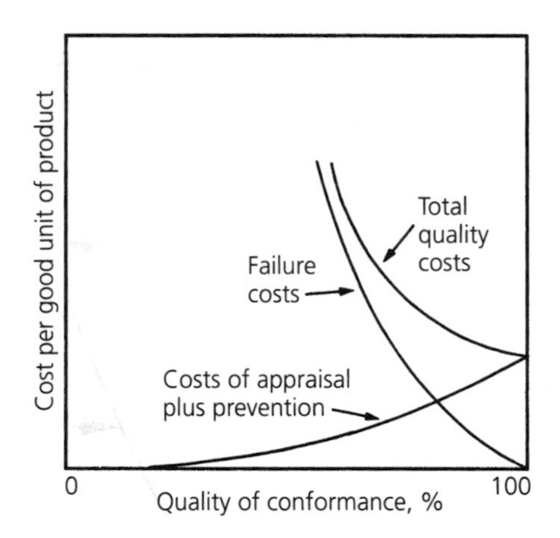

Figure 1.5. New model of optimum quality costs.

Both figures are reproduced from Juran's Quality Control Handbook, 4th ed. by J. M. Juran and Frank M. Gryna. New York: McGraw-Hill Book Co., 1988.

quality audits, and customer complaints as a measure of company performance and a source of determining cost reduction projects. This measurement is a basic and important part of quality management. The potential for improvement can be determined by a system of accurate and dependable quality cost measurement and analysis.

Since every dollar of quality cost saved can have a positive effect on profits, the value of clearly identifying and using quality costs should be obvious. By minimizing quality costs, quality performance levels can be improved.

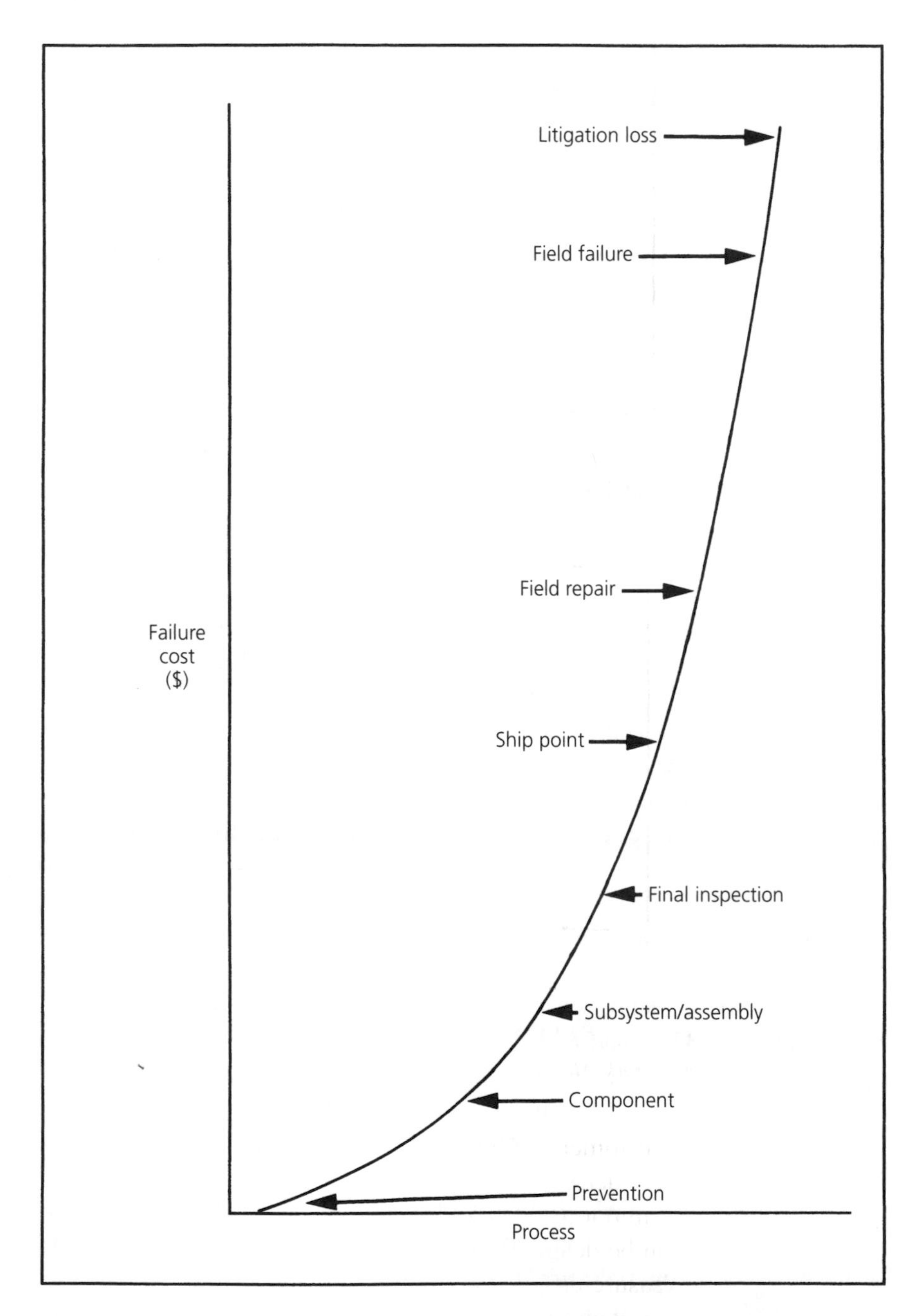

Figure 1.6. Failure cost as a function of detection point in a process.

THE TAGUCHI QUALITY LOSS FUNCTION (QLF) AND THE HIDDEN COSTS OF QUALITY*

Dr. Genichi Taguchi developed Taguchi Methods—combined engineering and statistical methods that achieve rapid improvements in cost and quality by optimizing product design and manufacturing processes. Taguchi Methods are both a philosophy and a collection of tools used to carry forth that philosophy.

Taguchi's philosophy can be summed up by the following statements:

1. We cannot reduce cost without affecting quality.
2. We can improve quality without increasing cost.
3. We can reduce cost by improving quality.
4. We can reduce cost by reducing variation. When we do so, performance and quality will automatically improve.

Taguchi disagrees with the "conformance to specification limits" approach to quality. The difference between a product barely within specification limits and a product barely out of specification limits is small, yet one is considered "good" and the other "bad." Rather, Taguchi Methods strive for minimal variation around target values without adding cost.

Taguchi defines quality as ". . . the loss imparted to society from the time the product is shipped." Fundamental to his approach to quality engineering is this concept of loss. When we think of loss to society, things that come to mind include air pollution or excessive noise from a car with a defective muffler. Taguchi views loss to society on a much broader scale. He associates loss with every product that meets the consumer's hand. This loss includes, among other things, consumer dissatisfaction, added warranty costs to the producer, and loss due to a company's bad reputation, which leads to eventual loss of market share.

The idea of minimizing loss to society is rather abstract and, thus, difficult to deal with as a company objective. When we consider loss to society to be long-term loss to our company, however, (and the two are equivalent), the definition may have more meaning.

As previously discussed, quality costs are usually quantified in terms of scrap and rework, warranty, or other tangible costs. As we saw, however, these constitute only the "tip of the iceberg" (see Figure 1.2).

---

*Material for this section was extracted from publications of the American Supplier Institute (ASI), Dearborn, MI.[7,8,9]

What about the hidden costs or long-term losses related to engineering/management time, inventory, customer dissatisfaction, and lost market share in the long run? Can we quantify these kinds of losses? Perhaps, but not accurately. Indeed, we need a way to approximate these hidden and long-term losses, because they're the largest contributors to total quality loss. Taguchi uses the Quality Loss Function (QLF) for this purpose.

The way the QLF is established depends on the type of quality characteristic involved. A quality characteristic is whatever we measure to judge performance (quality). There are five types of quality characteristics:

1. Nominal-the-best (achieving a desired target value with minimal variation, such as dimension and output voltage)
2. Smaller-the-better (minimizing a response, such as shrinkage and wear)
3. Larger-the-better (maximizing a response, such as pull-off force and tensile strength)
4. Attribute (classifying and/or counting data, such as appearance)
5. Dynamic (response varies depending on input, such as the speed of a fan drive should vary depending on the engine temperature)

The QLF will not be demonstrated for a nominal-the-best quality characteristic. From an engineering standpoint, the losses of concern are those caused when a product's quality characteristic deviates from its desired target value. For example, consider an AC/DC converting circuit in which the AC input is 110 volts and the circuit is to output 115 DC volts. The output voltage is the quality characteristic of interest, and its desired target value is 115 volts. Any deviation from 115 volts is considered functional variation and will cause some loss.

Suppose there are four factories producing these circuits under the same specifications, 115 ± 3 volts, and their output is as shown in Figure 1.7. Suppose further that all four factories carry out 100 percent inspection (let's even naively assume it's 100 percent effective), so that only those pieces within specifications are shipped out. If you're the consumer and wish to buy the circuits from one of the four factories, which would you choose, assuming that the price is the same?

While all four factories are shipping out circuits that meet the engineering specifications, Factory No. 4 appears to offer a more uniform product—that is, the variation around the 115-volt target is less at this factory than at the other three factories.

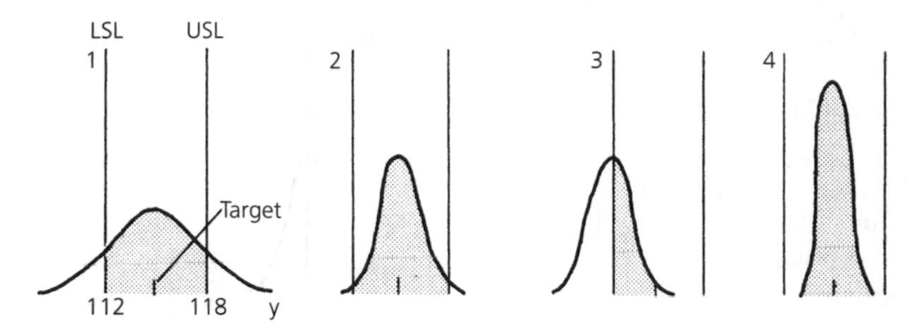

Figure 1.7. Output distribution from four factories.

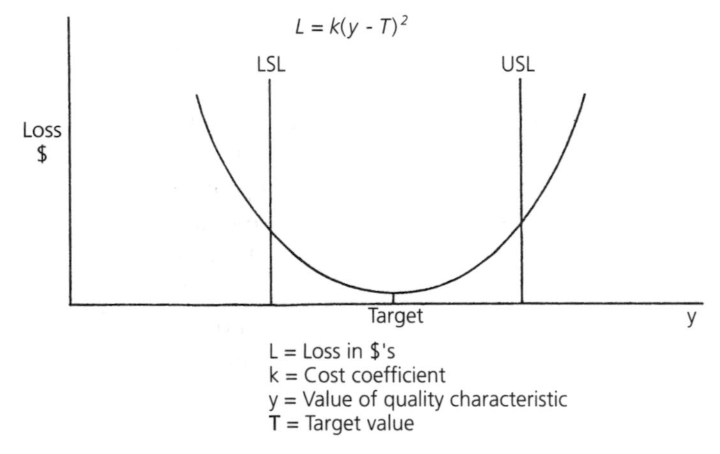

Figure 1.8. The quality loss function.

In this way of thinking, loss occurs not only when a product is outside the specifications, but also when a product falls within the specifications. Further, it's reasonable to believe that loss continually increases as a product deviates further from the target value, as the parabola (QLF) in Figure 1.8 illustrates. While a loss function may take on many forms, Taguchi has found that the simple quadratic function approximates the behavior of loss in many instances.

Since the QLF curve is quadratic in nature, loss increases by the square of the distance from the target value. Thus, if a deviation of 0.02mm from the target value generates a 20-cent loss, then a deviation of 0.04mm would cost 80 cents and a deviation of 0.06mm, $1.80, and so forth. In other words, if deviation is doubled, the loss is quadrupled. If it's tripled, the loss increases nine times. For smaller-the-better quality characteristics, such as part shrinkage, or larger-the-better quality characteris-

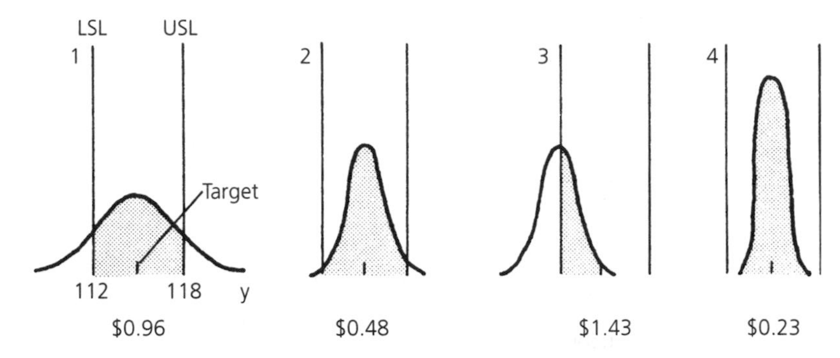

Figure 1.9. Average quality loss per piece.

tics, such as tensile strength, the QLF may become a half parabola. In any event, belief in the QLF promotes efforts to continually reduce the variation in a product's quality characteristics. Taguchi's quality engineering methodology is a vehicle for attaining such improvements.

The QLF was used to estimate the average quality loss from each of the four factories, as illustrated in Figure 1.9. Notice that the smallest average quality loss was obtained from Factory No. 4, the factory with the highest quality. In short, the QLF is a measure of quality in monetary units that reflects not only immediate costs, such as scrap and rework, but long-term losses as well.

QUALITY/ACCOUNTING INTERFACE

Some companies believe that a quality cost program will require extensive accounting system changes and additional staff. Others believe that their present cost accounting system is sufficient to identify all areas requiring management attention. Unfortunately, accounting systems were never designed to demonstrate the impact of the quality of performance (thought to be subjective measurement) on overall operating costs. That is why many of these costs have remained hidden for so long.

Identifying and collecting quality costs must be comprehensive if the system is to be effective, but it also must be practical. The collection and reporting of quality costs should be designed in conjunction with the basic company cost accounting system (see Appendix A, "Basic Financial Concepts"). If large elements of quality costs are incurred but not accurately identified within the cost accounting system (for example, scrap, rework, or redesign costs), estimates should be used until the system can be adjusted.

This will be necessary before a reasonable picture of total quality costs can be portrayed as a justification for improvement action. Also, if these quality-related elements are to become a prime target for cost reduction, they cannot be buried within other accounts. They must be clearly visible.

For all of the cited reasons, it is essential that both the in-house descriptions and the responsibility for quality cost collection, compilation, and reporting be a function of the controller's office—as a service to the quality management function. A controller's procedure for quality costs is necessary to provide company definitions or estimating technique, and location of elements within the company manual of accounts—that is, all that is needed to accurately portray total cost to the company. Holding the controller responsible for quality cost measurement will establish three important standards for the quality cost program:

- It will provide the stamp of financial validity to the program.
- It will assure that collection costs remain within practical limits.
- It will provide an opportunity for effective teamwork to develop between the controller and the quality function, with both organizations seeking cost benefits for the company.

In reality, it is reasonable to expect that the controller will not be eager to have a staff that is already overworked address an additional system for tracking costs. Therefore, the practical value of the quality cost system must be "sold" to the decision makers (see chapter 3, "Quality Cost Program Implementation").

Nevertheless, an internal quality cost procedure will direct the acquisition of specific quality cost data needed to support the company's quality improvement strategies and goals.

In developing the details of a quality cost system, there are two important criteria by which to be guided: (1) recognizing that quality costs are a tool to justify improvement actions and measure their effectiveness, and (2) including insignificant activities is not essential for effective use of quality costs.

If all significant quality costs are captured and used, the objective of the quality/accounting interface—quality cost improvement—can be justified and accomplished. Consistency and integrity will pay off. Comparisons with others are meaningless. Comparisons with your own past performance are what really matters. Incremental improvements in quality costs are what counts.

MANAGEMENT OF QUALITY COSTS

Managing quality costs begins with a general understanding and belief that improving quality performance, as related to product or service, and improving quality costs are synonymous (the economics of quality). The next step is to recognize that measurable quality improvement can also have a tangible effect on other business measures, such as sales and market share. The proviso, however, is that quality costs must be measured and must reflect cost or lost opportunities to the company.

It should be further understood that the cost of quality is a comprehensive system, not a piecemeal tool. There is a danger in responding to a customer problem only with added internal operations, such as inspections or tests. For service operations, this could mean more operators. While this may solve the immediate customer problem, its added costs may, in fact, destroy the profit potential. A comprehensive quality management program will force the analysis of all associated quality costs, making these added internal costs appear clearly as just one step toward the ultimate resolution—prevention of the root cause of the problem.

By now it should be obvious that a quality cost system has the potential to become an excellent tool in the overall management of a business. It can provide an indication of the health of management performance in many areas of a company. It will measure the cost of error-related activities in these areas. A quality cost program should, therefore, become an integral part of any quality improvement activity. Overall quality cost numbers will point out the potential for improvement, and they will provide management with the basis for measuring the improvement accomplished.

Aside from being an overall indicator of quality effectiveness, quality cost numbers are an important asset in the establishment of priorities for needed corrective action. Some companies continue to live with less-than-perfect performance levels because they believe that it would be more expensive to improve. Perhaps the greatest contribution of quality cost systems in this aspect of a business is showing the payoff for would-be corrective actions and justifying their accomplishment. For example, the real profitability of investment in an expensive new tool, machine, or computer system may be obscured by not having all the facts, such as the costs of inspection, sorting, rework, repair, and scrap and the risk of nonconforming product, service, or information reaching the customer.

An important part of managing quality costs is reducing the failure costs. For example, failure costs could be organized in Pareto fashion (the vital few as opposed to the trivial many) for elimination, starting with the highest cost items. If the basic quality measurement system of a company cannot provide the identification of defects or problems to which quality costs can be attached, the first corrective action required is to establish a system that does. Failure costs cannot be progressively reduced without a parallel system to assist in tracking down the defect causes for elimination. At best, without a defect or problem reporting system, only the most obvious problems, the so-called "fires," can be pursued. The not-so-obvious problems will remain hidden in the accepted cost of doing business. Identification and resolution of these otherwise hidden problems is the first major payoff of a quality cost program.

The next step in managing quality costs is to analyze the need for current appraisal costs. Are we taking too high a risk of excessive failure costs by not having a sufficient appraisal program? Or are we spending too much for appraisal, especially considering the improved levels of performance we have achieved? Quality cost analyses, in conjunction with risk analysis, have been used to set desired levels of appraisal activity. In a more constructive way, quality cost analyses also have been used to validate that appraisal activities are not a substitute for adequate prevention activities.

Like failure and appraisal costs, prevention costs of quality are managed through careful analysis leading to improvement actions. Prevention costs are an investment in the discovery, incorporation, and maintenance of defect prevention disciplines for all operations affecting the quality of a product or service. As such, prevention needs to be applied correctly, and not evenly across the board. Much improvement has been demonstrated through reallocation of prevention effort from areas having little effect to areas where it really pays off.

A quality cost program should always be introduced in a positive manner. If not, it can easily be misconstrued (in a negative sense), since it usually exposes a high degree of waste, error, and expenditures which are unnecessary in a company well managed for quality. For this reason, it is extremely important that all affected employees, starting with management, be carefully informed and understand that quality costs is a tool for improving the economics of operation. It doesn't matter what the starting numbers are. Variations in the application of quality costs, in the business itself, in accounting systems, and in overall performance, make each company unique. Therefore, comparisons with others are meaningless and must be avoided. The most important number, the very essence of quality cost objectives, is the amount of measurable improvement from year to year.

If the quality cost program is kept simple and practical, it will support the initiative to improve quality in all operations—the initiative of a quality- or excellence-driven management system. Therefore, when initially launching a quality cost program, care should be taken to plan it carefully to reach the desired objectives. A quality cost program need not identify all elements of quality costs (as described in Appendix B, "Detailed Description of Quality Cost Elements"); rather, it should concentrate on the quality cost elements most significantly affecting your company.

Judgment as to what is most significant depends on more than magnitude. It has been found that small expenses generated for some elements can be just as significant as huge expenses for other elements. In any event, the program must include all major quality cost elements, even if some have to be estimated. After the initial study, the program can be reevaluated and refined with additional details as necessary. For most companies, this initial approach will delineate many improvement opportunities. Managing quality costs means to act on these opportunities and reap the financial and reputational rewards, as well as quality improvements contained therein.

Total quality costs is intended to represent the difference between the actual cost of a product or service and what the cost would be if quality were perfect. It is, as previously ascribed to Juran, "gold in the mine," just waiting to be extracted. When you zero in on the elimination of failure costs and then challenge the level of appraisal costs, not only will you be managing the cost of quality, but you will also be mining gold.

QUALITY COSTS IN DEFENSE CONTRACTS

In December 1995, the Department of Defense (DOD) directed that changes of existing contracts be made, replacing military standards with accepted commercial standards. Through the DOD "Single Process Initiative", it was suggested that ISO 9000 be the alternative quality standard to MIL-Q-9858A.

For decades, MIL-Q-9858A, *Quality Program Requirements*[4] (initially published in 1963) had been the quality standard of choice for most complex products. It identifies quality program requirements for DOD contractors. It requires the establishment of a quality program to assure compliance with the requirements of the contract. Procedures, processes, and products are required to be documented and are subject to review by a government representative. The quality program is subject to the disapproval of the government representative whenever the contractor's procedures do not accomplish its objectives.

In general, paragraph 3.6 of MIL-Q-9858A requires that some form of costs related to quality be maintained by the contractor. Except for requiring the identification of the costs of "prevention and correction of nonconforming supplies," this specification provides little definition of a quality cost program's content. It allows the specific cost data to be maintained and used to be "determined by the contractor." Through the years, however, experience showed most government agencies and auditors to be looking for the type of quality cost system described in this book.

The concepts of the military standard are based on strong quality theory and withstood change, despite a radically changing manufacturing environment. In the establishment of the International Quality Standard ISO 9001, it is no coincidence that the member nations of the International Organization for Standardization (ISO) relied heavily on MIL-Q-9858A to create the base principles of ISO 9001.

However, the ISO recognized that, as more sophisticated options of ensuring quality became available and proven, government standards did not keep pace with change and often limited flexibility by prescribing methods of execution. Accordingly, the member nations approved a standard that provided all of the key requirements for having a sound quality system but did not provide specific instructions as to how to achieve their execution. This concept allows companies the flexibility to determine how all of the requirements can be satisfied.

As the government also recognized that MIL-Q-9858A required cancellation and that ISO 9001 is a legitimate alternative, the government risk in approving this proposal is low, as long as the contractor can ensure consistent compliance to the international standard.

As companies achieve ISO 9001 compliance, and have indicated by policy that they are dedicated to maintaining it, the risk to the government is extremely low that the company's quality system, regardless of method of execution, will stray far from the founding principles of MIL-Q-9858A. Continual audits are required to be conducted, both internally and by an independent registrar (if the company chooses to be registered by an independent third-party registrar) to ensure compliance and to maintain the registration. (It should be noted however, that at the time of this writing, the government is not requiring third-party registration and will continue using its system of oversight through the use of government auditors.)

Such dedication to the preservation of a viable quality system will ensure that products will continue to exhibit the highest integrity and that companies will continue to maintain the public trust. The flexibility that is now permitted by the international standard provides the base structure to continually improve processes.

MIL-Q-9858A continues to be the specification required on some Department of Defense contracts at the time of the publishing of this edition of *Principles of Quality Costs.* Some companies have not taken advantage of the "single process initiative" and continue with MIL-Q-9858A on multiyear contracts. When the contracts are satisfied, the requirement will gradually phase out and be replaced by an accepted commercial standard. The government has suggested ISO 9001, and current government contracts specify ISO 9001. For its effect on quality cost requirements, see ISO 9000 and Quality Costs, below.

ISO 9000 AND QUALITY COSTS

ISO 9000

One of the most striking and universal trends in the management of quality in the past few years has been the drive by businesses of all types to become certified to the quality system standard published by the International Organization for Standardization known as ISO 9000. The standard is identical (except for spelling differences) to the European standard EN-29000 and the American standard Q9000, published by the American Society for Quality. ISO certification is rapidly becoming a prerequisite for doing business, not only in the European Community but worldwide.

The ISO 9000 and related standards define and specify the elements of a quality system. The quality system can be viewed as the organizational structure, the documented procedures, and the resources that an organization uses to manage quality. The ISO 9000 standards require only that all the elements of the system be in place and working. The quality system may be highly effective or grossly ineffective. The ISO 9000 standards recommend, however, that the effectiveness of the quality system be measured. Although there are many measures possible, ranging from the counting of defects to sophisticated customer satisfaction surveys, the measures of most general interest are likely to be financial. Money is the universal language of business and is at least a consideration in most other enterprises. For this reason, the ISO 9000 Standards recommend a financial measurement of quality. As stated in Section 6.1 of ANSI/ASQC Q9004-1-1994, page 7, "It is important that the effectiveness of a quality system be measured in financial terms. The impact of an effective quality system upon the organization's profit and loss statement can be highly significant, particularly by improvement of operations, resulting in reduced losses due to error and by making a contribution to customer satisfaction.", and "By reporting quality system activities and effectiveness in financial terms, management will receive the results in a common business language from all departments."

Relevant ISO Documents

ISO 9001, 9002, and 9003 describe elements of quality systems pertaining to design/development, production, installation, and servicing that are intended to be contractual in nature and against which audits are to be conducted. These standards say nothing about quality costs. ISO 9004-1, on the other hand, is a guidance document providing detailed guidelines on overall quality management, as well as information relevant to implementing the contractual documents ISO 9001, 9002, and 9003. As of this writing, it is in this guidance document and in its follow-ons that quality costs are treated. This should in no way lessen the importance of quality costs in an effective quality management system. Indeed, the important areas of product safety, liability, and marketing are likewise handled in the same guidance document.

There currently are two relevant ISO documents pertaining to quality costs:

- ISO 9004-1:1994 *Quality Management and Quality System Elements—Guidelines*[10] Section 6 *Financial Considerations of Quality Systems.* This is identical to ANSI/ASQC Q9004-1-1994. It was revised from the original 1987 version.
- ISO10014 *Guidelines for Managing the Economics of Quality*—Draft International Standard, 1996.[11] This document has not been finally approved and issued as a standard, as of this writing.

Evolution of ISO Standards Pertaining to Quality Costs

To understand the relationship between these two standards, it is helpful to go back to the original 1987 version of ISO 9004-1 (ISO 9004) and compare it with the 1994 revision. It is apparent that an evolution has been taking place in how the ISO 9000 standards view financial aspects of a quality system. In the original document, the domain of economics of quality was limited to costs associated with achieving quality (Prevention and Appraisal Costs) and costs resulting from inadequate quality (Internal and External Failure Costs)—that is, to traditional costs of conformance and nonconformance. The latter were targeted for reduction. In the 1994 revision, the financial purview was extended from traditional quality costs to *all* costs incurred in fulfilling stated and implied needs of customers. Both costs of conformance and costs of nonconformance are targeted for reduction. ISO10014 extends the domain of "economics of quality" (see page 2) one step further to take into account increasing revenue or other desired beneficial effects, as well as the reduction of costs. Broader economic benefits are anticipated by increasing customer satisfaction, in addition to reducing costs. Financial tracking of both is recommended. An evolution of "economics of quality", compatible with Total Quality Management (TQM) philosophy, has occurred. An economics model depicting the ISO approach is shown in Figure 1.10.

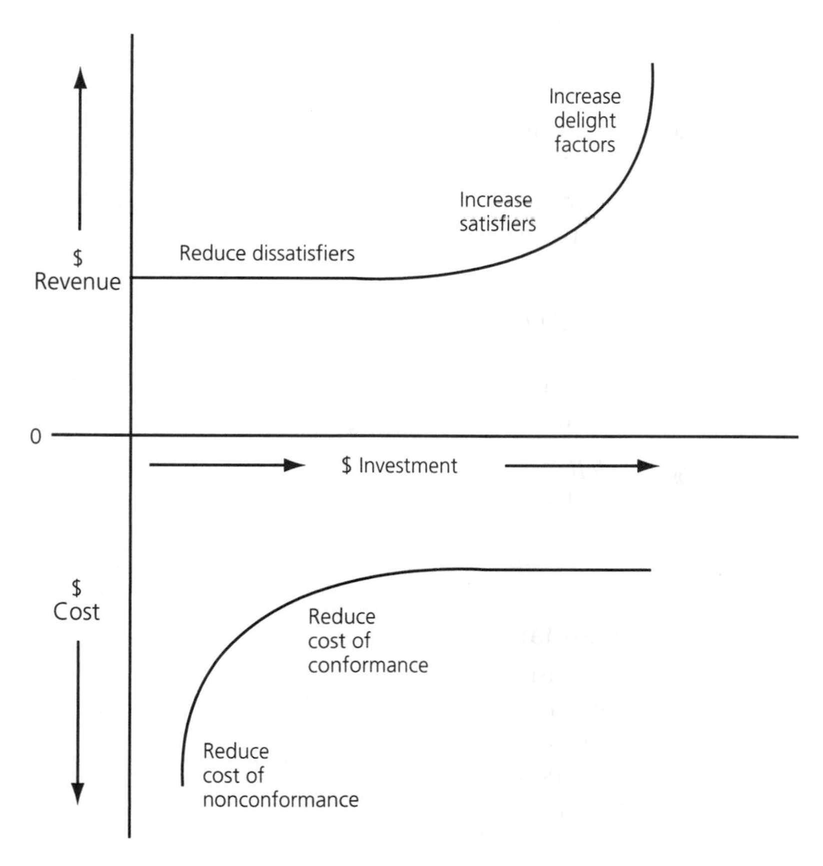

Figure 1.10. Economic model.

Collection and Reporting of Quality Costs

ISO 9004-1:1994 (the issue as of this writing) gives us three models for approaching quality costs and does not exclude others. Therefore, adaptations or combinations of the three are possible. In the words of the standard, they are the

- Quality-costing approach
- Process-cost approach
- Quality-loss approach

The Quality-Costing Approach. Quality-costing is the conventional approach of categorizing quality costs as prevention, appraisal, internal failure, and external failure costs (see chapter 2, page 31). It is thoroughly described elsewhere in this chapter and is well understood and backed by a wealth of experience. Prevention and appraisal costs (costs of conformance) are considered investments, while failure costs (costs of nonconformance) are considered as losses. Applying this approach normally involves investing in a relatively modest increase in the cost of prevention to realize a more significant reduction in the cost of failure, and ultimately a reduction in cost of appraisal as well, thereby substantially reducing the total cost of quality. In this approach, those costs are excluded which are part of the normal operation of the plant or service, e.g., cost of labor associated with making the product or delivering the service, cost of routine maintenance and repair, depreciation of equipment, carrying cost of inventory, and so on. Quality costs are usually reported as a percent of some base, such as sales or production costs (see chapter 2, page 34). This process is normally carried out for an entire organization but can also be applied to an individual process. It offers a rapid means of identifying "gold in the mine" (see page 19 in this chapter) and guides and motivates teams in quality improvement (see chapter 5, page 125). A quality cost program based on this conventional model will meet the guidelines recommended in the ISO standard.

The Quality-Loss Approach. The quality-loss approach, which we shall consider next, attempts to capture the intangible as well as the tangible costs, or losses, due to poor quality. The tangible losses are the commonly measured failure costs, such as scrap, rework, and warranty costs, shown as the tip of the iceberg in Figure 1.2, page 7. Intangible losses are the "hidden failure costs," such as lost sales due to customer dissatisfaction, shown as the submerged or hidden part of the iceberg. The best we can do is to estimate them. Although the ISO standard leaves it to the reader to decide how to quantify quality losses, multipliers, or the Taguchi Quality Loss Function, have been used to approximate the intangible quality losses. For a discussion on the "hidden costs of quality," see page 7. For the Taguchi Quality Loss Function, see pages 12–15.

Although the quality-loss approach permits only a rough estimate of quality costs and is much less rigorous than the other approaches, there are instances where it may be the only feasible method because of lack of available cost data. In other cases, even where such data are available, it may still offer some advantages. For processes running at a relatively low reject level, the impact of further improvement is often understated if only tangible losses are considered. Because the quality-loss approach comprehends intangible as well as tangible costs, a greater and more realistic impact of further improvement may be apparent.

The Process-Cost Approach. The process-cost approach looks at costs for a process rather than for a product or a profit center. The activities within an organization that are linked together and are directed toward fulfilling requirements of customers (both internal and external) can be considered a process. Of course the two previous approaches can also be used to generate quality costs for a process. However, the process-cost approach is unique in that it significantly changes the definition of cost of conformance and really changes the way quality costs are viewed. In the process-cost approach, the costs of conformance and nonconformance are defined as follows:

1. *Cost of conformance:* The costs incurred to fulfill all the stated and implied needs of customers in the absence of failure
2. *Cost of nonconformance:* The costs incurred due to failure of the existing process

Note that "cost of conformance" is significantly different from the traditional definition as used in the quality-costing approach. Cost of conformance in the conventional approach includes prevention and appraisal costs to assure that only good product or service reaches the customer but excludes normal production costs of running a process. The process-cost approach lumps together all costs incurred when a process is running without failure and calls them cost of conformance. Included are not only costs of assuring quality—such as costs of prevention; e.g., process control—but also costs of raw material, labor, energy, etc.

Cost of nonconformance is the traditional cost incurred due to failure of the existing process, such as scrap and rework. Defined in this way, greater cost saving opportunities may lie in reducing cost of conformance than in reducing cost of nonconformance. For example, great savings may be available from combining process steps or eliminating nonvalue-added steps. Both types of costs are depicted in Figure 1.10.

The following simplified example is intended to illustrate the differences between the quality-costing approach and the process-cost approach. Consider a process producing a specialty chemical powder that is running at a 96 percent yield. Assume the cost of production for this material is $8.00/lb. The traditional quality-costing approach would identify a cost of internal nonconformance of $.32/lb. Assuming only occasional customer complaints, automatic sampling and testing, and a minimum amount of engineering support, costs of external failure, appraisal, and prevention are even lower. The employee team estimating quality cost saving opportunities for this product see relatively small opportunity. They might struggle to raise the yield by one or two percentage points, but this would produce only a 1 to 2 percent cost improvement. This situation is not unusual.

Now consider a process-costing approach as previously described. Costs might be determined to be as in the "Before" column.

Process-Cost	Before	After
Cost of nonconformance	$0.32/lb.	$0.31/lb.
Cost of conformance		
Material	$2.00/lb.	$1.50/lb.
Labor	$1.50/lb.	$0.50/lb.
Energy	$1.00/lb.	$1.00/lb.
Overhead	$3.18/lb.	$1.59/lb.

The employee team estimating cost saving opportunities analyze the various steps in a flow diagram of the process to determine the contributors to cost of conformity and see a big opportunity in modifying or even reengineering the process. Eliminating nonvalue-added steps may reduce labor by $1.00/lb. and overhead by $1.59/lb. Using recycled raw material may reduce material costs by $0.50/lb. Costs shown in the "After" column are now realized. Instituting "just-in-time" procedures may reduce overhead even further by reducing inventory carrying costs and storage costs. Thus, analyzing the cost of conformity, and the process elements contributing to it, may result in a substantial cost reduction.

The process-cost approach appears to have some powerful philosophical and conceptual advantages. This is because it allows the tracking and reduction of costs normally associated with efficiency, in addition to those traditionally associated with quality (effectiveness). The process-cost approach may be particularly effective for organizations whose quality improvement efforts have matured to the point that tangible quality costs are relatively small and other tools of TQM are being used—for example, SPC, Just-In-Time procedures, cycle time reduction, etc.

One may argue that these are not really quality costs in the traditional sense. However, consider that most of the nonvalue-added steps in a process are there because of quality problems, introducing complexity into a process. Process simplification can come about only after reduction or elimination of errors. In order to reduce inventory, eliminate storage space, eliminate expediting of orders, and so on, a reduction of errors or an improvement in process quality is necessary. In such cases, increase in efficiency or productivity is a direct result of an improvement in quality. The costs that thereby are eliminated could be considered "hidden quality costs."

Future Directions

The new 10000 series of ISO standards move in the direction of TQM. They are concerned with quality technology and, like ISO 9004, are not universally applicable and are therefore nonmandatory. One of these standards, prepared by ISO/TC 176, was ISO 10014—*Guidelines for Managing the Economics of Quality.* Although for various reasons this document never advanced beyond the Draft International Standard (DIS) stage, it is likely that it will be issued as an ISO Technical Report, intended as an informative guidance document to organizations using related conformance and guidance standards. An examination of its contents gives an indication of the direction that "economics of quality" is taking among the international groups concerned with standards.

The document recommends a process for managing the "economics of quality" which contains dual paths to measure the economic effects of a process. One path (the organization's view) consists of the following steps:

1. Identify the main activities (steps) within the selected process.
2. Identify, allocate, and monitor costs at each step consistent with the organization's existing financial system. Any of the approaches listed in ISO 9004—that is, quality-costing, process-cost, or "other", such as life-cycle, value-added, may be used.
3. Produce a process-cost report.

The other path (the customer's view) consists of these steps:

1. Identify those factors causing customer dissatisfaction, customer satisfaction, and customer delight.
2. Monitor customer satisfaction.
3. Produce a customer satisfaction report.

The two paths then converge into the following single path:

1. Conduct a management review.
2. Identify opportunities. These could be in correction or prevention of nonconformances, in continuous improvement, or in totally new processes or products to improve customer satisfaction.
3. Conduct cost / benefit analysis of reducing costs or increasing customer satisfaction.
4. Plan and implement improvement.

While the approach outlined in ISO 10014 is philosophically appealing in that it considers opportunities as well as losses, in practical applications there is the risk that, in trying to measure all financial consequences, in the final analysis none may be measured satisfactorily. The traditional quality cost approach works as well as it does because it is so specific. There is a discipline in assigning costs to known categories. As we move to broader and broader concepts, such as total costs and finally to total benefits compared to total costs, we lose much of this discipline. The value of such concepts cannot be known until more experience is gained in applying them.

Conclusion

Although not required by mandatory standards, the routine measurement of financial consequences is recommended by ISO guidelines as a means of measuring the effectiveness of a quality system. Several measurement approaches are available. The quality-costing approach is a proven means of tracking, guiding, and motivating quality improvement. The other approaches are based on less experience but have their own advantages, particularly in situations in which it is desirable to include other TQM concerns, such as efficiency and customer satisfaction. The selection of the best approach ultimately will be based on maturity of quality efforts, type of organization or process, and other TQM tools applied concurrently.

QS-9000 AND QUALITY COSTS—THE AUTOMOTIVE INDUSTRY

QS-9000 quality system requirements define

> . . . the fundamental quality system expectations of Chrysler, Ford, General Motors, Truck Manufacturers and other subscribing companies for internal and external suppliers of production and service parts and materials.[12]

The approach taken was to have QS-9000 as a

> . . . harmonization of Chrysler's **Supplier Quality Assurance Manual,** Ford's **Q-101 Quality System Standard** and General Motors' NAO **Targets for Excellence,** with input from the Truck Manufacturers. ISO 9001:1994, Section 4 has been adopted as the foundation for **QS-9000** . . .[12]

QS-9000 applies to all internal and external sites supplying production materials, production and service parts, or finishing services to original equipment manufacturer (OEM) customers subscribing to it.

Other companies may adopt QS-9000, but Chrysler, Ford, and General Motors control the content, with the exception of ISO 9001, which is copyrighted by the International Organization for Standardization (ISO). A survey conducted jointly by the Automotive Industry Action Group (AIAG) and the Automotive Division of the American Society for Quality (ASQ) indicated an overwhelming vote of confidence in the value of the process and a substantial return on investment.

Cost of Quality

Clause 4.1.5 of the QS-9000, 3d edition, requires suppliers to document trends in the "Cost of Poor Quality", defined in the same standard as "The costs associated with production of nonconforming material. Typically quality management breaks down these costs into two categories: internal failure and external failure." It further explains that "Typically, information available through normal business financial reporting should be sufficient to identify and manage the cost of poor quality." In addition, it mentions that Cost of Poor Quality is "sometimes used interchangeably with Cost of Nonconformance." ISO 9004-1 is referenced for additional guidance.

Clause 4.2.5.2, Quality and Productivity Improvements, notes "Cost of Poor Quality" as an example of a situation which might lead to improvement projects. "Scrap, rework and repair" and "customer dissatisfaction" (other failure costs) are also listed among potential opportunities for quality and productivity improvement.

VDA 6.1—the German Automotive Quality Standard

In Europe, the Verband Der Automobilindustrie e.V. (VDA), an association of German automotive OEMs and suppliers to the German automotive manufacturers, has issued quality standard VDA 6.1, which includes as a requirement the cost of quality guides in ISO-9004-1:1994.[10] These requirements include not only the costs resulting from nonconformance—that is, internal and external failure costs—but also the costs associated with quality activity to assure conformance—that is, prevention and appraisal costs. Companies registered to VDA 6.1 must show evidence that a system is in place to collect and evaluate these costs and that the results are part of their Management Review.

Chapter 2
Quality Cost System Definitions

Almost every department of a company spends money on labor or materials that have specific impact on the quality of the product or service provided to customers. It's probably impossible to account for all of these costs, but attempts to do so have led to many different descriptions offered for the cost of quality. This chapter attempts to glean from these many efforts those elements of quality costs that have proven useful on a broad scale.

To assist the reader in determining the makeup of an individual quality cost system, a general description of quality cost categories will be presented. This will be reinforced by a detailed description of quality cost elements (see Appendix B, "Detailed Description of Quality Cost Elements") to be applied, as applicable and practical, to the development of an individual program.

QUALITY COST CATEGORIES

As discussed in chapter 1, quality costs have been categorized as prevention, appraisal, and failure costs. Failure costs are further divided into internal and external failure costs.

Prevention costs—the costs of activities specifically designed to prevent poor quality in products or services. Examples include the costs of new product review, quality planning, supplier capability surveys, process capability evaluations, quality improvement team meetings, quality improvement projects, quality education, and training.

Prevention costs could be misinterpreted in two ways: First, application of the definition of prevention costs could be unclear. Extra appraisal and failure costs may be incurred to *prevent* more expensive failure costs (for example, added inspections and rework to prevent newly found defects from reaching the customer). These clearly are not prevention costs. But, in the same sense, costs incurred to solve problems (corrective action or failure analysis costs) can be viewed as part of either the problem cost (failure cost) or the cost incurred to prevent the problem in the future (prevention cost). In this case, it doesn't really matter in which category the costs are accumulated, as long as there is consistency. The detailed descriptions (Appendix B) will attempt to identify elements that might be viewed this way.

The second way in which prevention costs could be misunderstood occurs whenever an individual is engaged in prevention activities as an integral but small part of a regular job assignment. In many cases, this may be a highly significant activity, such as control charting by the production operator, and part of the operator's cost could be considered prevention in the quality cost report. However, some consider this type of prevention activity as a desirable, built-in, self-discipline cost that is part of normal operating expense. This may also include allocations for automated mechanisms, such as a self-checking machine tool, automatic process control equipment, or an inspection edit built into the software for service processing by computer. On the other hand, individuals, such as engineers or analysts, may work full-time for short periods in activities (such as quality improvement projects) specifically to prevent defects or solve other quality problems further along in the process. This type of activity is clearly intended to be a part of prevention costs.

Appraisal costs—the costs associated with measuring, evaluating, or auditing products or services to assure conformance to quality standards and performance requirements. These include the costs of incoming and source inspection/test of purchased material; validation, verification, and checking activities; in-process and final inspection/test; product, process, or service audits; calibration of measuring and test equipment; and the costs of associated supplies and materials.

Failure costs—the costs resulting from products or services not conforming to requirements or customer/user needs–that is, the costs resulting from poor quality. Failure costs are divided into internal and external failure cost categories:

- **Internal failure costs** occur prior to delivery or shipment of the product, or the furnishing of a service, to the customer. Examples include costs of scrap, rework, reinspection, retesting, material review, and downgrading.

- **External failure costs** occur after delivery or shipment of the product, or during or after furnishing of a service, to the customer. Examples include the costs of processing customer complaints including necessary field service, customer returns, warranty claims, and product recalls.

QUALITY COST ELEMENTS

Quality cost *elements* are the detailed functions, tasks, or expenses which, when properly combined, make up the quality cost *categories.* For example, quality planning is an element of prevention, in-process inspection is an element of appraisal, rework is an element of internal failure, and customer returns are an element of external failure costs.

Although it is recommended that quality cost categories be used as defined herein, the elements making up these categories are different from industry to industry. Quality cost elements in health care, for example, differ significantly from those in manufacturing. Because of the extent of these differences and the many industries involved, such as banking, insurance, hospitality, etc., no attempt will be made to provide complete lists of these elements by industry. However, every attempt will be made to include examples from these industries wherever possible to help readers develop their own lists. Using the category definitions and examples as guidelines, the elements can be tailored to your organization.

In developing detailed elements for your organization, the approach taken is to describe the activities or work being performed which can be considered quality costs—that is, work that would not have to be performed if quality were, and always would be, perfect. Then, using the category definitions as a guide, fit these tasks into the proper categories. For example, if the task is being accomplished to prevent poor quality, the cost of the task is a prevention cost.

For the convenience of developers of individual quality cost systems, detailed descriptions of quality cost elements for each category of quality costs are provided in Appendix B and may be used as a guide. For further help, many excellent articles and publications on quality costs, in various service industries as well as manufacturing industries, are referenced in Appendix C, "Bibliography of Publications and Papers Relating to Quality Costs."

QUALITY COST BASES

In working out the details of an individual quality cost system, it is important for the quality manager and the controller to work together—to mesh their two different sources of knowledge into one integrated system. Since the costs involved may be incurred by any department, function, or cost center, a customized internal quality cost procedure is required. This procedure will describe the sources of data to be reported from the account ledgers in terms of existing account, department, and cost center codes. It will describe how any required estimates are to be prepared and where to use associated labor benefits, allocated costs, and labor burdens, and it will provide the measurement bases against which quality costs may be compared.

While actual dollars expended is usually the best indicator for determining where quality improvement projects will have the greatest impact on profits and where corrective action should be taken, unless the amount of work performed is relatively constant, it will not provide a clear indication of quality cost improvement trends. Remember, the prime value of a quality cost system is in identifying opportunities for improvement and then providing a measurement of that improvement over time. Since the volume of business in total, or in any particular product or service line, will vary with time, real differences (improvements) in the cost of quality can best be measured as a percent of, or in relation to, some appropriate base. Total quality cost compared to an applicable base results in an index which may be plotted and periodically analyzed in relation to past indices. The base used should be representative of, and sensitive to, fluctuations in business activity.

For long-range analyses, net sales is the base most often used for presentations to top management. For example, total cost of quality may be scheduled for improvement from 9 percent of sales to 8 percent during a given business plan year. While this measurement may be important from a strategic planning point of view, it would not be practical and could be misleading for the day-to-day, week-to-week, month-to-month needs of the practitioners who are commissioned to make it happen.

In industries such as aircraft manufacturing, the failure to ship just one aircraft in the quality cost report period could severely impact sales for that period. Sales for the period would drop significantly, thereby causing a rise in the quality cost index, although, in fact, quality performance may not have changed at all. Going one step further, the sale of that aircraft in the following period might inflate that period's sales figures, thereby causing a misleading but significant quality improvement trend when compared to the previous period.

In general, in industries in which sales may vary significantly from one quality cost reporting period to another, net sales do not make a good short-term comparison base. However, these short-term sales variations should even out over the long term, and the use of net sales for a long-range comparison base is excellent.

Short-range bases should be directly related to quality costs as they are being incurred and reported. They should relate the cost of quality to the amount of work performed. For short-range use, appropriate bases for quality costs are best determined from a review of data already in use in work areas and, thereby, already understood by the people who will have to learn to use quality costs. In fact, the best bases are those which are already key measures of production. Typical examples include overall operating costs, total or direct labor costs, value-added costs, and the actual average cost of a delivered product or service. The basic idea is to use a meaningful, on-line, and well-known base relating to the amount of business activity in each area where quality cost measurements are to be applied in support of performance improvement.

For effective use of a quality cost system, it may be preferable to have more than one base. Usually, for long-range planning purposes, total quality costs as a percent of net sales is used. There may be no better common denominator than net sales for year-to-year planning and measures of accomplishment according to top management. For current, ongoing applications, however, several bases can be used. The bases selected should be related to the management emphasis already being placed on specific areas for improvement. The following examples are typical indices that incorporate this feature:

- Internal failure costs as a percent of total production/service costs
- External failure costs as an average percent of net sales
- Procurement appraisal costs as a percent of total purchased material costs
- Operations appraisal costs as a percent of total production/service costs
- Total quality costs as a percent of production/service costs

There is no limit to the number of indices or the level of detail that an effective quality cost system can have. More danger exists in oversimplification—such as using only one base for all purposes. There is no perfect base. Each base can be misleading if used alone. This can easily lead to confusion and disinterest. It's important to the success of quality cost use that bases for individual progress measurements not appear to be unnatural to the parochial intent of the area. Instead, they should be seen as complementary to that intent (for example, rework costs as a percent of area labor costs). They could also be used to provide indices that may have shock value—to get the corrective action juices flowing (for example, "Hey, did you know that, for every dollar expended in your area, fifty cents results from poor quality?").

To help in the selection process, consider the following types of normally available bases:

- A labor base–such as total labor, direct labor, or applied labor
- A cost base–such as shop cost, operating cost, or total material and labor
- A sales base–such as net sales billed or sales value of finished goods or services
- A unit base–such as the number of units produced, the number of services performed, or the volume of output

Other Considerations Pertaining to Bases

The previous discussion focused on the appropriateness of available financial bases to quality costs viewed in terms of ratios, indices, or percentages. There are additional factors which can influence application of these bases:

- *Sensitivity to increases and decreases in production/service schedules.* Most manufacturing and service operations have a level at which efficiency is highest. Additions and subtractions from the workforce, maintenance of equipment, and the use of backup suppliers may influence both quality costs and built-in prime costs. If the influence is substantial, an attempt should be made to quantify these factors and recommend changes to minimize adverse effects. In these days of serious competition, successful companies are using many techniques to overcome such adverse influences, including flexible manufacturing systems, intensive formal training, and Just-In-Time quality programs with suppliers.

- *Automation.* With productivity and quality as national goals in the world-class competition for business, successful companies have turned to robotics and automation to reduce direct and indirect costs. Here again, the effects on ratios such as scrap, rework, or appraisal versus direct labor costs may be substantial. Obviously, application of quality cost principles dictates that we be able to measure the (presumed) favorable influence of automation on appraisal or failure costs and, more broadly, on the ability of a business to influence customer perceptions and actual experience concerning quality.
- *Seasonal product sales.* Some companies, such as department stores, have high seasonal sales. External failure costs, such as customer complaints, may be seasonally grouped and quality costs adjusted accordingly. A four-quarter moving average of the ratio between external failure costs and net sales billed is an appropriate technique to use in these circumstances.
- *Oversensitivity to material price fluctuations.* The law of supply and demand still prevails, and raw material costs may experience wide fluctuations. If internal failure or appraisal are ratios resulting from the application of prime costs, this may have a dramatic effect. In such cases, the use of direct labor, rather than prime costs, may be appropriate.

TREND ANALYSIS AND THE IMPROVEMENT PROCESS

Quality costs alone cannot do anything for a company except to illustrate what is being expended in specific areas related to quality and to highlight opportunities for cost improvement. To put quality costs to use, they must be organized in a manner that will support analysis. As previously noted, one way to achieve this is to look at quality costs in ratio with known costs. Use them to raise questions such as

- Did you know that for every $100 spent for production, $14 are lost in internal failure costs?
- Did you know that for every $100 spent for material purchases, $3 have to be spent for supplier goods inspection?

Questions such as these immediately show the value of quality costs in direct relation to known cost expenditures. The next logical step is to assemble and examine these ratios over time to determine whether the situation being depicted is getting better or worse. Failure costs, in particular, lend themselves to this type of analysis. Supplementing the initial analysis with the best empirical explanations of what can be achieved will become the first step in the projection of reasonable improvement goals. Each individual trend analysis can then be extended into the future, first as a plan with specific goals and then to monitor actual progress against the plan.

As indicated in the discussion of quality cost bases, there are two types of quality cost trend analyses: long-range and short-range. The long-range analysis normally views total quality costs over a long period of time. It is used principally for strategic planning and management monitoring of overall progress. Short-range trend charts are prepared for each company area where individual quality cost improvement goals are to be established. The approach to short-range targets can be to assign one for each general operational area, or it can become as detailed and sophisticated as the quality management system will support.

Figure 2.1 is a composite example of a long-range quality cost trend chart for a typical organization with sales in the range of $100 million to $200 million. It shows total cost of quality as a percent of net sales over a period of ten years. It also shows prevention, appraisal, internal, and total failure costs separately as a percent of sales (external failure costs are shown as the difference—the shaded portion—between internal and total failure costs). The first two years show quality cost history without any knowledge of, or emphasis on, its reduction. The third year is the start of quality cost measurement and use. Years four through nine show actual progress accomplished. Year 10 is a projection of the expected continued progress.

To determine exactly where to establish short-range quality cost trend charts and goals, it is necessary to review the company's basic quality measurement system. To actually reduce quality costs, it is necessary to find the root causes of these costs and eliminate them. Real improvement depends on actions within the basic quality measurement and corrective action system, enhanced by the use of quality costs as an important support tool. Specific uses of quality costs, therefore, must be correlated to specific quality measurement target areas for improvement.

A minimum quality measurement system should include summary appraisal results from all key operational areas. These include receiving

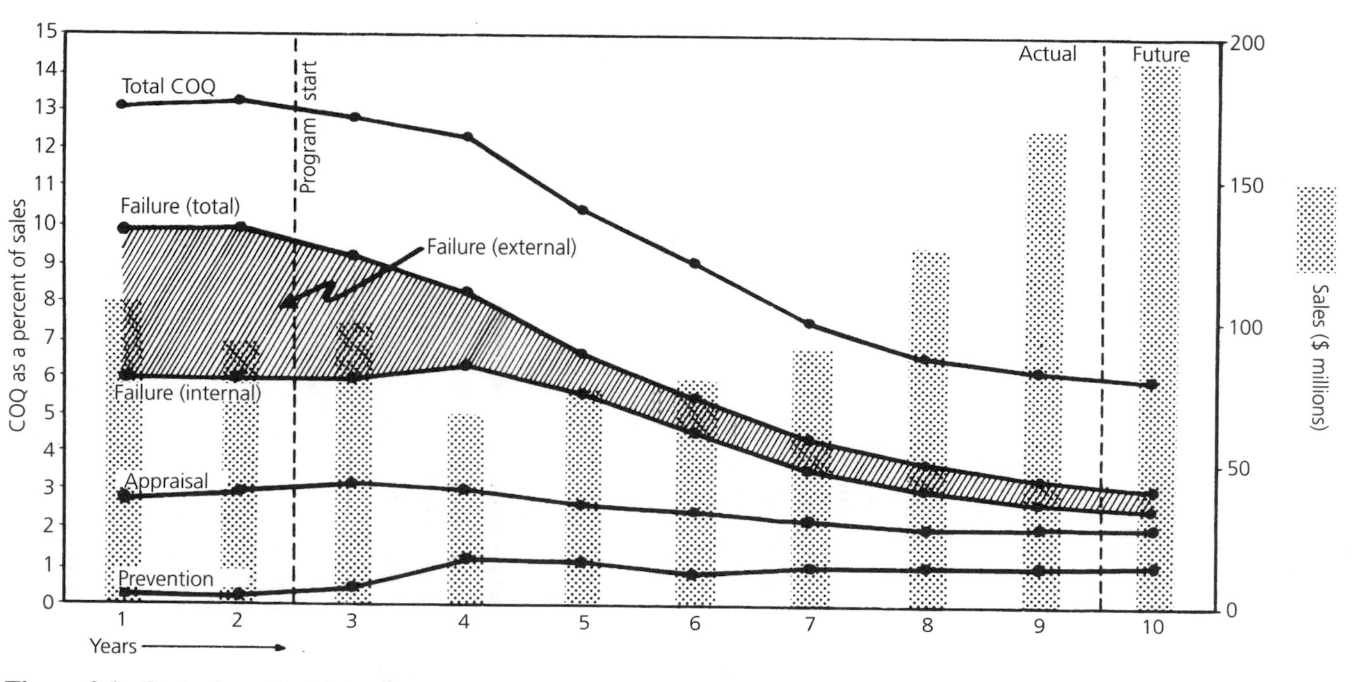

Figure 2.1. Cost of quality history.

inspection, fabrication inspection, final assembly inspection and test, and field failure reports. The summaries are usually presented as trend charts to indicate and make people aware of the current levels of quality performance. Quality cost trend charts, when correlated, will supplement these performance charts with viable cost data to support the improvement effort. This is the essence of their use together (see Figure 2.2).

It should be noted that there is normally a time lag between basic quality measurement data and quality cost data. Quality measurement data are always current (usually daily), whereas quality cost data are accumulated after-the-fact, as most cost accounting reports are. It is important, therefore, to understand that quality costs are used to support improvement (before-the-fact) and to verify its accomplishment (after-the-fact), but actual improvement originates as a result of using current quality measurement data in the pursuit of cause and corrective action.

There is also a time lag between cause and effect—that is, quality improvements do not show immediate reductions in quality cost because of the time lag between the cause and its effect.[1] This lag can be observed on a quality cost trend chart. For this purpose, it may be desirable to indicate on the chart when quality improvements were made.

Figure 2.3 is a simplified quality cost trend chart marked to indicate the start of a quality improvement activity. The note enables us to see the reason for the steady improvement over the past five months—in April, training programs were initiated.

The first effect was an increase in the quality cost index due to the cost of the programs (prevention cost increased but failure costs remained the same). After a cause-and-effect lag of about two months, the value of the training began to become evident, as shown by a steady reduction in the quality cost index (failure costs decreased while prevention costs remained the same). By November, a 45 percent reduction was indicated.

Obviously, the training programs were a worthwhile investment. Had no improvement been indicated after a reasonable amount of time, some action would have been necessary. The programs would have had to be reevaluated and either revised or dropped in favor of some other course of action.

Actual quality improvement begins with the preparation of a cumulative frequency distribution of defect types for each quality performance trend chart used. A cumulative frequency distribution can be shown as a simple bar chart using the totals for each defect type for the

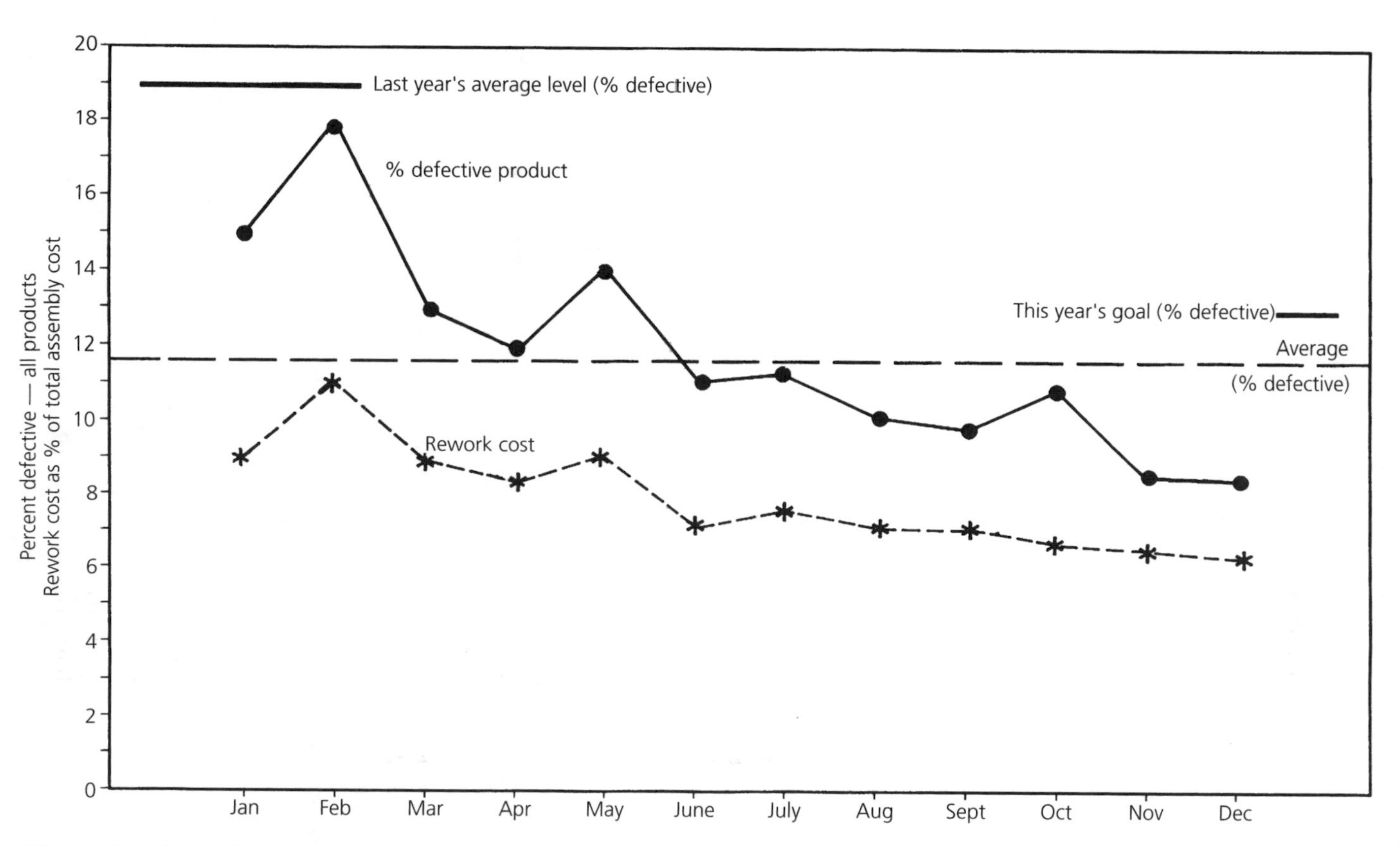

Figure 2.2. Assembly area quality performance.

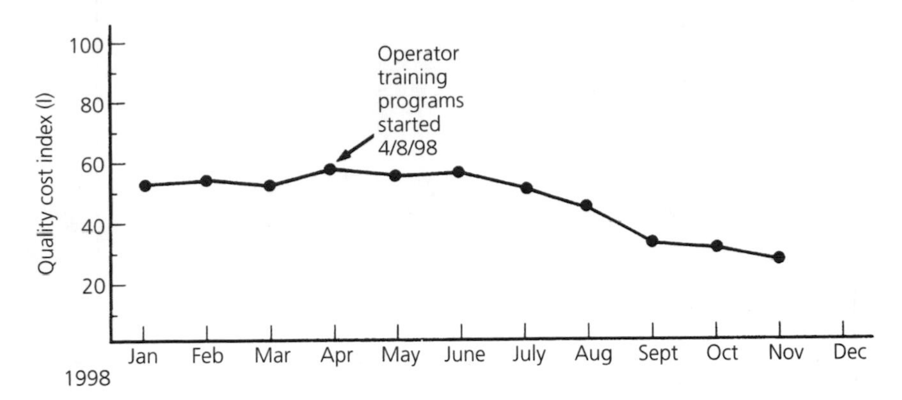

Figure 2.3. Quality cost trend.

same time period as the trend being depicted, or a shorter period, as desired. Reorganization of these data in accordance with the Pareto principle (displayed in descending order of significance) will show that only a few of the many contributing types will be responsible for most of the undesired results (see Figure 2.4). These "vital few" are identified for investigation and corrective action. In the example shown, 93 percent of the defects occurred in the drill and tap, plating, and deburring operations. Corrective action concentrated in those operations will have the greatest impact on quality improvement. As each most significant contributor to failure costs is eliminated in descending order, the related failure costs of quality will descend in a like manner. As each new level of performance is achieved, associated appraisal costs may also be reduced to some degree.

The foregoing description of short-range quality cost usage defines a simple, straightforward, basic approach needed by any quality cost program to make it effective. Actual programs can become more complex or sophisticated as required. Fundamentally, if quality costs can be measured and related to an area where basic quality performance data exist, the quality cost improvement process can begin.

In summary, an effective quality cost program consists of the following steps:

- Establish a quality cost measurement system.
- Develop a suitable long-range trend analysis.

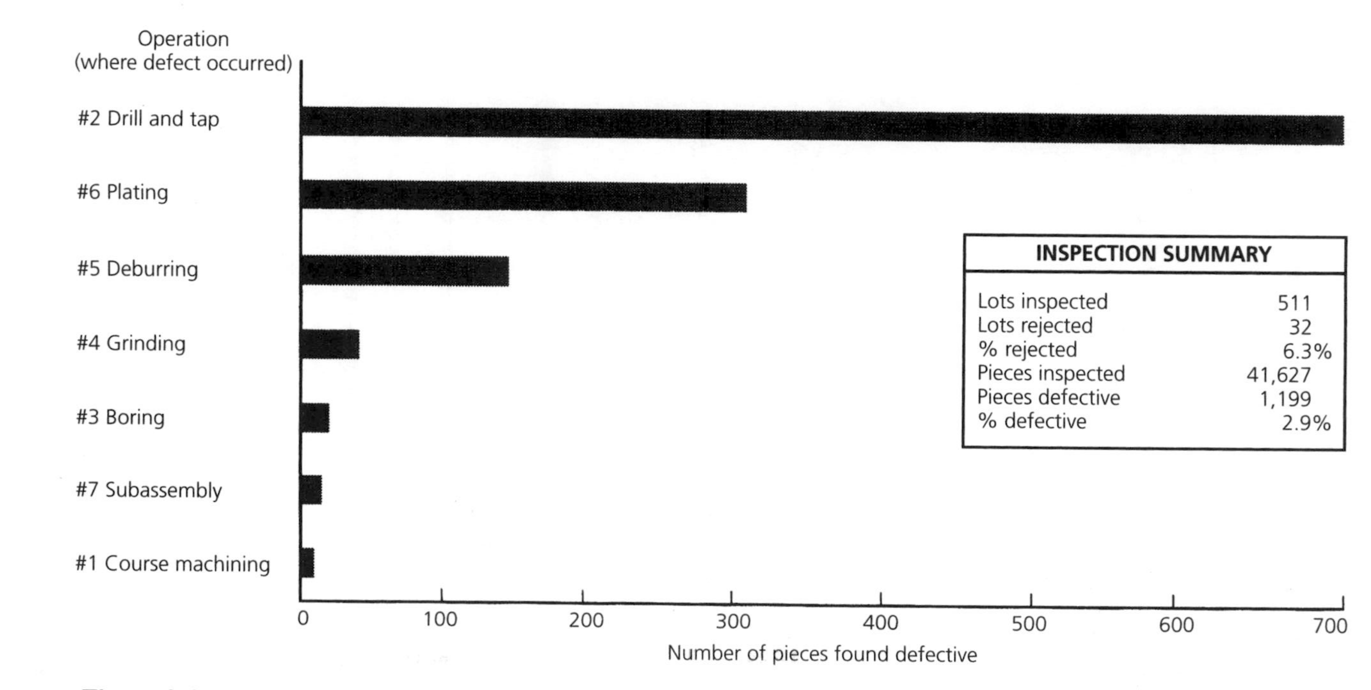

Figure 2.4. Pareto analysis–machine shop.

- Establish annual improvement goals for total quality costs.
- Develop short-range trend analyses with individual targets which collectively add up to the incremental demands of the annual improvement goal.
- Monitor progress against each short-range target and take appropriate corrective action when targets are not being achieved.

Chapter 3
Quality Cost Program Implementation

HOW TO GET STARTED

Like many good things in life, a quality cost program will not occur by itself. Its implementation requires an advocate and champion within the company. While this person normally is the quality manager (or senior quality function representative), it can be anyone. The only requirements are knowledge of quality cost systems, a clear view and belief in their application and value to the company, a desire and willingness to be advocate and leader, and the position and opportunity (within a company) to meet the imposed challenges.

The first step to be taken is to verify with factual costs that a quality cost program can be beneficial to the company. This is necessary to attract management's attention and interest. To do this, a review and analysis of financial data must be conducted in sufficient detail to determine the general levels of quality costs as they exist today. It's the major costs, however, that are important for this purpose. Most likely, much of the data required is presently and readily available. If not, some of these costs may even be estimated. The point is that this step should be relatively easy and does not have to account for *all* quality costs. If readily available and easily estimated costs are included and represent the major costs of quality, then sufficient data will have been obtained to present to management. These data should justify the effort and interest management in participating in the program. Be careful, however, to locate any major increments of quality cost that may be hidden in large accounts, (e.g., significant rework costs buried in normal operating cost accounts.

Once the quality cost levels are determined, the opportunity for improvement should be obvious. The results should be sufficient to sell management on the need for the program. It is not uncommon to find initial quality cost estimates of more than 20 percent of sales. While direct comparisons cannot be made, some manufacturing companies with extensive quality improvement program and quality cost experience are demonstrating that total quality costs can be reduced to as little as 2 percent to 4 percent of sales. The reduction is pretax profit.

The next step is to determine whether management is ready to accept and support a quality cost program. Here an internal judgment is required. The real question is whether management is truly open to new ideas in the operations area of the company. Unfortunately, a quality cost program can never succeed from the bottom or the middle of the organization upward. It needs the backing and support of top management to have any chance for success.

When it has been determined that top management will be receptive, the next step is to plan the sales pitch needed to achieve its acceptance and support. For this purpose, in addition to the general levels of overall quality costs already determined, a more detailed example will be required. That is, a specific, incremental area of the operation must be exposed to management in sufficient detail to show how actual quality costs can be calculated and eliminated through analysis and corrective action. Thus, management's understanding of the full cycle of quality cost opportunity and accomplishment will be complete. A logical approach to finding the right example for top management is to conduct a survey looking for specific areas with high failure costs. Then the areas with the most obvious opportunity for improvement are selected. Final selection of the area to be used as the example, and probably for the pilot run of the ensuing program, should be influenced by the cooperative attitude of the area management team. The best example should provide not only the right opportunity but also a high probability of instant success when the program begins.

At this point, the champion of quality costs is ready to develop an overall plan and schedule for quality cost program implementation. Essential ingredients of the plan should include

- The management presentation, designed to identify the overall opportunity, to show an example of how the program will achieve its benefits, and to accomplish management acceptance and support for the implementation plan and schedule

- Conduct of the planned pilot program
- Education of all functions to develop awareness and interest in participation in the quality cost program
- Development of the internal quality cost accounting procedure
- Overall collection and analysis of quality cost data
- Quality cost reporting and use (integration with the quality management system and quality improvement program)

THE MANAGEMENT PRESENTATION

Before undertaking any large-scale attempt to implement a quality cost program, management must be convinced of the value of the program and the use for which the system is intended. Any proposed need for additional efforts in the important business of cost accumulations and use is likely to be challenged. Thus, a comprehensive presentation to management is needed to elicit its understanding and interest, and to justify the proposed effort.

Companies not already engaged in quality cost programs are unaware of the actual magnitude of the quality cost dollar and its direct impact on their total business. This is where the previous evaluation of the general levels of quality cost comes into play. Those figures show not only the previously unknown levels of quality cost, particularly failure costs, that are being incurred, but also the potential cost improvement opportunity. This should whet management's appetite to hear more and allay fears that the proposed benefits may not be real.

Like any selling proposition, a positive attitude must permeate this presentation. Benefits to management must continually be stressed. Not only will current expenses, unproductive work, and pure waste be reduced, but customer relations, market share, employee satisfaction, and profit will be enhanced. There is not a top management team in existence that does not want to improve quality, but there are many that don't know exactly how to proceed or are not sure if their companies can afford it. The message of cost of quality could be exactly what is needed to justify their pursuit of a sound quality improvement program.

The presentation should contain a clear description of the detailed intent of the program and how it will be accomplished. It should describe the extra cost data to be gathered (the investment). The quality costs arrived at earlier and the detailed example previously chosen should clearly illustrate that failure costs being incurred could be almost totally prevented (the return on investment). The picture presented should be one of gold nuggets just sitting there, waiting to be plucked from the operation. The clarity and authenticity of this portion of the presentation will go a long way toward alleviating whatever fears management may have about the program's validity.

Once management is sold on the genuine value of the program, it can then be educated in the basic concepts of quality costs (chapter 1) and the need for teamwork among all involved functions. Emphasis should be placed on the fact that quality-related costs are not solely generated by the quality function. They encompass significant costs generated by design, purchasing, operations, and various support groups. It is, indeed, a companywide program.

Finally, the presentation should describe the quality cost program implementation plan and schedule, the results that can reasonably be expected, and a clear indication that there will be an extraordinary return on investment. Before the meeting is concluded, management should give its approval, support, and commitment to participate.

THE PILOT PROGRAM

A pilot program is recommended, because it will

- Prove the ability of the system to produce cost-saving results
- Resell management on the continued need for the program
- Limit the initial scope of implementation—both people and area
- Allow system debugging prior to full implementation

Because of its importance to the ultimate success of quality cost implementation, the pilot program needs a full-time leader—one who knows quality management and the company and who is willing to learn about accounting (a co-leader from accounting would be ideal but is not mandatory). The principal investments in the entire quality cost program are the leader/advocate and the quality cost collection system. This is a relatively small investment in a program that can have far-reaching benefits. It is, however, a point that should have been raised and committed to at the management presentation.

Selection of the pilot area, as discussed previously, should be strongly influenced by the area's opportunity to produce quick and significant results. Depending on actual circumstances, it may be advisable to work with a unit as small as a single program or product line within a facility, a typical plant or office in a multifacility company, or an entire company division. There are no hard and fast rules, but the following guidelines should apply. To assure a high probability of success, the unit selected for the pilot program should

- Be as typical of the company's operation as possible
- Contain costs in all categories of quality cost measurement, although some elements may have to be estimated
- Present obvious improvement opportunities
- Have a cooperative local management

Before starting the detailed planning for the pilot area, a key person from the accounting department should be selected to work with the leader/advocate (if a co-leader from accounting was not previously assigned). This person will help bridge the gap between current accounting information and the needs of the pilot quality cost program—and will later develop the companywide quality cost accounting procedure. It is advisable to select someone who is a progressive thinker and a quality-minded person. Select an individual who knows not only how the books *should be kept* but, more important, exactly how they are kept.

Then the leader/advocate, the accounting representative, and a local area management representative can form a team to pursue the pilot quality cost program objectives. All the expertise needed to assure success exists in this team. From this point on, it's a matter of effort, patience, and perseverance.

The actual steps of the pilot program involve

- Measurement of quality costs and appropriate bases
- Tie-in with basic quality measurements
- Establishment of key trend analysis charts
- Identification of improvement opportunities and goals
- Leadership and support of problem identification, analysis, and solution
- Strict enforcement of necessary corrective actions
- Summary reporting of progress

As the pilot program progresses, it should be documented as a case history for use with quality cost program implementation on a companywide basis. If timing could be such that pilot program progress could be achieved before the end of a fiscal year, the stage would be set to allow for companywide implementation to start at the beginning of a new fiscal year.

QUALITY COST EDUCATION

After management approval of the quality cost program and concurrent with the start of the pilot program, key members of each department should be educated in the concepts of a quality cost system and the detailed program plan for implementation. Emphasis should be placed on the involvement of all functions, the importance of teamwork, and the real opportunities for performance and cost improvement that exist in many functional areas. The importance of examples here cannot be overstressed. The ultimate objective of this education is agreement on the benefits of the program and a commitment to cooperation or participation as required.

Departments should be given the opportunity to review the entire program as planned and see exactly where they fit. As they come to recognize the contributions or participation that will be expected of them, they can begin to evaluate the program's benefits and impact on their individual departments. It is very important at this point in program development that all department representatives be encouraged to make program suggestions from their expert viewpoints—that is, solicit quality cost elements peculiar to each department. Ask them to prepare a list of those tasks or functions performed by their departments that can be considered quality costs—work that would not have to be performed if quality were and always would be perfect. Then, using the definitions provided in chapter 2 as a guide, fit these tasks into the proper categories—prevention, appraisal, and internal or external failure. For example, if a function was performed because a product or service did not conform to requirements or customer/user needs, its cost is considered a failure cost. Further, if the nonconformance was discovered prior to delivery or shipment of the product, or the furnishing of a service to the customer, the failure cost is an *internal* failure cost. (See "Quality Costs Elements," page 33; Figure 3.1; and Appendix B for help in this process.) The tasks or functions listed and categorized are their departments' quality cost elements. Adoption of these elements into the program, along with any other worthwhile suggestions, will not only help to refine the

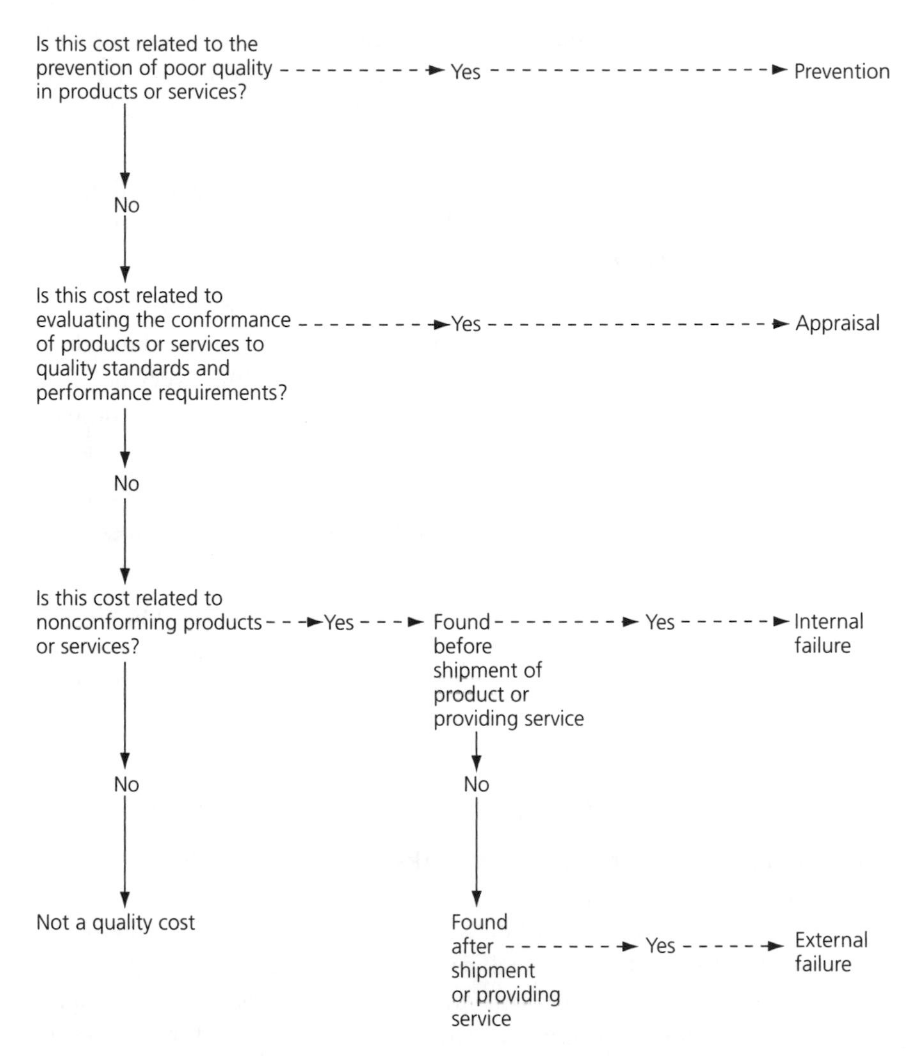

Figure 3.1. Assignment of cost elements to quality cost categories.

details of the program but also will allow each department to become a part of the program's development.

The quality cost education of key representatives of involved functional organizations also provides an opportunity to stress their support role to overall quality management, the benefits they will gain from improved quality, and some of the pitfalls that hinder success. The following items should always be included in the quality education of other functions.

- Remember that, without a quality management system and quality improvement program to support, there is no need for quality costs. Emphasize the twofold benefits of quality improvement—improved customer satisfaction at less cost.
- Remember that there can be no improvement, cost or otherwise, without corrective action. Each department must be committed to all required corrective action.
- Remember that the objective of the quality cost program is to identify areas where cost improvements can be achieved through the betterment of quality performance. Don't insist that every definable element of quality cost be tracked. If it's not truly significant, don't argue about it. Throw it out.
- Don't complicate the bookkeeping because of quality costs. Relate to it as it is. Change it only if the knowledge gained proves that it should be changed (from a business viewpoint).
- Don't try to move too quickly from the pilot program into all other areas—even when the pilot program is expected to be very successful. Remember that quality cost progress is a journey, not a destination.

INTERNAL QUALITY COST PROCEDURE

Concurrent with the progress of the pilot program, the company quality cost procedure can be developed. It will already have been discovered that many of the needed quality cost data are not readily available from the cost accounting system. In a typical service business, for example, many appraisal and internal failure costs are considered a normal part of operations. As such, these costs are not segregated and available for use. In other cases, what is accounted for in the accounting books may not be the same as the quality cost definition. Rework in manufacturing, for example, may be accounted for as a variance against a standard allowance. Discrepancies such as these, coupled with expected variations in individual cost accounting systems, clearly signal the need for a detailed, internal quality cost procedure for each company involved in a quality cost program.

The internal quality cost procedure is necessary to describe each element of quality cost to be used and to define how and when the actual cost data are to be estimated or collected, and assembled. It also defines the comparison bases to be included. To assure accuracy, in terms of actual cost to the company, the procedure should also define the application of fringe benefit costs, overhead burdens, and other accounting adjustments to each defined element of quality cost. Finally, the procedure should establish responsibilities for execution of its requirements, and it should provide a reporting format for the quality cost data to be presented for use (see Figure 3.3, page 57, for an example of a summary report).

To assure the integrity of the quality cost data and their acceptance by all who may be affected by the data, the internal procedure should be authorized by the controller or chief accountant. The procedure can be prepared with the help of the quality cost leader/advocate, but it should be implemented through accounting. If the collection of quality cost data is related to the quality function, it will not have the validity required to command attention. In fact, it might easily slip into that realm of accommodations viewed as "belonging to the quality department."

A good place to start in preparing this procedure is the company's manual of accounts, which should provide a description of what each account contains. Add to this the "Detailed Description of Quality Cost Elements" included in Appendix B and the element lists arrived at by the individual departments during the quality cost education phase discussed earlier in this chapter. Then begin the judgments that will match accounts with quality costs. An obvious match will occur if the account exists only because of less-than-perfect work, such as a rework account. More often than not, the match will not be so obvious, and practical judgments will have to be worked out. Internal definitions should use terms that make sense to the users. Simplification and clarity, rather than magnitude, is the rule of thumb that should be applied. Don't make a "program" out of the collection system.

In preparing the internal procedure, there is no need to agonize over the proper category for any questionable increment of quality cost. Remember that the ultimate aim is to reduce all elements of quality cost consistent with the goals of the company's quality improvement program. With this in mind, increments of quality cost measurements can be allocated to those categories that best fit the needs of the company. This is particularly applicable when a person's normal activities fall into more than one quality cost category, such as a tester who, in addition to acceptance testing, works part-time troubleshooting and part-time retesting because of failures. In this case, a company must decide whether to include the tester's total cost in the appraisal category or to separate out the failure increments of cost (troubleshooting and retesting), based entirely on its value to the company quality cost program. The decision is not nearly as important as consistency in execution.

Another problem that may be faced during procedure development is the soundness of key, related cost accounting practices. For example, if some waste (scrap) is accounted for but significant amounts are not, the company may decide to tighten up on the definition or practice. If significant costs are being expended because of customer problems, and not separately accounted for, the company may decide that now is the time to start accounting for them. Development of each quality cost procedure will provide some unique opportunities to refine the cost accounting details for improved financial management.

These improvements in cost reporting may actually cause quality costs to show an increase in the early phases of the program. This must be understood from the beginning to preclude disappointment on management's part, since it may be expecting a windfall cost reduction (see the discussion on cause-and-effect lag on page 40 and Figure 2.3 in chapter 2).

Internal company quality cost definitions should be approached in a practical manner. Using Appendix B, "Detailed Description of Quality Cost Elements," as a guide, each company should tailor these definitions to meet its own needs (see discussion on quality cost elements in chapter 2, page 33). With experience, quality cost elements can be created, deleted, or combined. There is no panacea for quality cost systems. Each system should harmonize to the greatest extent possible with the company cost accounting system, and it should be sufficient only to the actual quality improvement opportunities within the company.

QUALITY COST COLLECTION AND ANALYSIS

Preparing and officially issuing the internal quality cost procedure is a company's key commitment to the implementation and use of a quality cost system. This is one of the best things that could happen for the quality management program—and for the quality manager. Now the real work can begin.

Quality Cost Collection

Ideally, the internal quality cost procedure includes a complete system of cost elements, generated as discussed in the previous two sections of this chapter. These cost elements (or accounts) should be coded in such a way that the costs of prevention, appraisal, and internal and external failures could be easily distinguished and sorted. The cost elements described in Appendix B are coded in such a fashion. This is easily seen in the detailed quality cost element summary (Figure B.1) in Appendix B.

Using such a coding system, if all cost element codes beginning with 1. were sorted and totaled, the sum would be the total prevention cost. In a like manner, the sum of the 2's would be the total appraisal cost, and so on. If more detail is desired, the second digit in the cost element code could represent a breakout of further significance. For example, all the 1.3 codes in Appendix B represent prevention costs pertaining to purchasing. Additional digits could be added to the codes, depending on the level of detail desired.

Collection of quality cost labor becomes relatively easy with a system such as the one just described. Applicable quality cost element codes are entered on a labor distribution, charge, or time card, together with the hours expended against the cost elements represented by the codes. The labor hours are subsequently converted to dollars by data processing. An exception to this is scrap for which the labor hours cannot be collected on a real time basis for obvious reasons—you don't know you are making scrap while you are making it. The work must first be inspected, rejected, and dispositioned before it becomes scrap. In many companies, existing scrap reporting documents are forwarded to the estimating department, where the labor and material costs expended to the stage of completion of the scrapped items are estimated. This differs from what is generally termed "replacement cost," or the cost of the work if the job had been completed. We are only interested here in the labor and material dollars actually lost in the work accomplished up to the time of the work being scrapped.

Quality Cost Analysis

With the system of collecting quality costs implemented, a spreadsheet is prepared, listing the elements of quality cost to be collected against a spread of the departments, areas, and/or projects where the costs will occur (see Figure 3.2). Microsoft Excel®, Lotus 1-2-3®, or Quattro Pro® can be used to simplify this effort. This is set up to be used by accounting for each reporting period and will show what quality cost elements are being reported (or not being reported) by each reporting area. The next step is to collate the collected costs onto a second sheet, one designed to summarize the data in exact accordance with plans for use (see Figure 3.3). It is in these forms that the quality cost data will normally be presented to the quality department for use.

Element: Code	Element: Description	Accounting	Administration	Engineering	Estimating	Field services	Manufacturing engineering	Marketing	Procurement	Production	Production control	Quality	Receiving	Shipping	Totals
1.1.1	Marketing research														
1.1.2	Customer/user perception surveys/clinics														
1.1.3	Contract/document review														
1.2.1	Design quality progress reviews														
1.2.2	Design support activities														
1.2.3	Product design qualification test														
1.2.4	Service design — qualification														
1.2.5	Field trials														
1.3.1	Supplier reviews														
1.3.2	Supplier rating														
1.3.3	Purchase order tech data reviews														
1.3.4	Supplier quality planning														

Figure 3.2. Quality cost data spreadsheet.

QUALITY COST SUMMARY REPORT
FOR THE MONTH ENDING _______
(In thousands of U.S. dollars)

Description	Current month			Year to date		
	Quality costs	As a percent of		Quality costs	As a percent of	
		Sales	Other		Sales	Other
1.0 Prevention costs 1.1 Marketing/customer/user 1.2 Product/service/design development 1.3 Purchasing prevention costs 1.4 Operations prevention costs 1.5 Quality administration 1.6 Other prevention costs						
Total prevention costs						
Prevention targets						
2.0 Appraisal costs 2.1 Purchasing appraisal costs 2.2 Operations appraisal costs 2.3 External appraisal costs 2.4 Review of test and inspection data 2.5 Misc. quality evaluations						
Total appraisal costs						
Appraisal targets						
3.0 Internal failure costs 3.1 Product/service design failure costs 3.2 Purchasing failure costs 3.3 Operations failure costs 3.4 Other internal failure costs 4.0 External failure costs						
Total failure costs						
Failure targets						
Total quality costs						
Total quality targets						

Base data	Current month		Year to date		Full year	
	Budget	Actual	Budget	Actual	Budget	Actual
Net sales						
______________ Other base (specify)						

Figure 3.3. Quality cost summary report.

Initially, the data presented will be analyzed over a sufficient period of time, in conjunction with basic quality measurement data, to determine and verify current opportunities for improvement. It is expected, then, as part of overall quality improvement efforts, that these opportunities will be presented to the organizations involved for their understanding and commitment to problem identification, cause determination, and necessary corrective action. At this point, improvement targets can and should be established.

Remembering that quality costs are a support tool to the quality management program, it should be clear that further uses of quality cost data will be integral to the prime quality management or quality improvement program. Normally, the data will be used to develop individual trend charts to depict the initial opportunity, the targets for improvement, and the actual progress against the targets (see Figure 3.4). The data are also used to prepare overall progress charts (usually monthly or quarterly) for subsequent use with quality management reports (see Figure 3.5).

One of the biggest pitfalls to avoid in the implementation of a quality cost program is approaching it from a stand-alone point of view. Quality cost reports, even total quality costs, can have no meaning without the benefit of a meaningful dialogue about actual company performance—except, perhaps, as an act of flag waving.

ACTIVITY-BASED COSTING

Although quality costs can be identified and collected within the framework of any financial accounting system, one accounting method is particularly compatible with quality cost methodology and objectives—namely, Activity-Based Costing (ABC). The aim of Activity-Based Costing is to improve overall cost effectiveness through a focus on key cost elements. Quality cost methodology seeks to assign quality-related costs to specific activities, products, processes, or departments, so that these costs can be targeted for reduction. The use of ABC techniques makes it easier to find and assign these costs. The level of detail and the information content inherent in conventional accounting practices are often insufficient for adequate quality cost analysis and application to continuous improvement. ABC, on the other hand, because of its more detailed cost database, is better suited to these needs.

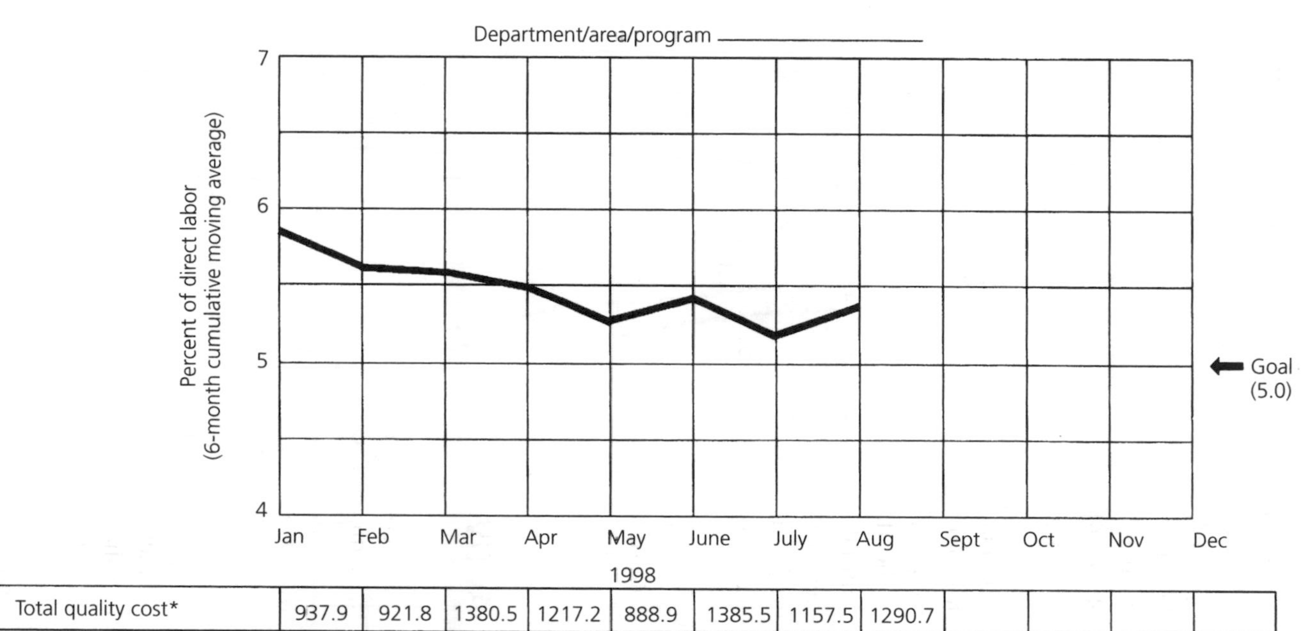

	Jan	Feb	Mar	Apr	May	June	July	Aug	Sept	Oct	Nov	Dec
Total quality cost*	937.9	921.8	1380.5	1217.2	888.9	1385.5	1157.5	1290.7				
Direct labor*	16,429	18,984	25,028	21,051	18,562	25,363	24,546	20,943				
% of direct labor	5.7	4.9	5.5	5.8	4.8	5.5	4.7	6.2				
6-month moving average	5.8	5.6	5.6	5.5	5.3	5.4	5.2	5.4				

*In thousands

Figure 3.4. Total quality costs.

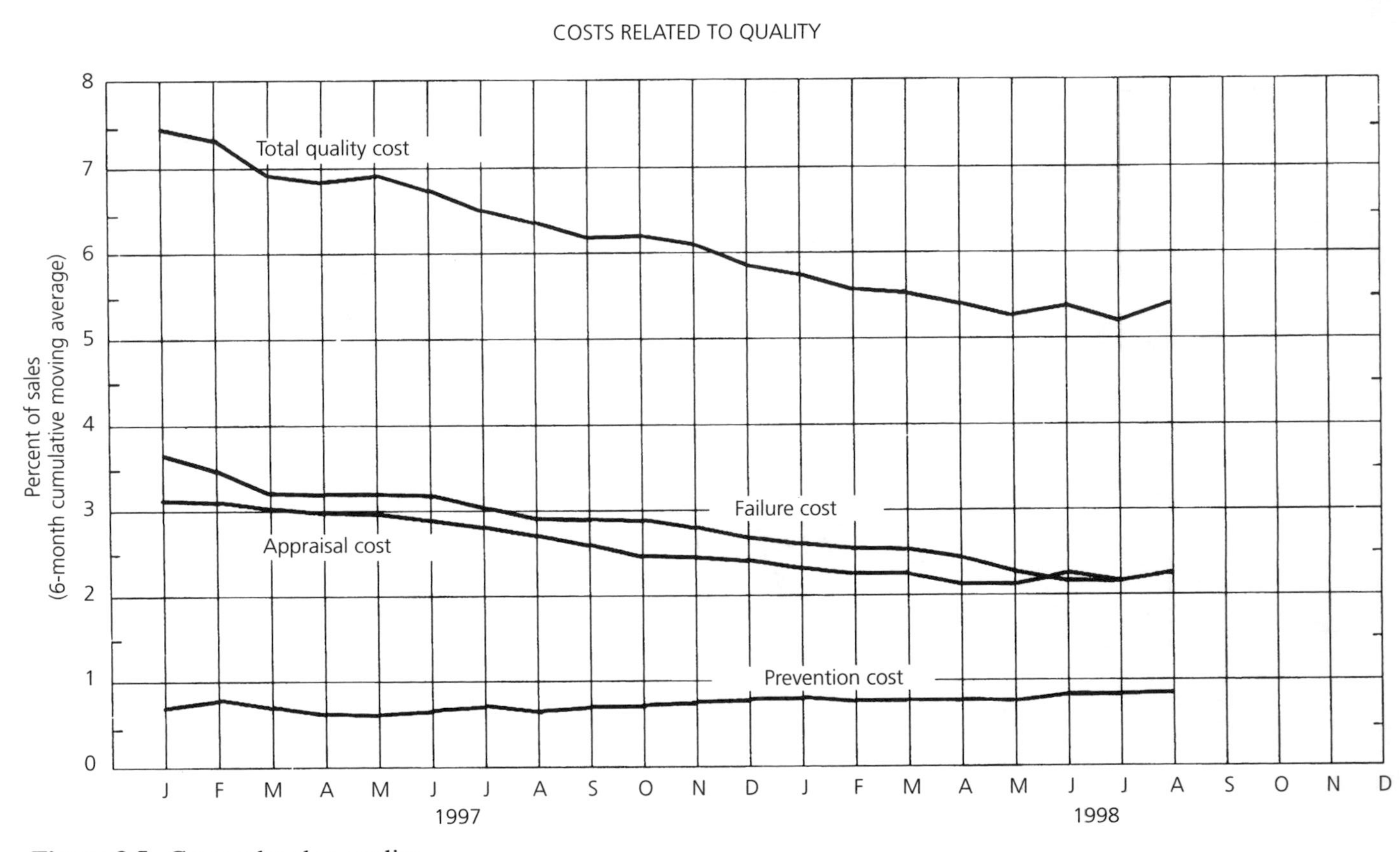

Figure 3.5. Costs related to quality.

Activity-Based Costing is an accounting procedure for allocating the cost of indirect and overhead expenses (the cost of an organization's resources) to specific activities in proportion to the use of a given resource by that activity. This is in contrast to conventional accounting practice, which allocates indirect and overhead expenses in proportion to direct costs incurred by an activity. In the sections that follow, we shall see, through examples, the implications of this accounting difference and how ABC can facilitate the use of quality costs to achieve continuous quality improvement.

Quality Costs and the Accounting Department

Once an organization decides to identify, collect, and monitor its quality costs, it usually turns to the accounting department and says in effect, "Find me all the costs of quality" or "Tell me what we are spending on prevention, appraisal, and failure." The accounting department normally comes back and says, "Wait a minute! That's not the way we collect our costs. We don't have accounting buckets called 'prevention', 'appraisal,' or 'failure'. We don't collect costs in such categories." So the next job is usually for a quality specialist to sit down with a member of the accounting department and together scan the existing accounting categories to identify those accounts that represent or contain costs that are quality-related. Sometimes this is relatively simple and straightforward. For example, there may be an inspection department whose total budget may represent appraisal activities, or there may be cost variances or overruns caused by failure to meet a deadline due to a quality problem. But in the vast majority of cases quality costs lie buried and must be uncovered. They are typically buried in the standard cost. Standard cost is the average planned cost expected to be incurred in a given year in the manufacture of a given product or the delivery of a given service. It consists of direct labor, direct materials, and overhead (see Appendix A). For example, a standard cost for a product may be based on a historical 90 percent yield, which means about 10 percent of the standard cost represents scrap. A 10 percent scrap level is planned. The cost of scrap would show in the accounting ledger only if it exceeded the planned 10 percent and would appear as a cost overrun. The quality specialist and the representative of the accounting department must devise new accounting categories to identify the real cost of scrap or rework.

On the other hand, the standard cost may represent a process whose cycle time and labor content is grossly inflated by the inclusion of nonvalue-added steps, such as waiting for missing assembly parts to arrive or waiting for information to fulfill an order in a retail operation. In these examples, the quality specialist and the accounting representative must break down the labor costs for assembling a product into those representing activities that are essential, such as soldering a lead, and those that do not add value, such as moving a batch of circuit boards into storage. In these examples, the direct labor or material costs included in the standard are separated into material or labor costs that are associated with an ideal product or process and those that represent waste. Note that we are dealing in these examples with direct costs. The breakout of quality costs, while not always easy, is at least conceptually sound. While the greater level of detail in ABC may make the cost separations easier, they can nevertheless be carried out with conventional cost accounting data, accompanied by judicious decisions as to what constitutes waste. However, the situation changes when it comes to overhead costs. Conventional accounting procedures often lead us into doing some things that really don't make sense in assigning overhead costs.

How Overhead Costs Are Assigned to Products or Services

To what costs are we referring when we speak of overhead and indirect costs? Figure 3.6 shows how costs can be incurred at various levels in an organization manufacturing a product. Similar considerations apply for delivering a service.

Some costs can be assigned directly to specific units of product or service. These typically are costs of the labor hours expended or the cost of incoming materials or energy consumed to produce a unit of output. These are called "direct costs" and at one time represented by far the largest frac-

Unit	Direct labor	Direct materials
	Machine hours	Energy usage
Batch	Setup	Material handling
	Scheduling	Shipping and receiving
Product support	Redesign	Engineering changes
	Bill of materials	Complaint investigation
Facility support	Property taxes	Insurance
	Depreciation	Maintenance

Figure 3.6. Levels at which costs are incurred.

tion of the cost of a product or service. Other costs, such as cost of setting up production for a batch of product or shipping or receiving multiple lots of product, are not assignable at the unit level, since they may depend on batch or lot size. A way must be devised to spread these costs over the units produced. There are still other activities that fall into the category of support services for several products or services. An example is complaint handling; another is purchasing. Finally, there are expenses that are incurred at the facility level that must be paid, whether or not there is any output—such expenses as property taxes, depreciation of plant, and insurance. Except for those costs incurred and assigned at the unit level, all the other costs shown in Figure 3.6 are overhead costs.

Overhead costs are those costs incurred to support product manufacturing or service operations (see Appendix A, p. 179 and 181). They consist of three parts:

1. Indirect material costs—These are the costs of supplies consumed in operations but are not directly a part of the end product, such as, shipping materials and perishable tools.
2. Indirect labor—These costs normally represent the wages of employees who do not work on the end product or on delivering the prime service but who support the production or service process, such as supervisors, operations support personnel, and maintenance people.
3. Fixed and miscellaneous expenses—These include depreciation, taxes, rent, warranties, and insurance.

Overhead costs in conventional accounting practice are incorporated into the standard cost and are done so in proportion to the amount of direct labor (or sometimes in proportion to machine hours or direct materials) already contained in the standard cost, i.e., consumed in providing a unit of output. The more direct labor involved in providing a product or service, the more overhead expense is assigned to that product or service. In the case of using direct labor content to apportion overhead costs, the direct labor can be said to be a "cost driver".

Let's consider an example of a plant that manufactures two products, "shafts" and "housings", and see how an indirect expense—namely, "material handling"—is assigned using conventional accounting methods and using Activity-Based Costing. The basic parameters of the problem are summarized in Figure 3.7. The data represent a single month.

Direct labor hours = 10,000
Total direct labor cost @ $15 per hour = $150,000
Labor content of shafts and housings = 0.25 hours

Number of loads transported = 1200
Material handling expense @ $10 per load = $12,000
Material handling requirement:
Shafts = 2 loads per 100 piece lot
Housings = 4 loads per 100 piece lot

Figure 3.7. Material handling monthly expense data.

The monthly material handling expense is $12,000. Since there are 10,000 hours of direct labor expended in the plant each month, each direct labor hour also carries a material handling overhead charge of $1.20 per hour.

[$12,000 / 10,000 hours = $1.20 per hour]

The direct labor content of these two products is identical, at 0.25 direct labor hours; each shaft and housing, therefore, is allocated $0.30 material handling charge.

[0.25 hours x $1.20 per hour = $0.30 (shaft or housing)]

This is true despite the fact that, in reality, there is more material handling involved in transporting the shafts (4 loads for housings vs. 2 loads for shafts).

Enter Activity-Based Costing

ABC assigns costs of resources to activities in proportion to the use of the particular resource by each activity. Hence, in the example, the $12,000 monthly cost of material handling is allocated as $10.00 to each load.

[$12,000 / 1200 loads carried = $10.00 per load]

The number of loads transported becomes the "cost driver," in contrast to the direct labor content. Since the housings require four loads at $10.00 per load, or $40.00, to transport a 100-piece lot, as opposed to only two loads at $10.00 per load, or $20.00, to transport a 100-piece lot of shafts, a material handling cost of $0.40 is allocated to the cost of producing a housing, whereas a cost of $0.20 is allocated to the manufacture of a shaft.

[$40.00 / 100 housings = $0.40 per housing]

[$20.00 / 100 shafts = $0.20 per shaft]

This is a more accurate assignment of costs than in the case of conventional accounting practice.

Now you will note from Figure 3.7 that the labor rate is $15.00 per hour and 0.25 hours is required to manufacture a shaft or housing—that is, $3.75. You could argue that it doesn't make a great deal of difference if an additional $0.20, $0.30, or $0.40 is added for material handling. And you would probably be right, especially since in the case of this overhead item the overhead rate is only an average of 8 percent. This is why conventional accounting methods have worked in the past. Overhead has represented only a small proportion of direct expense. But, in today's world, with automation and computer-controlled processes, the direct costs are overwhelmed by indirect costs and other overhead expenses.[1] It is not uncommon for overhead rates to be several hundred percent of direct labor costs. Under these circumstances, it is vitally important how we assign overhead costs if we are to have a hope of controlling and reducing them.

In the example, material handling, and specifically the number of loads transported, is a cost driver. In reality, there are many cost drivers, such as purchase orders, machine setups, complaint investigations, maintenance calls, engineering changes, and lost items. For each cost driver, an overhead rate is determined by dividing total costs for the driver (for example, total costs for all complaint investigations) by the number of driver events (for example, the number of complaints investigated). The results might be, for example, $70 per machine setup, $650 per complaint investigation, and $65 per maintenance call. These rates can then be applied to specific products or services, recognizing that different products use various components of overhead at different levels or, in some cases, may not use them at all. For example, if it costs $650 to investigate a complaint, and there are ten customer complaints associated with shafts in a given month, then ABC requires an assignment of $6500 of the overall customer complaint expense to shafts for that time period.

All of this seems like a lot more work for the accounting office. At one time, that would have been true. However, with the computerization that now exists in all state-of-the-art accounting departments, it is only the initial setup of the accounts that requires more accounting work. After that, everything is automatic, and, assuming proper data entry, accurate detailed cost information is available on request.

Using Activity-Based Costing to Identify and Analyze Quality Costs

While ABC makes possible more accurate assignment of all overhead costs and can lead, for example, to more correct product or service pricing, it offers a special benefit in the area of quality costs—namely, the better identification of those activities that can lead to quality improvement. For example, in the case of customer complaints, we are already talking about a quality cost (external failure). It is important for purposes of problem solving and continuous improvement that we know what portion of the customer complaint cost is assignable to shafts as opposed to housings.

In conventional accounting practice, we can always get this information by going to the customer service department and sorting through its complaint records. The problem is that this effort gets multiplied many times over when we consider the number of different products and the number of different types of quality costs with which we are confronted.

In addition, this task would have to be repeated at regular intervals, such as, every month, whereas in Activity-Based Accounting, this breakout has already been done for us. Moreover, the process that identifies and quantifies the many cost drivers in an organization provides a database that not only lets us find and properly assign quality costs but also helps us to take apart these quality costs, so that we can go from costs to cost drivers, from cost drivers to drivers of cost drivers, and ultimately to root causes.

In theory, we should be able to assign a quality cost to a root cause of a quality problem. This proves extremely valuable, since we can then calculate the return on investment and the payback time for investing to fix a root cause. The following example will illustrate this type of analysis.

From Cost Drivers to Root Causes

In an organization using Activity-Based Costing, an internal failure cost of $24,000 has been identified for a given year associated with the manufacture of its two products, shafts and housings. This internal failure cost is a result of reworking product, which accounts for $9600, or 40 percent of the internal failure cost, and of scrapping product, which accounts for $14,400, or 60 percent of the internal failure cost. For various reasons, different percentages of shafts could be reworked as compared with those of housings; hence, the percentages scrapped are also different for the two products. Rework and scrap are cost drivers in ABC terms.

Figure 3.8 shows how costs are assigned to the two products, shafts and housings, in proportion to the extent that each product consumes that

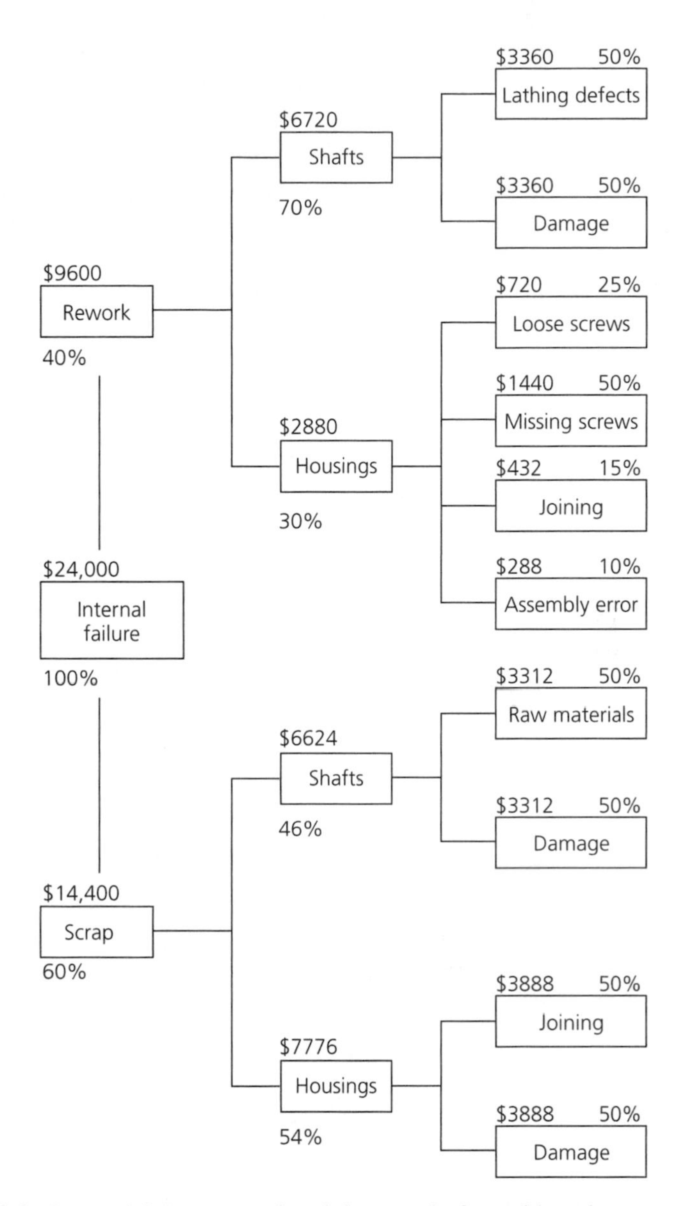

Figure 3.8. Internal failure costs breakdown—shafts and housings.

driver—that is, uses rework resources or accounts for scrap. But the analysis need not stop here, because we can and should ask what the causes for rework and scrap are, in the case of both the shafts and housings. These causes are also shown in Figure 3.8. These are drivers of drivers, or second order drivers. We see a total of seven causes distributed among the two products accounting for either rework or scrap. We essentially divide the costs of rework and scrap into the costs associated with the factors responsible for the rework and scrap.

The costs attributable to each cause are shown in Figure 3.8 and are summarized in Figure 3.9, where they are also displayed in Pareto fashion. From a quality improvement perspective, the biggest payback would result from finding the causes of "damage" and correcting them. This might require the identification of another level of causes and cost drivers. Perhaps some of these drivers will prove to be root causes.

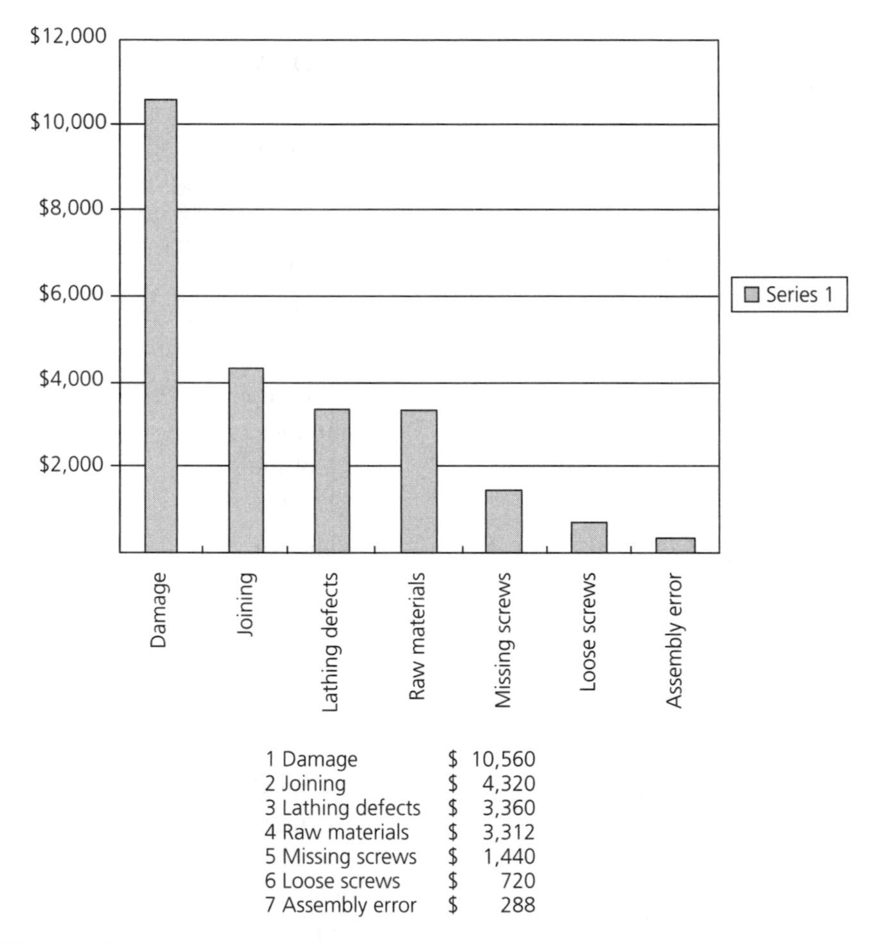

1 Damage	$	10,560
2 Joining	$	4,320
3 Lathing defects	$	3,360
4 Raw materials	$	3,312
5 Missing screws	$	1,440
6 Loose screws	$	720
7 Assembly error	$	288

Figure 3.9. Causes of failure.

Given the level of cost detail available from ABC, it is possible to estimate the cost impact of fixing a cause. In the example cited, $10,560 is a result of "damage" to both shafts and housings. If 75 percent of the damage could be eliminated through identifying and correcting root causes, a savings of $7920 per year would result. The estimated savings can then be compared to the required investment. In the example, if an investment of $4000 is required, the payback period for the investment can be calculated—in this case, $4000/$7920, or approximately six months. The level of detail inherent in Activity-Based Costing, thus—enables cost-benefit analysis and provides for sound investment decision making for continuous quality improvement.[2]

Using ABC to Identify Quality Costs

A five-step process has been recommended by D. W. Webster[3] for using Activity-Based Costing to identify the costs of poor quality:

1. Identify all activities, (appraisal and prevention), and results (internal and external failures).
2. Determine the activity costs associated with prevention and appraisal tasks, and with internal and external failures.
3. Identify the activities that benefit from prevention and appraisal activities and that cause internal and external failures.
4. Assign the Activity-Based Cost of quality as appropriate. Assign the cost of prevention and appraisal to the activities that benefit from prevention and appraisal. Assign the costs of internal and external failures to the activities identified as the root causes of these failures.
5. Adjust the calculated costs of products and services to reflect these additional costs of quality.

Conclusion

The use of Activity-Based Costing in conjunction with quality cost analysis offers several advantages:

1. Overhead costs, which may represent by far the largest portion of the cost of a product or service, can be accurately broken down and assigned to the product, department, process, or activity that is responsible for these costs. The computerization of cost systems has greatly reduced the cost of obtaining more accurate information characteristic of Activity-Based Costing.

2. A great many quality costs are in the overhead category, rather than in the direct category. This is particularly true of "hidden" quality costs—that is, those intangible costs that do not fit the conventional categories of rework, scrap, warranties, etc. (See the discussion of hidden quality costs on page 7). With ABC, they may be accurately assigned.
3. With the proper assignment of overhead costs, the calculation of the cost of poor quality changes and often affects the identification of the vital few areas for quality improvement. This impacts project selection and investment decisions.
4. Distinctions between high-performing departments or processes and low-performing departments or processes, with respect to quality, become more obvious when overhead is properly allocated.
5. The changes in quality costs over time can be more realistically gauged when the artifacts of arbitrarily assigned overhead costs are eliminated.
6. Nonvalue-added and noncost-effective activities can be more readily identified and eliminated, thus leading to improvements in cycle time, as well as in quality and costs.

Chapter 4
Use of Quality Costs

QUALITY IMPROVEMENT AND QUALITY COSTS

Once the quality cost system is installed, its principal use is to justify and support quality performance improvement in each major area of product or service activity. Performance improvement starts with the identification of problems. In this context, a problem is defined as an area of high quality cost. Every problem thus identified is an opportunity for profit improvement, because every dollar saved in the total cost of quality is directly translatable into a dollar of pretax earnings.

Chapter 5, "Quality Improvement and Quality Cost Reduction," describes techniques for using quality cost data in programs to improve quality, reduce costs, and thereby improve profits. Chapter 5 clearly identifies that the effective use of quality costs means full integration with the quality measurement and corrective action system. Fundamentally, quality cost measurements are established for each major product/service line or cost center within the total operation. As these measurements become an integral part of the quality measurement system, coupled with the identification and elimination of the causes of defects, they have logically come to provide the language for improvement potential and goals.

Actual progress in quality improvement and quality cost reductions cannot be legislated. It must be earned through the hard work process of problem solving. There are many methods for the analysis of quality data, but it also requires knowledge of company operations and the processes involved. Knowledge of basic statistics and problem-solving techniques are also important. Once a cause in need of correction is identified, the action necessary must be carefully determined, and it must be individually justified on the basis of an equitable cost trade-off, for example, a $200 per week rework problem versus a $5000 solution. At this point, experience in measuring quality costs will be invaluable in estimating the true payback for individual corrective action investments. Cost benefit justification of corrective action is an ongoing part of the quality management program.

It should be recognized that the generation of errors and defects is not limited to operations personnel. Errors that result in waste and rework are often caused by product/service and process design engineers, by the designers and fabricators of tools and operating equipment, by those individuals who determine process capabilities, and by those who provide the written instructions for the operator. Also, errors that affect product or service can be caused by the calibration technician, the maintenance person, or even the material handlers. Clearly, almost anyone within the total operation can contribute to failure costs. Effective corrective action, therefore, can and will take many avenues throughout the operating organization.

Some problems have fairly obvious solutions and can be fixed immediately, such as the replacement of a worn machine bearing or a worn tool. Others are not as obvious, such as a marginal condition in design or processing, and are almost never discovered and corrected without the benefit of a well-organized and formal approach supported by related costs. Marginal conditions often result in problems that become lost in the accepted cost of doing business. Having an organized corrective action system justified by quality costs will cause such problems to surface for management's visibility and demand for action.

The thing to remember about corrective action is that you only have to pay for it once, whereas failure to take corrective action may be paid for over and over again.

Another important use of quality costs is its use as an integral part of quality management reporting. Quality management reports are used to report quality progress and to focus attention on areas needing improvement. They are used to inform management of overall status and, in a more direct manner, to promote and support needed action in each major area. Without quality costs as a focal point for demanding action and reporting progress, quality management reporting would be a more difficult task. There is no better way to measure the overall success of the quality improvement program. If improvement is being achieved, problems are being resolved and quality costs are being reduced.

When quality costs are being used in quality management reports, caution should be exercised in attempting to compare different product/service lines or operations areas. People inexperienced in the ways of quality costs probably have a tendency to compare complex operations with relatively simple ones and expect similar results. This can never be. Areas pushing the state of the art and new activities in general will have higher quality costs as a percentage of some base than will mature, well-performing operations. There is always a danger in comparing quality costs. It pays to keep the focus on reduction, regardless of starting level.

QUALITY COSTS AND THE STRATEGIC BUSINESS PLAN

One mission of the quality management function is to educate top management about the long-range effects of total quality performance on the profits and quality reputation of the company. Management must become convinced that strategic planning for quality is as essential as planning for any other functional area. Unless the ingredient of quality is truly built into company operations from the first concept of a new product or service to the ultimate satisfaction of its users, all of which may take years, a company cannot be truly confident about the degree of actual customer satisfaction that will be achieved.

The strategic planning process focuses on costs. It is management's way of substantiating future profits. Because it is cost-oriented, the cost of quality allows the quality function to readily meet the challenge of inclusion in this important planning activity for the company. Quality costs allow the effect of the management of quality to be cost quantified. It further allows quality costs to be considered in the plans and budgets for each department or area where they occur. Thus, quality cost systems can be viewed as the breakthrough that allows the quality function to become a bona fide member of the company's (cost-oriented) management team.

The strategic planning process involves, in general, a review and an analysis of past performance and present position; the establishment of business objectives based on actual current or anticipated conditions; the election of specific, strategic action plans to achieve the objectives; and the implementation and monitoring phase. The quality function's role in this process should be to

- Analyze major trends in customer satisfaction, defects or error rates, and quality costs, both generally and by specific program or project. These trends should also be used to provide inputs for setting objectives
- Assist other functions to ensure that costs related to quality are included in their analyses for setting objectives
- Develop an overall quality strategic plan which incorporates all functional quality objectives and strategic action plans, including plans and budget for the quality function

There is no better way for the quality management function to "put its stake in the ground" than to develop a strategic quality plan substantiated by quality costs and to have this plan committed to in the overall company business plan.

SUPPLIER QUALITY COSTS

Supplier quality costs, if tracked, can be significant and can be good indicators of problem areas. A system of managing and tracking supplier quality costs follows the methods discussed for quality costs in general. They, too, are categorized as prevention, appraisal, and failure costs, as defined in chapter 2, pages 31–33. Supplier quality costs include prevention cost elements, such as the cost of supplier quality surveys; appraisal cost elements, such as the costs of receiving and source inspection; and failure cost elements, such as the cost of dispositioning nonconforming purchased material, the costs of scrap and rework of supplier-caused nonconformances, and the cost of site visits to correct supplier service problems.

Hidden Supplier Quality Costs

There are supplier quality costs that are apparent and relatively easy to identify and assign to various suppliers by the buyer, such as those examples just mentioned. However, there are also hidden supplier quality costs, just as there are hidden quality costs in any quality cost system (see page 7).

Hidden supplier quality costs are divided into three parts:

- Those incurred by the supplier at the supplier's facility
- Those incurred by the buyer in solving problems at the supplier's facility
- Those usually not allocated to suppliers but incurred by the buyer as a result of potential or actual supplier problems

Quality costs incurred by the supplier at their facility are unknown to the buyer and, therefore, hidden. Even though the magnitude is hidden, the types of costs are not. They are the same types of quality costs the buyer incurs. For example, the supplier certainly has prevention efforts. If they make a product, they have expenses related to the quality engineering of the product. Even if the supplier is a small shop, this task must be done by someone and may very well be handled by the production supervisor if the plant lacks a quality engineering staff. Certainly, effort is expended in the appraisal area, even by the smallest suppliers. Someone must inspect the product or service prior to delivery. (In a one-person shop, this is done by the person who made the item.) Also, each shop, whether it is large or small, has failure costs. When the supplier makes a mistake in manufacturing, they must either rework the item or scrap it, causing an internal failure cost. If the supplier sends it to the buyer, it may be rejected, creating an external failure cost for the supplier. If the supplier is performing a service and the buyer is not satisfied, the supplier can either redo the work or replace the original product with a new one (for example, a dry cleaner ruining a garment), both external failure costs.

The second type of hidden cost, that which is incurred by the buyer in solving problems at the supplier's facility, is usually not specifically allocated to suppliers. Except for an awareness of troublesome suppliers, there is usually no tabulation of the cost of the effort or the travel expenses involved. Therefore, the actual expense is hidden. An example is the cost to the buyer of sending a quality engineer to a supplier to resolve a crisis.

The last type of hidden quality cost occurs at the buyer's facility. This type of cost may include the following:

- Specifying and designing gages that must be used by the buyer's receiving inspection and, perhaps as well, by the supplier prior to shipping
- Designing appropriate specifications that the supplier must follow in the manufacture of the product or the performing of the service
- Adding special inspection operations and quality control effort in the buyer's production line related specifically to a supplier product
- Reviewing test and inspection data on supplier material to determine acceptability for processing in the buyer's facility

- Calibrating and maintaining equipment necessary in the quality control of supplier material
- Losing production time due to unavailability of good material
- Field engineering required to analyze and correct a problem caused by a supplier

It must be remembered that this discussion of the types of supplier-related hidden costs is by no means exhaustive. There are many more, some of which may be significant in an individual situation.

Application of Quality Costs to Supplier Control

Initially, the buyer, in order to reduce supplier-related quality costs, must determine what costs are important. Comparing the relative magnitudes of quality costs by category and element should be the first step. The company's quality cost program could be an invaluable aid to accomplishing this analysis. For example, assume a situation in which purchased material rejections are the buyer's biggest problem. If the buyer has reason to believe that quality costs will be lowered through improvements in the purchased material rejection rate, then this is the important item for this company.

The next step is to do a Pareto analysis (see chapter 5) to determine which suppliers are causing the problem. Very likely, then it will be found that relatively few suppliers are causing most of the problems. Then the buyer can focus effort on the "vital few" suppliers and take appropriate action.

What is appropriate action? The buyer might convince the vital few suppliers to institute quality cost programs, if practical for them. Discretion must be exercised before insisting on this. Some companies may be too small to support a quality cost program. Special circumstances may exist in other companies that would prohibit this action. However, if a supplier finds that launching such a program is feasible, the costs most visible to the buyer most likely will be reduced by doing so. If these costs are reduced, the hidden costs expended by both the buyer and the vital few suppliers should also be lowered. The result will be that the quality of both the supplier's product/service and the buyer's product/service will improve. This should increase profits for both. Also, improved profitability for the supplier may eventually result in lower prices for the buyer in a competitive market.

What other action can be taken if we know the magnitude of the supplier quality costs? It is possible that these costs can be incorporated into a buyer's supplier rating system. Besides the traditional inputs of price, delivery, and incoming rejection rate, the supplier rating system should also incorporate supplier quality costs as described in the following example.

A Supplier Rating Program Using Quality Costs

One successful application of quality costs in a supplier rating program has been in operation for several years by an electrical products manufacturer. Although not theoretically perfect, this system has proven its effectiveness in improving supplier quality, and it is certainly an outstanding example of a practical and workable approach. The company actually uses a dual supplier rating system. The first portion is quite traditional in that it tracks price and delivery, and it will not be discussed here. The second part, however, evaluates supplier quality cost performance for each supplier, using an index based on the following formula:

$$\text{QCPI} = \frac{\text{Supplier Quality Cost} + \text{Purchased Cost}}{\text{Purchased Cost}}$$

No attempt was made to include all supplier quality costs because of the administrative problems involved. Therefore, those costs that were important for this particular company were identified.

Cost of Processing Incoming Rejections. Through a special study, it was determined that each rejected lot of material required approximately $100 of expense to document and return to the supplier. Therefore, the total cost of a supplier's rejected shipments over a period of time was estimated to be the number of rejected lots for the supplier multiplied by $100.

Example

$$2 \text{ Rejected Lots} \times \$100/\text{Rejected Lot} = \$200$$

Cost of Complaint Investigations. As one might anticipate, a special study of the time needed to investigate complaints showed that this could not be estimated to any degree of accuracy. Therefore, each engineer was asked to document the investigation time required for each supplier. The total cost of complaint investigations was estimated to be the investigation time for that supplier multiplied by the average hourly wages and fringe benefits of an engineer.

Example

$$10 \text{ Hours Investigation Time} \times \$20 = \$200$$

Cost of Processing in Receiving Inspection. Because this company had labor standards in receiving inspection, this cost could be estimated by using the appropriate labor standard, the average hourly wages and fringe benefits of a receiving inspector, and the number of lots processed for a particular supplier.

Example

1.00 Std. Hour/Lots × $15/Hour × 50 Lots = $750

Cost of a Defective Product after Receiving Inspection. This was the most difficult to evaluate, because a defective product could be either reworked or scrapped. If scrapped, the cost might not be recovered from the supplier, depending on how clearly responsibility could be assigned. Also, when a defective part is found, sorting the remaining parts in the lot might be the best alternative. Fortunately, a special study indicated that, no matter what action was taken, the purchased cost of that part provided an acceptable estimate of the quality costs incurred. Therefore, this cost was estimated for each supplier by multiplying the number of defective parts found after receiving inspection by the initial purchase price of the part.

Example

100 Rejected Parts × $1.80 Purchased Price/Part = $180

Caution: This method of estimating the cost of a defective product should not be adopted before verifying by a special study that it is reasonable under your specific circumstances.

Supplier Quality Cost. This company's supplier quality cost for the supplier in question equals the sum of its costs of

Processing incoming rejections	=	$200
Complaint investigations	=	200
Processing in receiving inspection	=	750
Defective product after receiving inspection	=	180
Supplier quality cost	=	$1330

A ranking of suppliers supplying similar parts by quality cost performance index follows.

Supplier	Supplier Quality Cost ($)	Purchased Cost ($)	Index (QCPI)
A	2410	99,928	1.024
B	1950	40,000	1.049
C	2800	43,643	1.064
D	2500	12,230	1.204
E	7000	7,631	1.917

Example of index calculation for supplier A

$$\text{QCPI} = \frac{\text{SQ Cost} + \text{Purchased Cost}}{\text{Purchased Cost}} = \frac{\$2410 + \$99{,}928}{\$99{,}928} = 1.024$$

The company also developed a method of interpreting the quality cost performance index to assess each supplier. A perfect supplier would have no quality costs, since there would be no rejections, there would be no complaint investigations, and receiving inspection would be unnecessary. Therefore, the index for a perfect supplier would be

$$\text{QCPI} = \frac{\text{SQ Cost} + \text{Purchased Cost}}{\text{Purchased Cost}} = \frac{0 + \text{Purchased Cost}}{\text{Purchased Cost}} = 1.000$$

The actual assessment used by this company was

Index (QCPI)	Interpretation
1.000–1.009	Excellent
1.010–1.039	Good
1.040–1.069	Fair
1.070–1.099	Poor
1.100+	Immediate corrective action required

Using this assessment, first priority for this company was to obtain immediate corrective action for suppliers D and E. Results for the overall program were encouraging, with the percentage of total suppliers rated good or better increasing from 75 percent to 80 percent and supplier quality costs reducing 8.5 percent, in the first year.

Many variations and innovations can be developed for using quality costs to evaluate supplier performance. How it is done is less important than the recognition of the size and impact of the supplier-related quality costs. Once these are recognized, planned steps can be developed for measuring, comparing, and analyzing so that improvement can be made.

A Return on Investment Analysis Using Supplier Quality Costs

The previously discussed firm also developed a return on investment and analysis strategy using supplier quality costs. Supplier E had a quality performance index (QCPI) of 1.917. This was interpreted to require immediate corrective action on the part of the buyer company.

First thoughts of the company centered on canceling the contract with supplier E and transferring the tools to either supplier A, B, or C, all of which had much better quality performance indices. A closer look at the situation revealed that supplier A, B, or C may not do much better initially, since this was a new generic product that was undergoing significant start-up expenses. A trip to supplier E revealed that, although the company did not have a staff of problem solvers, its quality system and manufacturing equipment were adequate.

The buyer then considered the idea of sending a problem solver in its company to supplier E for two weeks to expedite the reduction of start-up difficulties. In making this decision, the return on investment (ROI) concept was used:

$$\text{ROI} = \frac{\text{Savings} \times 100}{\text{Investment}}$$

Savings would be the reduction in supplier quality costs anticipated through this approach. In time, the purchased cost probably would be reduced as well. The investment for doing this would be the wages, fringes, and travel expenses of the problem solver. For this situation, a potential reduction of $6000 in quality costs was estimated for an investment of $1500 to provide help to supplier E. The return on investment was

$$\text{ROI} = \frac{\$6000 \times 100}{\$1500} = 400\%$$

Obviously, this is a good idea, if the objectives can be achieved.

COST OF QUALITY IN SMALL BUSINESS

This section discusses quality costs in the small business sector. It will present the results of research at four small firms and will provide recommendations on making a cost of quality study in a small manufacturing or service firm.[1]

The Companies Studied

Four companies were interviewed to gather information regarding the cost of quality in small businesses. The companies include two manufacturing concerns and two from the service sector.

The first of the manufacturing companies makes plastic packaging for use in the food industry. Plastic film on rolls is bonded together to form bags, and these go through a rolling process in which the customer's logo is printed on the outside of the bag. The product is then cut to the specified size. The company employs from 100 to 249 people and has annual sales of between $20 and $50 million.

The second manufacturing company makes electrical surge protectors. The casings for the protectors are purchased from outside sources, and the company makes and assembles the inner components. The firm employs from 100 to 200 people and has annual sales between $2 and $8 million.

The first of the service industries provides computer programming services and prepackaged software. This company is involved with computer software analysis and the design and development of database decision system software. It employs 90 to 110 people and has annual sales of approximately $14 million.

The last company interviewed is a managed health-care services company. The firm acts as an intermediary between insurance companies and the insured. It employs approximately 500 people, and its annual revenues are between $25 and $50 million.

Results of the Study

A summary of the research results is presented in Table 4.1. For each of the four categories of the cost of quality (prevention, appraisal, internal failure, and external failure), the table specifies the elements of cost which the companies reported as applicable (indicated by an *X*). In addition, the "Yes/No" notation refers to the capturing of data: "Yes" means that the firm currently records the data; "No" means that the data is not currently being recorded but could be.

Table 4.1. Summary of categories.

Category/Element	Manufacturing 1		Manufacturing 2		Service 1		Service 2	
Internal Failure								
1. Scrap	X	Yes	X	Yes	X	Yes		N/A
2. Rework	X	Yes	X	Yes	X	Yes	X	Yes
3. Analysis	X	No	X	No	X	No	X	No
4. Supplier	X	Yes		N/A	X	No	X	No
5. Sorting		N/A	X	No		N/A	X	No
6. Downgrading	X	Yes	X	Yes		N/A		N/A
External Failure								
1. Warranty		N/A	X	No	X	No		N/A
2. Complaint Adjustment	X	No	X	No	X	No	X	No
3. Returned material	X	Yes	X	Yes		N/A		N/A
4. Allowances	X	Yes	X	Yes	X	No	X	No
Appraisal								
1. Incoming	X	No	X	No	X	No	X	No
2. In-process	X	No	X	No	X	No	X	No
3. Final	X	No	X	No	X	No	X	No
4. Quality audit	X	No	X	No	X	No	X	No
5. Equipment test	X	No	X	No	X	No		N/A
6. Materials and Service		N/A	X	No	X	No		N/A
7. Inventory		N/A	X	No		N/A		N/A
Prevention								
1. Quality plan	X	No	X	No	X	No	X	No
2. Products review	X	No	X	No	X	No	X	No
3. Process plan	X	No	X	No		N/A		N/A
4. Quality audit	X	No	X	No	X	No	X	No
5. Supplier evaluation	X	No		N/A	X	No	X	No
6. Training		N/A	X	No		N/A	X	No

X—Indicates element applies to company
Yes—Indicates data is currently captured
No—Indicates data is not currently captured but could be

Internal Failure Costs. In all of the companies interviewed, the element of rework is an applicable cost of quality, and in all cases each company is currently capturing this figure from basic data now recorded. Scrap applies to three of the four companies; however, one of the service companies is a hybrid, and scrap is tracked in the manufacturing area of the company. It appears that scrap may not apply in the service industries. All of the companies answered "Yes" to the area of failure analysis, but none of them is currently capturing the amount spent in this area (each indicated that this amount could be determined by using time estimates from time cards and then converting the time data to dollars). No pattern was observed across firms with respect to the supplier area or 100 percent sorting (two of the companies indicated that this applies, two indicated that it does not). The manufacturing companies indicated that they do lower prices because of a product downgrade and are able to capture this amount; this area does not apply to the service firms.

External Failure Costs. One area, Complaint Adjustment, applies to all companies. None of the firms is currently capturing the costs in this area, but each company indicated that these charges could be captured. The methods for estimating the costs vary, but all of the methods are based on some method of determining or collecting the actual hours spent on the adjustment of complaints. Also, since the companies are small, most of the complaints are handled by middle or upper-level management. These individuals indicated that their time could be determined through better records of the time and money spent in this area.

Another element that applies to all companies is Allowances. Each company indicated that concessions are made to customers when they accept substandard products. The manufacturing companies are capturing these costs using data that are currently being recorded. The service companies, however, are not currently capturing these costs. Both service companies indicated that these costs could be determined using current data (either penalties charged by the customer or the amount of fees waived because of the problem encountered).

Appraisal Costs. Incoming, In-process, and Final Inspection and Testing; and Product Quality audits apply to all of the companies surveyed. However, none of the companies is currently capturing these costs. All companies indicated that these costs could be determined if their labor reporting were more specific—that is, if time cards were used for each individual action performed by employees. This is a pervasive theme throughout this analysis; the use of more definitive labor reporting would allow most of the costs of quality to be captured and dollarized. None of the other areas of Appraisal applies to all of the companies interviewed; nor is there any pattern, such as "Yes" for manufacturing and "No" for service.

Prevention Costs. The areas that apply to all of the companies are Quality planning, New Products review, and Quality audit. All companies indicated that these costs are not currently being captured but could be. Once again, the overriding factor seems to be that the more efficient use of time cards would serve as a means of determining the costs in these areas. No pattern is evident in the other areas in this category.

Overview. Two themes seem to be basic to all of the companies. First, since the firms are small, a great many quality problems are handled by management, often without understanding the extra costs incurred throughout the honeycomb of the firm. Each company indicated in its own way that the costs of correcting problems could be captured if the individuals involved would keep records of the costs incurred in solving problems and pacifying customers.

The other issue pervasive across companies is that the costs of quality that apply but are not being captured could be captured or estimated through the use of some method of time-capturing device, for example, time cards indicating the amount of time spent on specific areas of inspection, testing, etc. Also, since the companies are small, management is able to talk out problems with one another. The time spent solving problems is also a cost of quality. This cost could also be estimated from meeting minutes, better recordkeeping by the individuals involved, and so on.

The Impact of Quality on Sales Revenue

Traditionally, the measurement of the cost of quality has focused on the costs of nonconformances—that is, defects or errors in the goods or services delivered to external or internal customers (external and internal failure costs). An important cost that is not usually measured is lost sales due to poor quality. This is referred to as a hidden cost (see discussion on page 7), because it has not been measured. These lost sales are due to customer dissatisfaction with the goods or services provided. This dissatisfaction may result in a loss of current customers—"customer defections"—and an inability to attract new customers because of a tarnished quality reputation.

This loss is difficult to measure, although, if sufficient market research information is available, it can sometimes be used with other information to estimate the loss of sales revenue due to poor quality.[2] In any event, the impact of quality on sales revenue should be considered, at least by identifying the areas of customer dissatisfaction and by taking action to improve the retention of current customers and to create new customers.

Recommendations for Making an Initial Cost of Quality Study

One approach follows these steps:

1. In monetary terms, introduce management to whatever data are available. The effect will be to indicate how big the problem potentially is in terms that will get their attention.
2. Propose that a committee be formed to gauge the cost of quality. Ideally, someone from management should chair this committee, and it should include additional personnel from major line functions.
3. Adapt the elements comprising the costs of quality to fit the firm. This list can be prepared by a quality manager or a finance manager, with input from accounting and other functions.
4. Have upper-level management affirm the definitions and assign duties based on these definitions, including an agenda for data collection.
5. Collect, summarize, and analyze the data. The analysis should identify the "vital few" failure costs. Specific improvement projects should then be proposed to determine and remove the root causes.
6. Select one improvement project and pursue it using modern problem-solving tools of quality improvement.[3] This first project should be carefully selected to learn and demonstrate the effectiveness of the problem-solving tools.
7. Review the full study and select additional improvement projects to pursue.

This approach provides an opportunity for upper management to demonstrate leadership on quality, and it also assures the involvement of functions so that the study receives priority and the results are recognized as credible.

In defining the costs of quality, the following guidelines should be kept in mind:

1. Customize the definition for your own organization. The failure, appraisal, and prevention categories presented here have proven useful in practice. As a possible starting point, use that framework, along with the elements reported in Table 4.1 for a manufacturing or a service firm. Review Appendix B for additional elements that may apply to your organization. Create a draft of the definitions of categories and show it to various functions, asking their input on additional elements or changes in wording. What results from all this are the "right" definitions for your firm. Whether these definitions conform to the literature is not critical.
2. Obtain agreement of the executive management team on the elements of cost to be included before any data are collected. Sometimes, summarized data on one or two key elements, such as scrap and rework, can gain management's attention and stimulate the need for a full study. The accountant could be asked to review this paper and other literature to prepare a draft of definitions of elements. The executive team could then review and discuss the draft and finalize the definitions.
3. Don't limit the definitions to only costs that directly involve the goods or services sold to customers, such as scrap, rework, and complaints. Poor quality is now viewed as applying to any activity in the company. Any work that must be discarded or reprocessed should be viewed as a failure cost of quality. Thus, when information is missing from a document, the time spent in retrieving the missing information contributes to the cost of quality.
4. Don't accept as inevitable certain camouflaged costs that are routinely incurred but are really part of the cost of quality. In manufacturing, some examples are costs of redesigning a product because it fails to meet customer needs or costs of changing processes because they are unable to meet product specifications. In the service sector, watch for activities that are described with such words as *rework, check, expedite, correct, adjustment,* and *shrinkage.*

Focus on the internal and external failure cost categories, because these provide the major opportunity for the removal of causes of customer dissatisfaction and reduction in costs of quality. These costs should be attacked first—"that's where the money is." Determining the root causes and removing them will require some level of diagnosis, but the investment of time and resources in diagnosis can achieve a benefit-to-cost ratio of between 5 to 1 and 10 to 1.

Appraisal costs are also an area for potential reduction, but not until the causes of the failure costs have been identified and removed, thereby reducing the need for appraisal.

In the initial study, cost data are collected from different sources:

1. *Established accounts.* Examples are scrap or rework accounts that quantify the costs incurred in these areas, and price reductions due to product downgrades.

2. *Analysis of ingredients of established accounts.* Check to make sure that only the costs of quality are included in the analysis. For example, customer returns will probably include returns for reasons other than product defects. These should not be quantified in the analysis. It may be necessary to view the source documents to determine the reason for the return.

3. *Basic accounting documents.* For example, inspection costs incurred in the operations area could be quantified by obtaining the names and associated payroll data of the employees responsible.

4. *Estimates.* Several approaches may be needed:

   a. *Temporary records.* For example, some production workers spend part of their time repairing defective product. Timekeeping devices could be used to establish temporary records to capture costs incurred to repair defective products. These could help to estimate total repair costs.

   b. *Work sampling.* This random sampling approach determines the percentage of time spent in each of a number of predefined tasks. This percentage could then lead to an estimate of the costs incurred in these areas.

   c. *Allocation of total resources.* For example, in the shipping department, part of the employee's time is spent on inspecting before packaging the product. There may be, however, no provision for capturing this cost. To quantify this time and cost, ask each employee to estimate time spent on inspection while packaging the product.

d. *Unit cost data.* Determine the cost of correcting a single error. This cost can then be multiplied by the estimated number of errors of the same type that are expected per year. Examples include billing errors and scrap.

Reporting the Cost of Quality

Reporting the cost of quality can take three forms:

1. Special reports to support activities on quality improvement projects
2. Periodic reports to summarize current status on selected elements of the cost of quality
3. Comprehensive reports similar to the initial study described earlier

As structured quality improvement teams using the project-by-project approach have emerged as a strong force, reporting on the cost of quality has focused on supporting activities for quality improvement projects. These reports should include information to help diagnose the problem, and information to track the change in costs as a problem-solving remedy is implemented. What data is needed is determined by the team, and the team often collects its own data.

Although some companies have used a quality cost scoreboard to periodically give the status of key elements of the cost of quality, the trend is for the cost of quality and other quality-related information to become integrated into the overall performance reporting system of organizations. A limited number of measures would be reported, including the cost of quality and any information on the impact of quality on sales revenue.

Periodically—say, annually—a comprehensive report on the cost of quality is useful to summarize and consolidate the efforts and results of project teams and other quality improvement activities. Such a report should

1. Reflect the results of improvement efforts
2. Provide guidance to identify major areas for future improvement efforts

Additionally, the report should be expressed in terms that are meaningful to management. The cost of quality can be related to several other measures. To determine what measures might be used, see the section on Quality Cost Bases in Chapter 2.

The comparative base used will determine the effect that the results of the study will have on the attitude of management. For instance, the executives interviewed in the four firms discussed earlier thought that costs as a percentage of sales revenue, as a percentage of profit, and as dollars per unit of product produced, were meaningful measures.

Conclusions

Several promising conclusions emerge from this research.

First, small firms can estimate the cost of quality easier than large firms. The smaller number of personnel and fewer lines of communication in small firms make it easier to trace and determine the costs of events that lead to poor quality.

Second, analyzing the components of the cost of quality spotlights where most of this loss exists and, thus, defines the areas where improvement efforts should be focused to improve quality and reduce the extra costs of poor quality.

Finally, addressing the major contributors to the cost of quality by finding and eliminating the root causes furnishes a golden opportunity for a firm to provide customers with better value. These days, all firms claim to have products with the "best value" but this claim can be made tangible by using the savings in cost of quality (achieved by a quality improvement effort) to:

1. Finance additional product features without raising prices, or
2. Lower prices for products with existing features. Either route to increased value will, of course, lead to higher sales income for the firm.

For many firms, estimating the cost of quality can be the catalyst to fuel action-oriented steps to achieve quality improvement.

SOFTWARE QUALITY COSTS

Software is the computer programs, associated procedures, documentation, and data pertaining to the operation of a computer system. As a purely intellectual product, it is among the most labor-intensive, complex, and error-prone technologies in human history. Differentiated from computer hardware, the physical machines on which software works, many types of software products and systems exist today. These are often characterized either by business domains, (for example, information systems) or by relationship to other software layered between the user and the computing machinery, (such as programs embedded in microprocessors to create intelligent devices and appliances).

The Development and Economics of Software

To highlight software's distinctive characteristics, it is helpful to contrast the development of software with that of manufactured products:

- Software is an intellectual, rather than a physical, product, so its development is subject to human and logical constraints, rather than physical laws.
- One cannot assume that a software specification is stable. Changing requirements is expected behavior in software development.
- Productivity levels vary widely (more so in individuals than in teams).
- Product defects are results of human misunderstandings and mistakes, not deficient materials.
- Manufactured goods are valued for their features, but software is also valued for its interactive functionality.
- The economics of software quality hinges on the process of understanding requirements.
- This process of understanding requirements, more so than conformance, is commonly responsible for the value of a software product.
- The costs of the manufacturing phase of software production are insignificant. The bulk of software development costs are in the design, implementation, and testing disciplines.
- Statistics cannot be applied to replications, because software products are usually one of a kind.
- The cost of ownership is accounted differently, because software assets are not capitalized and depreciated.

What Is Software Quality?

Although there is no single comprehensive standard definition of software quality, descriptions and terms are found in sources such as *ISO 9000-3, IEEE Software Engineering Standards,* and various books on the subject. The following are definitions of software quality from several distinct perspectives:

- *Level of satisfaction.* The degree to which a customer or user perceives that a software product meets his or her composite needs and expectations
- *Product value.* The value of a software product relative to its various stakeholders and the competition
- *Key attributes.* The extent to which a software product possesses a desired combination of properties
- *Freedom from defects.* The degree to which a software product works correctly in target user environments, free from operational flaws
- *Process quality.* In relation to the development process by which the product is produced, it is the extent to which people do the right things in an effective way

Every application/business domain faces a specific set of software quality issues, and software quality must be defined accordingly. For example, life critical applications have very stringent operational needs, whereas typical information system applications must focus on measures of customer satisfaction.

For each software development project, a specific level of software quality must be defined during the planning phase. Such a definition both contributes the basis for practical measures of quality progress and delineates readiness for release to customers.

Why Is the Cost of Software Quality (CoSQ) Important Now?

As shown in Figure 4.1, if improving business success through software quality is a corporate goal, then we need answers to a few simple questions, questions that are too often not asked in today's software development situations. These questions are:

- How much does software quality cost?
- What are the benefits of good quality software?
- How good is our software quality?

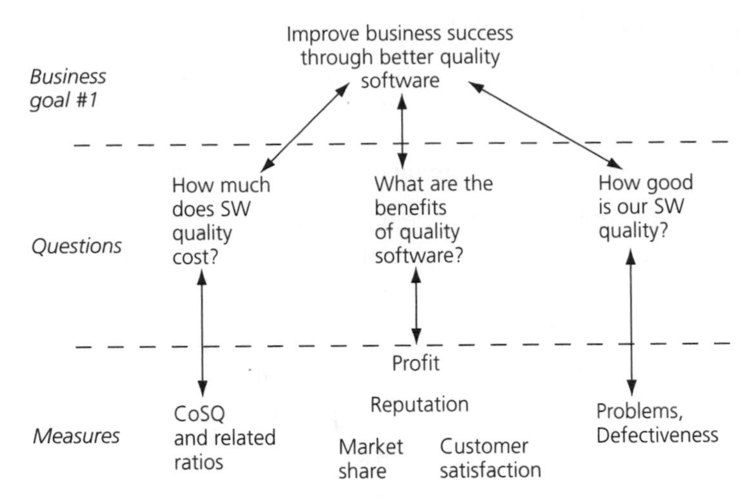

Figure 4.1. Cost of Software Quality (CoSQ) in context.

Once the answers to these questions are known:

- The costs can then be compared to overall software production costs and software product sales.
- The costs can be compared to benchmarks and norms.
- Deeper analysis can lead to actions taken to improve the competitive situation.
- The bottom-line effect of improvement actions can be measured.
- The economic trade-offs involved with software quality become visible, thus leading to better decision making.

The Application Cost of Quality Principles to Software

Table 4.2 lists the four Cost of Quality (CoQ) categories with typical costs of software quality. Most prevention costs are in the development cycle, except for organizationwide costs, such as process definition and metrics collection and analysis.

Cost of Software Quality

While the costs of software quality assurance and process improvement have been a topic of concern for more than twenty years and the Cost of Quality categories have often been used broadly in discussions of software

Table 4.2. Typical costs of quality for software.

Category	Definition	Typical Costs for Software
Internal failure	Nonconformances detected prior to product shipment	Defect management, rework, retesting
External failure	Nonconformances detected after product shipment	Technical support, complaint investigation, defect notification, remedial upgrades and fixes
Appraisal	Discovering the condition of the product	Testing and associated activities, product quality audits
Prevention	Efforts to prevent poor product quality	SQA administration, inspections, process studies and improvements, metrics collection and analysis

quality, very limited data has been available in the open literature for discussing the cost of software quality (CoSQ). Knox's model[4] and the Raytheon studies[5,6] are notable exceptions in that they explicitly use the cost of quality model.

Due to the limited amount of data available on CoSQ, Knox used the emerging CoQ model developed in manufacturing environments, extending it across the Software Engineering Institute's Capability Maturity Model (SEI CMM)[7] to produce a theoretical CoSQ model (see Figure 4.2). The SEI CMM specifies requirements for software organizations according to five levels of process maturity (see Table 4.3).

Starting with the total CoSQ (TCoSQ) at 60 percent of development costs (based on two industry figures) for CMM Level 1 organizations, Knox used manufacturing experience to hypothesize that CMM Level 5 organizations can cut this CoSQ by about 67 percent. He then rationalized the four component costs at each CMM level. His model suggests that, for Level 3 organizations, CoSQ is about half of development costs.

The same year that Knox's paper appeared, Dion[5] used the CoQ model as one means of interpreting the results of quality initiatives undertaken at Raytheon's Electronic Systems Group (RES). More recently, Haley[6] updated this study. The CoSQ results are shown in Figure 4.3. (Appraisal and prevention costs were shown separately in the Dion paper but were combined in the Haley paper.)

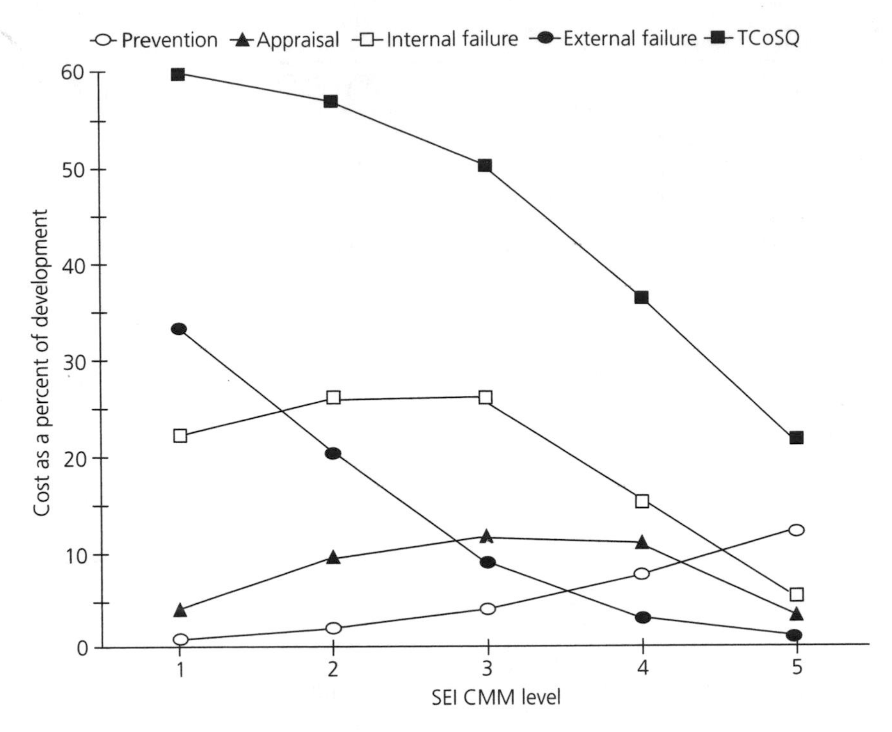

Figure 4.2. Knox's theoretical model for cost of software quality.

Table 4.3. Levels in the Software Engineering Institute's capability maturity model.

SEI CMM Level		Description
1	Initial	Software processes are undefined and depend on individual efforts.
2	Repeatable	SQA and basic project and configuration management enable repeatability.
3	Defined	Processes are documented, standardized, and integrated into the organization.
4	Managed	Process and product quality are managed using detailed measures.
5	Optimizing	Continuous process improvement is enabled by quantitative process feedback.

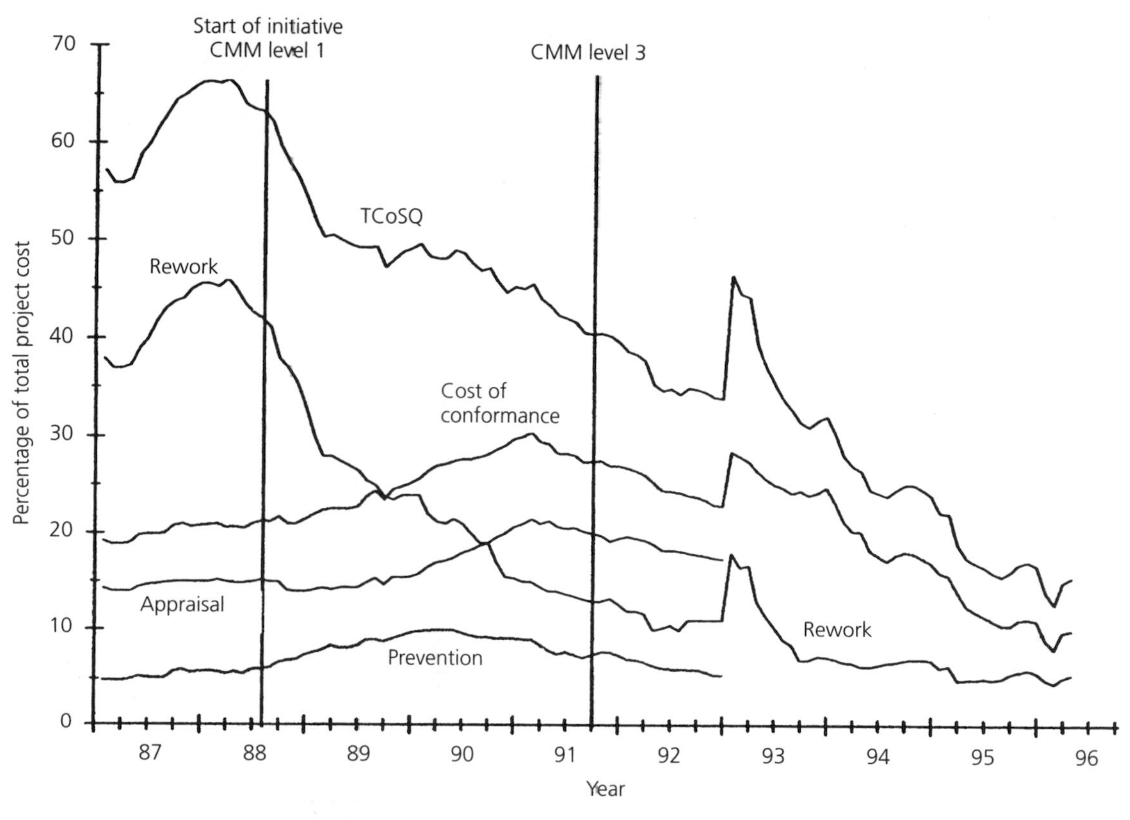

Figure 4.3. Cost of software quality for 15 projects at RES[5,6].

Starting at CMM Level 1, RES introduced a software process improvement program in August 1988. Using the results of tracking fifteen projects, they achieved CMM Level 3 practices in a little over three years. Their results agree well with Knox's model; in the Level 1 stage, RES's total CoSQ fluctuated between 55 percent and 67 percent of total project costs, and, by the time of reaching Level 3 process maturity, their total CoSQ had dropped to approximately 40 percent. By 1996, this organization's total CoSQ was approximately 15 percent of total project costs and the rework due to both internal and external nonconformances had been reduced to less than 5 percent. (For a more extensive discussion of CoSQ at RES, see the CoSQ case study, page 169.)

A third source of CoSQ data is a Price Waterhouse study that analyzed the costs and benefits of software quality standards from a survey of nineteen United Kingdom (UK) software suppliers.[8] The study estimated the cost of conformance (prevention and appraisal costs) to be 23 percent to 34 percent of development effort. The study also estimated nonconformance (failure) costs at 15 percent of development effort for a total CoSQ of 38 percent to 49 percent of development effort. It must be noted that this study excluded the costs of unit testing and rework because the suppliers could not separate these costs. With increases in the estimates to account for this exclusion, CoSQ in a software organization with a quality system can range from 40 percent to 55 percent of development costs, with a conformance costs to nonconformance costs ratio ranging from 1.5 to 2.

As compared to the RES graph, these figures generally agree with a period late in 1990, when RES was approaching CMM Level 3: RES's CoSQ was about 45 percent of development, and its ratio of conformance to nonconformance costs was about 1.5 (conformance~27/nonconformance~18). Knox's model predicted that a CMM Level 3 organization would have a total CoSQ of 50 percent, but with a conformance $(3 + 11 = 14)$ to nonconformance $(50 - 14 = 36)$ cost ratio of approximately 0.4 (14/36). It appears that Knox's model is a fair predictor of CoSQ for maturing software organizations but that actual conformance costs are much higher and nonconformance costs much lower than what the model predicts.

From this data, we can expect CoSQ, with the present state of software engineering practice, to range from 20 percent to 70 percent of development costs. Even accounting for the margin between production costs and sales, CoSQ appears to be roughly twice manufacturing CoQ.

Potential Benefits of Using CoSQ

The works of Knox and RES demonstrate one of the benefits of measuring and using CoSQ, that is, justification for quality initiatives. Examples of return on investment (ROI) in quality improvement initiatives speak most clearly to managers responsible for maintaining a profitable organization. However, CoSQ can be used for a number of other benefits. It can:

- Provide cost data for motivational purposes by demonstrating the relationship of employee efforts to the bottom line
- Provide a basis for budgeting the quality operation
- Compare process improvements and identify the most cost-effective ones
- Provide a measure of comparing the success of projects
- Be used to identify quality improvement candidates

Elements of a CoSQ Effort

Several points can be made with regard to measuring and using cost of quality information specifically for software process improvement. These are accounting and gathering of quality cost data, quality metrics collection, data analysis, and the presentation of the results.

Accounting. Gathering quality cost data assumes that costs have been accounted using task and expense elements that can be summed into the four major categories of quality costs. Many software organizations track costs in a manner amenable to quality costing, but many others do not. In the latter case, a preliminary step of defining and installing such a chart of accounts is required. A sample of such a chart of quality costs is provided in Table 4.4. The quality elements in a software organization's chart of accounts must be tailored to reflect its software process. To realize the full benefit of CoSQ, the chart of accounts must also allow for the addition of process improvement tasks.

In the best cases, quality costs can be taken directly from departmental accounting reports. In other cases, it may be necessary to resort to basic accounting and engineering records, such as schedules, time reports, defect reports, and purchasing records. In the worst cases, one may fall back on interviews with members of the software organization in order to construct estimates of each quality cost element. A controlled scientific study is unlikely; incomplete data can suffice in beginning a software cost benefit analysis.

Table 4.4. A sample CoSQ chart.

1. Prevention Costs
- 1.1 Requirements
  - 1.1.1 Marketing research for customer/user quality needs
  - 1.1.2 Customer/user quality surveys
  - 1.1.3 Product quality risk analysis
  - 1.1.4 Prototyping for customer review
  - 1.1.5 User requirements/ specification reviews/ inspections
- 1.2 Project
  - 1.2.1 Project quality planning
  - 1.2.2 Project process validation
  - 1.2.3 Quality assessment of development platform and tools
  - 1.2.4 Platform and tools development for quality
  - 1.2.5 Developer quality training
  - 1.2.6 Quality metrics data collection
  - 1.2.7 Design for quality: software component reuse
  - 1.2.8 Formal inspections/ peer reviews
  - 1.2.9 Project configuration management
  - 1.2.10 Project change management
  - 1.2.11 Supplier capability assessment
- 1.3 Reuse library
  - 1.3.1 Salaries
  - 1.3.2 Expenses
  - 1.3.3 Training
  - 1.3.4 Platform and tools
- 1.4 Configuration management administration
  - 1.4.1 Salaries
  - 1.4.2 Expenses
  - 1.4.3 Training
  - 1.4.4 Platform and tools
- 1.5 SQA administration
  - 1.5.1 SQA salaries
  - 1.5.2 SQA expenses
  - 1.5.3 Software process and standards definition and publication
  - 1.5.4 Metrology: data maintenance, analysis, and reporting
  - 1.5.5 SQA program planning
  - 1.5.6 SQA performance reporting
  - 1.5.7 SQA education/training
  - 1.5.8 Process improvement
  - 1.5.9 SQA process compliance audits

2. Appraisal Costs
- 2.1 Supplied product testing
- 2.2 Project appraisal costs
  - 2.2.1 Verification and validation activities
  - 2.2.2 Testing: planning, platforms, setup, test data generation, test execution and logging, reporting, test data evaluation
  - 2.2.3 Product quality audits
- 2.3 External appraisals
  - 2.3.1 Process maturity evaluation
  - 2.3.2 Field performance trials
  - 2.3.3 Special product evaluations

3. Internal Failure Costs

- 3.1 Product design defect costs
  - 3.1.1 Causal analysis and reporting
  - 3.1.2 Design corrective action
  - 3.1.3 Rework and retest due to design corrective action
  - 3.1.4 Work products wasted due to design changes
- 3.2 Purchased product defect cost
  - 3.2.1 Defect analysis cost
  - 3.2.2 Cost of obtaining product fix
  - 3.2.3 Cost of defect work-arounds
  - 3.2.4 Rework
- 3.3 Implementation defect costs
  - 3.3.1 Defect measurement and reporting
  - 3.3.2 Defect fixing
  - 3.3.3 Causal analysis and reporting
  - 3.34 Project process corrective action
  - 3.35 Fix inspection
  - 3.36 Retest and integration

4. External Failure Costs

- 4.1 Technical support for responding to defect complaints
- 4.2 Product returned due to defect
- 4.3 Maintenance and release due to defects
- 4.4 Defect notification costs
- 4.5 Upgrade due to defect
- 4.6 Service agreement claims (warranty expense reports)
- 4.7 Litigation costs and liability claims (insurance and legal reports)
- 4.8 Penalties (product contract reports)
- 4.9 Costs to maintain customer/user goodwill due to dissatisfaction (sales reports)
- 4.10 Lost sales/market share due to quality problems (field salesperson reports)

Sources of quality cost data: Ordinarily, quality cost data for the majority of categories would be obtained from salary and expense reports. Exceptions are in the external failure category and are shown here in parentheses.

One of the pitfalls of a CoSQ program is "controversial cost elements." Usually, the question is about which costs are normal operating costs and which are quality costs. An example is the cost of producing a project management plan. While this plan is produced for the sake of managing a project's expenses and schedule, it also influences product and process quality. It is helpful to keep in mind the following points:

- Arguments over controversial elements have been known to sabotage cost of quality programs.
- The largest quality costs are those that are most easily discerned, such as reviews, software quality assurance, testing, and rework.

Therefore, it is often safe to exclude controversial elements without unduly affecting the total CoSQ.

- Consistency throughout a CoSQ program is more important than thorough inclusion of quality costs, because consistency allows for clear identification of improvements as well as candidates for improvement.

Concerns may also arise as to how quality costs should be categorized. Again, consistency is important. For example, in Table 4.4, the costs associated with formal inspections (peer reviews) are treated as prevention costs rather than as appraisal costs. This is a matter of interpretation, depending on when a work product is considered ready for appraisal. Although manufacturing inspections are conducted on pieces after they are produced, in software production, inspections may be incorporated in the production process per the peer reviews key process area for the SEI CMM Level 3. For documentation, this means that a document is not complete until it has undergone a peer review and has been revised. The same is true for code, especially when code inspections precede unit testing, clearly an appraisal activity.

Quality Metrics Collection. The CoQ has been used primarily in a fundamental approach to quality—that is, focusing on defect rates (manufacturing) or service problem reports (service industries)—rather than broader approaches that would take into account such factors as usability, testability, and maintainability. The fundamental approach has the advantages of straightforward measurement and ease of understanding. It also allows comparison of dissimilar products. Most software producers take a fundamental approach to quality, concentrating on defect measurement, prevention, and removal.

A defect collection system for collecting both defect metrics and the failure portion of quality costs would provide data having the added advantage of aiding in root cause analysis and of identifying the most costly defects (see discussion in chapter 1, pages 10 and 18). Defect measurement is a good place to start with measuring CoSQ improvements. Specifically, CoSQ can be plotted against the number of product defects at the completion of system testing. This metric may be obtained from defect reports during testing and for a specified time period, for example six months, following product release. It could also be generated statistically based on postrelease defect reports for previous products from the same organization.

CoSQ Analysis and Dynamics. Plotting CoSQ against a quality measure (e.g., product defects) provides the CoSQ curve and, plotted against time, reveals trends in an organization's quality processes. This addresses most of the goals of quality costing: justification, motivation, budgeting, and process improvement cost effectiveness. However, Pareto analysis, based on the principle that quality costs are localized (80 percent of the quality costs are incurred by 20 percent of the quality nonconformances), can be used to identify candidates for process improvement (see Chapter 5, page 112). When CoSQ is categorized by product and process sources, typically one or two sources will be shown to incur much higher costs than the others.

In analyzing CoSQ data, the dynamics of the model must be taken into account. The following are some of the factors that affect CoSQ over time:

- Advances in software technology—for example, the prevalence of graphical user interfaces—create new demands on software producers.
- Growing user sophistication creates demands for increased functionality and better support (documentation, training, technical services).
- Better applications and systems set new standards for performance and reliability.
- Better software production technology—for example, in testing and configuration management—supports higher quality goals.
- Reduced cycle time and time to market increase competition in the marketplace and may be accompanied by changes in actual or perceived quality.

These factors may shift the point of diminishing returns, usually to the right, over time. For example, either better software production technology or growing user sophistication can effect a shift in the optimum CoSQ toward a higher level of quality.

CoSQ Presentation. Relationships that have the greatest impact on management are:

- Quality costs as a percent of sales
- Quality costs compared to profit
- Quality costs compared to the magnitude of the current problem

In addition to these, showing CoSQ as a percent of total development costs is appropriate to software for several reasons. First, sales and profit may not have a direct relationship to the actual cost of a software product, since software pricing is often dictated by market forces. Second, all but a small percentage of software development costs can be measured in labor hours, so the costs can be readily shown in either hours or dollars. Third, the state of the art in software development is such that comparing quality costs to development costs illustrates the magnitude of the current challenge.

Conclusions

CoQ is a proven technique in manufacturing and service industries, both for communicating the value of quality initiatives and for identifying quality initiative candidates. CoSQ offers the same promise for the software industry, but it has seen little use to date. Initial uses of CoSQ indicate that it represents a very large percentage of development costs—60 percent and higher for organizations that are unaware of improvement opportunities. CoSQ use can, however, demonstrate significant cost savings—such as Raytheon's fourfold reduction in rework—for software organizations willing to undertake quality improvement initiatives. Perhaps what is more important, the use of CoSQ enables an understanding of the economic trade-offs that accompany activities and expenditures made for improving the quality of delivered software.

Chapter 5

Quality Improvement and Quality Cost Reduction

This chapter is intended to provide guidance to company management and to professionals engaged in quality program management to enable them to structure and manage programs for quality cost reduction. It describes techniques for using quality costs in programs to reduce costs and, thereby, improve profits. Although most of the examples and discussions to follow relate to manufacturing industries, the techniques and methods described are just as applicable to the various service industries and may be used by management in banking, insurance, health care, retail, etc.

In reading this chapter, it must be understood that improving quality results in lower total quality costs. Total quality costs include elements incurred in marketing, design, purchasing, manufacturing, and service. In short, every part of the product cycle typically generates some quality costs, and programs for identifying and improving cost must be comprehensive enough to involve all these functions.

THE QUALITY COST IMPROVEMENT PHILOSOPHY

It is a fact, too often unrecognized, that every dollar saved in the total cost of quality is directly translatable into a dollar of pretax earnings. It is also a fact that quality improvements and quality cost reductions cannot be legislated by management demand—they must be earned through the process of problem solving. The first step in the process is the identification of problems; a problem in this context is defined as an area of high quality costs. Every problem identified by quality costs is an opportunity for profit improvement.

This chapter discusses a quality program that is *not* confined to the control of quality in manufacturing. Most people recognize that quality is determined by many factors outside of manufacturing, but many quality programs do not concern themselves with these factors. In some cases, quality program efforts have been attempts at not allowing things to get any worse (control) instead of striving to make things better (improvement). As a result, things have deteriorated in many places, simply because controls are not, and never can be, 100 percent effective. Improving quality is similar to improving product costs. It is everybody's job and everybody is for the idea, but, until there is management commitment to improve and a formal program for forcing improvement, it just doesn't happen.

This chapter describes what each company function must do to improve quality, through the involvement of people in marketing, design, purchasing, accounting, manufacturing, and quality assurance. It describes ways to find problems and correct their causes. It tells you how to use the costs associated with quality and how to reduce these costs.

Quality improvement results in cost improvement. Designing and building a product right the first time always costs less. Solving problems by finding their causes and eliminating them results in measurable savings. To cash in on these savings, the quality performance must be improved. This chapter describes ways to do that.

Figure 5.1 illustrates how quality cost analysis bridges the gap between the elements of a prevention-oriented quality program and the means used by company management to measure performance—the profit and loss statement. The chart shows the flow of quality cost information from the working quality assurance level to the total cost of quality level, and ultimately to the profit and loss statement. Every dollar saved because of improved quality has a direct impact on profit.

QUALITY COSTS AND THE PROFIT CENTER

Quality costs for a profit center consist of costs incurred in several activities. Figure 5.2 shows the buildup of costs from all functional departments into an overall quality cost analysis for the entire profit center.

As can be seen, quality costs are incurred by all major functions in an organization, so problem areas can exist anywhere. Careful analysis must be done to find the most costly problems, and programs must be developed to attack them. Many times, a strategic program is necessary. When this need exists, a strategic quality program should be developed, using input from all functions, and it should become a part of the profit center's overall strategic program. Figure 5.3 shows the relationship between the

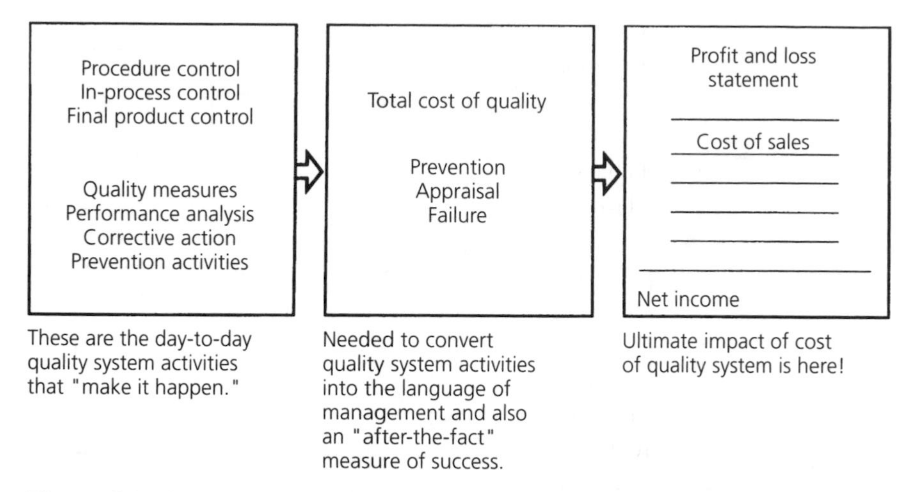

Figure 5.1. Quality cost system.

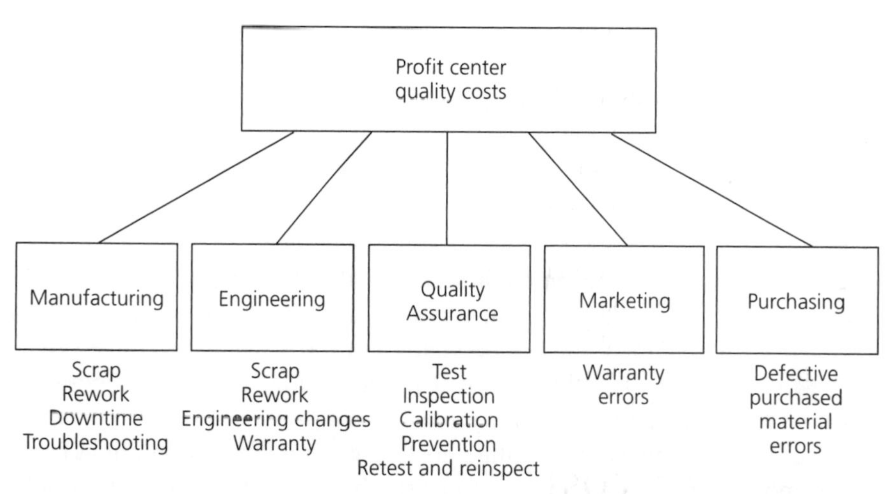

Figure 5.2. Profit center quality costs.

overall strategic program and the quality program. (For a discussion on quality costs and the strategic business plan, see page 73.)

PROGRAMMING IMPROVEMENT

The strategic quality plan describes a management commitment to quality and quality cost improvement. The quality cost data indicate areas that are candidates for improvement. When the highest cost areas are analyzed in greater detail, many improvement projects become apparent. For example,

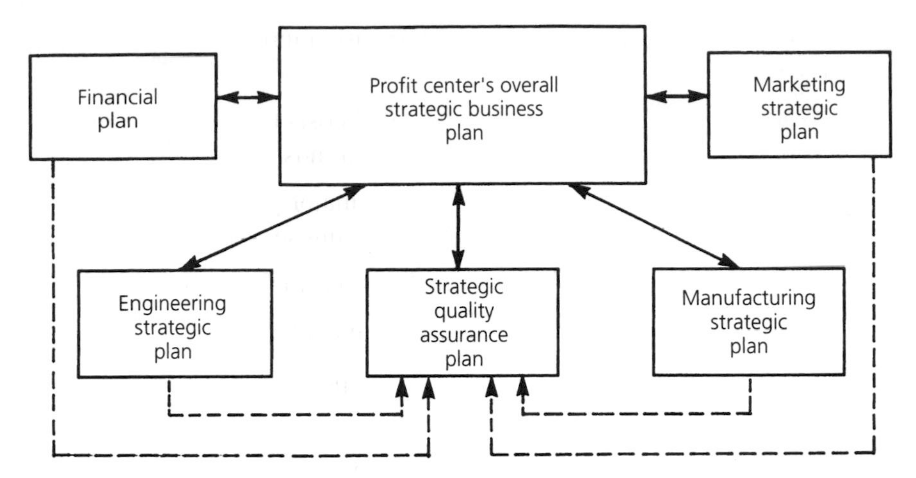

Figure 5.3. Profit center's overall strategic business plan.

high warranty costs are a trigger to rank customer failure problems for detailed investigation, with the aim of investigating product design, process control, or inspection planning for solutions to the highest cost problems. Regardless of what the high quality cost element may be, the mere act of identifying it should lead to actions to reduce it.

It is of major importance for management to understand that there are no general solutions to quality problems—that is, high quality cost areas. These problems are not solved by organizational manipulations, new management techniques, or even quality cost analysis. The quality cost information simply identifies problem (opportunity) areas. Once the problem area has been identified, the detailed nature of the problem has to be investigated and appropriate actions taken. *The entire process of quality improvement and quality cost reduction is pursued on a problem-by-problem basis.*

Because of high external failure costs, a natural temptation might be to place more emphasis on appraisal efforts, but this approach may simply convert some external failures to internal failures (such as scrap and rework) and bear an increased inspection burden. Similarly, it may be tempting to increase product engineering efforts in a generalized attempt to prevent defects, but a generalized effort may not be very effective. Usually, the improvements are obtained by actions in the prevention category. Effective prevention actions are those aimed at very specific problems—problems that can be spotlighted by the quality cost studies. To put it succinctly, the process of quality and quality cost improvement depends on understanding cause-and-effect relationships; the study of total quality costs is perhaps the most effective tool available to management to obtain this understanding.

In summary, to effectively establish quality improvement efforts, it is necessary to

- Recognize and organize quality-related costs to gain knowledge of magnitude, contributing elements, and trends
- Analyze quality performance, identify major problem areas, and measure product line and/or manufacturing section performance
- Implement effective corrective action and cost improvement programs
- Evaluate the effect of action to assure intended results
- Program activities for maximum dollar payoff and maximum effective manpower utilization
- Budget quality work to meet objectives

FINDING THE PROBLEM AREAS

When quality costs are displayed to managers who have not been exposed to the concept, the initial question is likely to be "How much should they be?" or "How does this compare with other organizations or products?". Unfortunately, it is not practical to establish any meaningful absolute standards for such cost comparisons. A quality cost system should be tailored to a particular company's needs. This is necessary to perceive significant trends and furnish objective evidence for management decisions as to where assurance efforts should be placed for optimum return. While the search for industry guidelines or other standards of comparison is natural (in fact, benchmarking encourages this), it is quite dangerous, since it leads to quality cost emphasis of "scorecarding" rather than use as a management tool for improving the status quo.

The futility of establishing meaningful absolute quality cost guidelines is more apparent if you consider

1. Inherent key variations in how companies interpret and capture quality cost data
2. Critical differences in product complexity, process methods and stability, production volume, market characteristics, management needs and objectives, customer reactions, and so on
3. The awkwardness or inappropriateness for many companies of the most prevalent form of quality cost measure (percent of net sales billed), considering the effect of time differences between time of sales billing and the incurrence of actual quality costs

This last factor is particularly important for periods involving an expanding or a contracting product volume or mix, unstable market pricing, shifting sales/leasing revenue ratios, or changing competitive performance criteria. Accordingly, it is much more productive to abandon efforts to compare your quality cost measurements with other companies' in favor of meaningful analysis of the problem areas contributing most significantly to *your* quality costs, so that suitable corrective actions can be initiated.

Analysis techniques for quality costs are as varied as those used for any other quality problems in industry. They range from simple charting techniques to complicated mathematical models of the program. The most common techniques and examples of their use will be discussed in this chapter. They are trend analysis and Pareto analysis by quality cost category, element, department, product, service, or other grouping.

Trend Analysis

Trend analysis is simply comparing present cost levels to past cost levels. It is suggested that costs be collected for a reasonable amount of time before attempting to draw conclusions or plan action programs. The data from this minimum period should be plotted in several ways.

Costs associated with each quality cost category (prevention, appraisal, internal failure, and external failure) should be plotted periodically, such as monthly or quarterly, as both total dollars and as a fraction of one or more measurement bases thought to be appropriate for future use as indicators of business activity. Elements contributing a high proportion of the costs within a quality cost category should be plotted and analyzed separately. Figure 5.4 contains a plot of total quality costs in a hypothetical company and plots of costs expressed as dollars per unit produced and as a percentage of sales. The graphs show that total quality costs are increasing but that total quality costs as related to units produced and sales are not changing significantly.

Figures 5.5 and 5.6 are graphs plotting quality cost categories as total dollars (Figure 5.5) and related to the same two bases (Figure 5.6). Figure 5.5 shows increases in the total dollars spent in all cost categories. Costs are stable, however, when related to the measurement bases (Figure 5.6), except for internal failure. The internal failure costs have increased slightly over the twelve-month period. This indicates that further analysis of internal failure costs should be made. The technique most often used for further analysis is Pareto analysis.

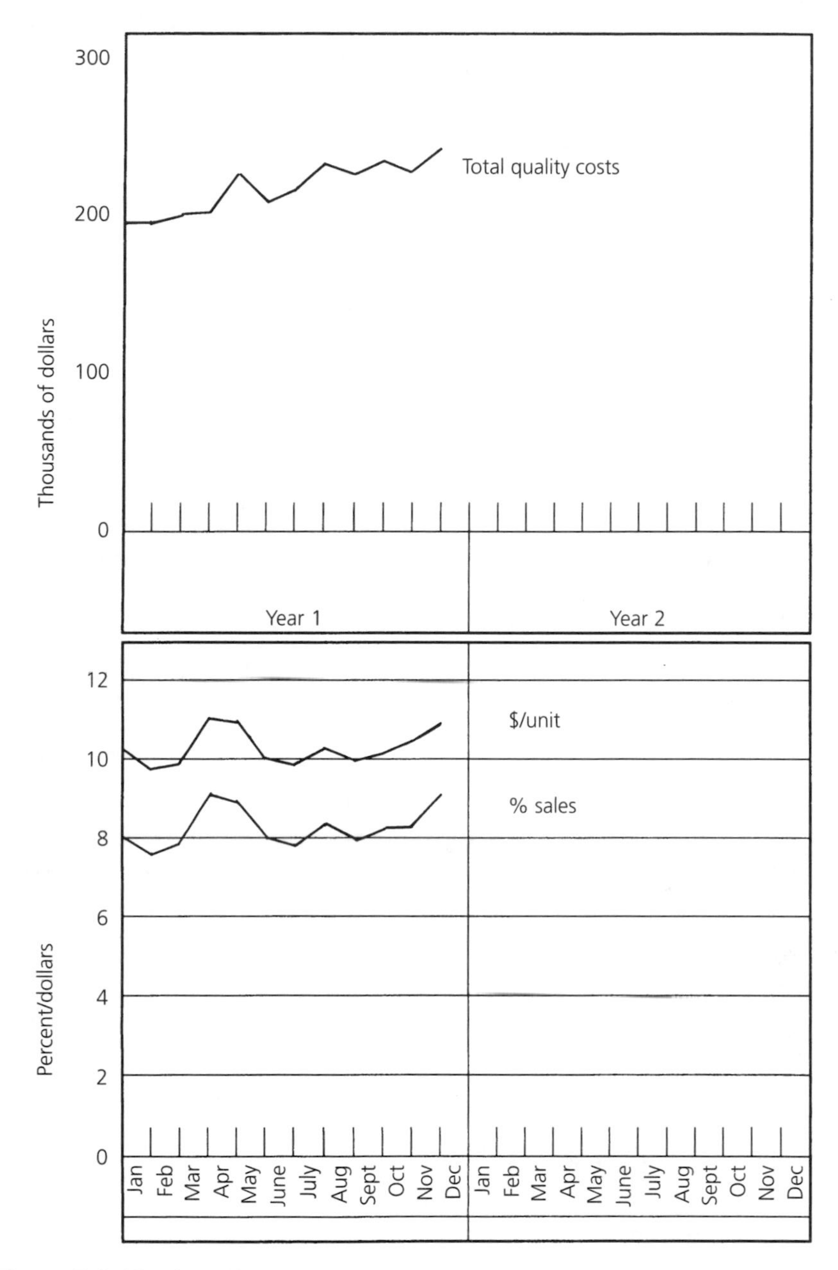

Figure 5.4. Total quality costs.

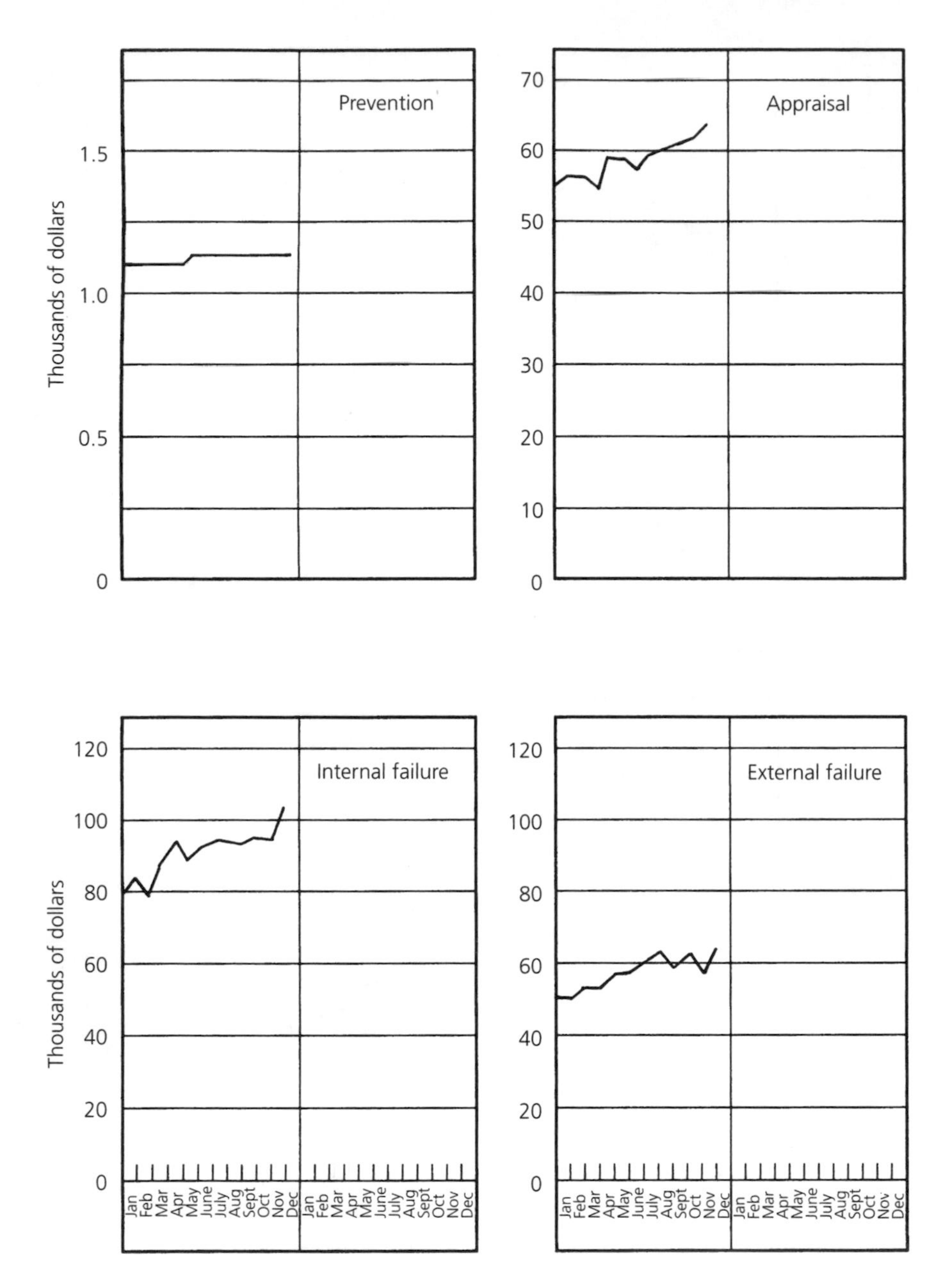

Figure 5.5. Quality costs—total dollars.

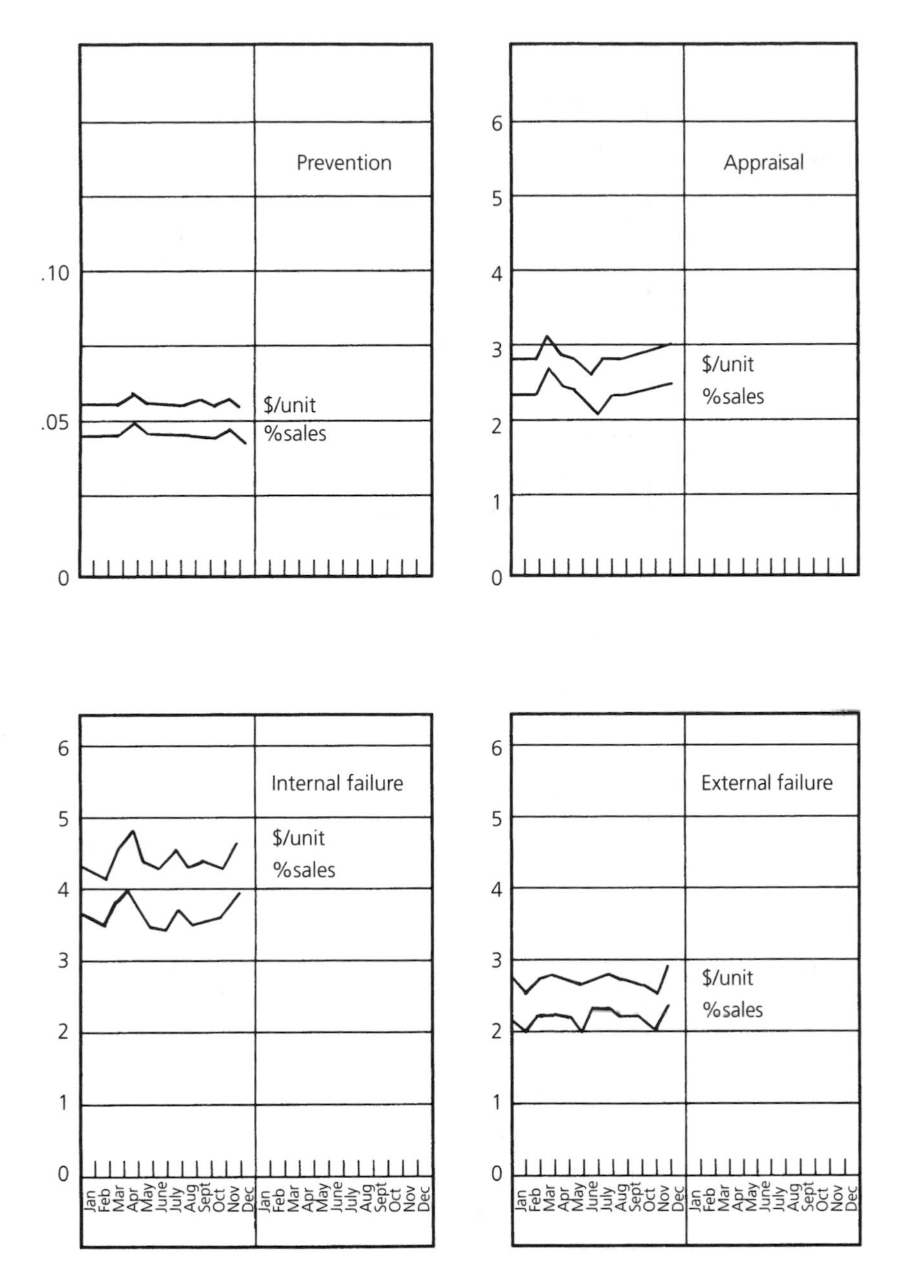

Figure 5.6. Quality costs related to bases.

Pareto Analysis

The Pareto analysis technique involves listing the factors that contribute to the problem and ranking them according to the magnitude of the contributions. In most situations, a relatively small number of causes or sources will contribute a relatively large percentage of the total costs. To produce the greatest improvement, effort should be expended on reducing costs coming from the largest contributors. In the example, the largest contributor to the total costs and the one showing an increasing trend is internal failure (see Figure 5.6). Figure 5.7 is a Pareto distribution showing the costs contributed by each element included in internal failure costs.

Two elements, scrap and remedial engineering, account for 69 percent of total internal failure costs. Pareto analysis can be used to determine where the scrap and remedial engineering costs originate. The distribution in Figure 5.8 shows that two departments in the shop account for 59 percent of the scrap charges. Figure 5.9 shows that 83 percent of the remedial engineering charges are being generated by two design engineering sections.

These distributions are typical of ones which could be found in any company. Using this sequence of techniques, high cost contributors can be identified and targeted for corrective action attention. In this example, a 10 percent reduction in internal failure costs by only the two highest cost contributors would mean a $75,000 cost reduction:

[$450,000 (scrap) + $300,000 (remedial engineering)] x 10% = $75,000

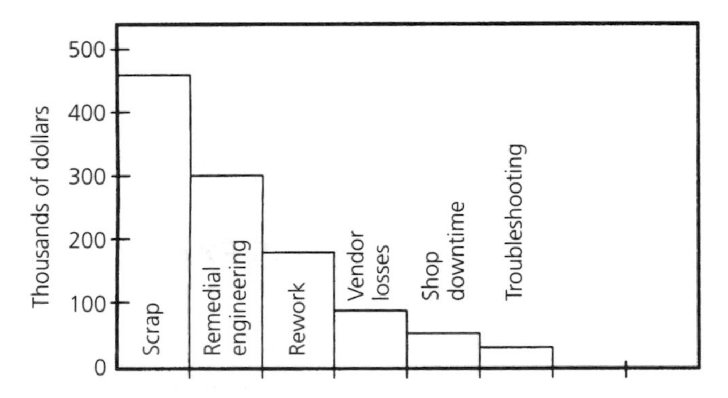

Figure 5.7. Pareto distribution of internal failure.

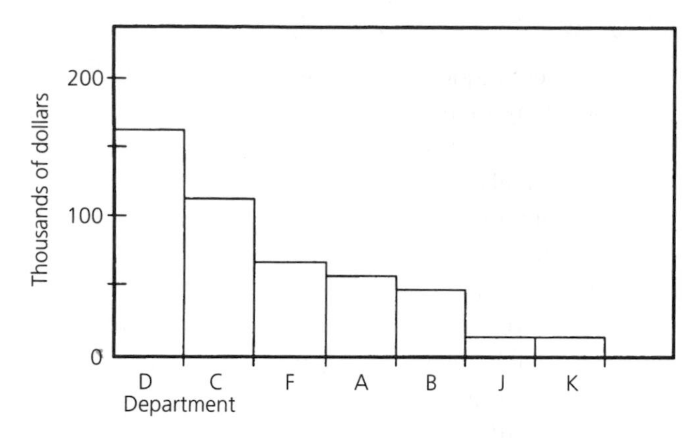

Figure 5.8. Pareto distribution of scrap.

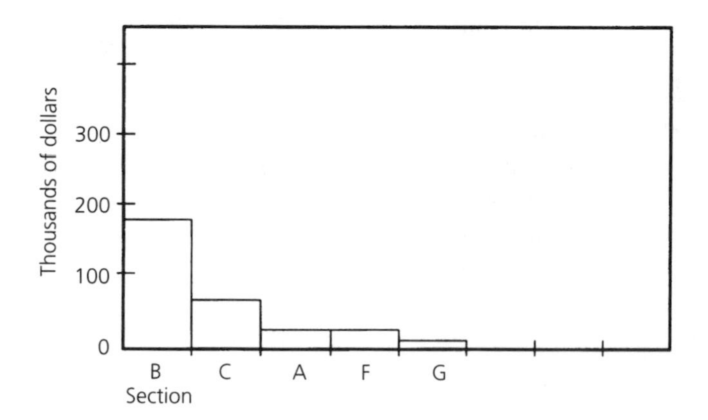

Figure 5.9. Pareto distibution of remedial engineering.

Objectives such as this are realistic and can be obtained if you know where to look. The Pareto analysis technique will reveal this information.

QUALITY COST ANALYSIS EXAMPLE

About the Operation

Last year, sales for the Transmotor Division of PDQ Company were approximately $25 million, consisting of about 90 percent industrial customers and 10 percent government contracts. Profits after taxes were $1.2 million.

Sales increased steadily from $1.5 million in January to $2.6 million in December. This increase was due to the introduction and wide acceptance of a new product design. The new product was not only more reliable but less costly to produce. With a sizable amount of the new product in inventory at the start of the last year, the production rate was not increased until the second quarter.

During the year, a recently hired quality engineer started working on an analysis of the quality program. He was able to improve systems and procedures, but, since the middle of last year, high rejection rates on the new product (both at final assembly and on parts) forced him to spend most of his time attempting to solve some of the problems that were causing the high rejection rates.

The division's quality manager, Carl Harris, has heard about the quality costs management technique and wants to see if it can benefit his division. Carl has attended several ASQ conferences and seminars and was able to talk with quality control managers of companies that make a product line similar to his. From what he can determine, it appears that quality costs between 4 percent and 6 percent of net sales billed are common in companies making similar products. He is not sure, however, which cost elements are included in his competitor's quality costs. A rough calculation of his division's costs for last year's month of October reveals the following figures:

Prevention	$1,000
Appraisal	100,000
Internal failure	36,000
External failure	27,000
Total quality cost	$164,000

Carl's first attempt at establishing a quality engineering program began over a year-and-a-half ago, with the hiring of an ASQ Certified Quality Engineer. Improvement of inspection methods and solutions to a few chronic quality problems have since enabled Carl to reassign several inspectors and cover the increased production load without increasing the number of inspectors in the last three quarters of the previous year. To date, a considerable amount of 100 percent inspection is still being done, however, and Carl believes that more of the inspection process can be eliminated by upgrading the efficiency of the manufacturing process.

The cause of the present high rejection rate on the new product is not really known, and there is a considerable amount of fingerpointing going on. Manufacturing blames a faulty design and the purchase of bad material; design engineering claims that the existing tolerances are not being met and that parts are being mishandled before they get to the assembly area. Carl decides to determine which departments are the high cost contributors by setting up a quality cost program.

Starting the Program

The first decision the quality manager must make is which unit will be covered by the study. Since there is no breakdown by profit center within the division, it is decided that the entire division will be included in the study.

The next thing the quality manager does is discuss the concept and proposed program with the controller and request her aid in the initial study and future reporting. The controller is skeptical of the program, but she does agree to provide costs on those elements which are compiled and used for other purposes. The controller also agrees to provide personnel to aid in compiling other element costs as needed.

This done, the elements to be studied must be selected. The elements shown in Figure 5.10 are selected as those most representative of the Transmotor Division operation. It is found that there are no separate accounts for some of the elements and that estimates must be made for those items. In some cases, this requires splitting amounts in a general account according to an estimated fraction of that account which should be charged to the element. Some estimating can best be done by counting the number of people performing such tasks as rework and sorting. Work sampling is also a valuable technique for such estimating. After determining the cost sources to use for each element, a detailed first study can be made. For the Transmotor Division, it was decided to collect data for the entire preceding year. These data are shown in Figure 5.10. The actual costs for each category are plotted in Figure 5.11.

Internal failure, appraisal, and the total costs show an upward trend, as would be expected in a period of increasing activity. Prevention costs haven't changed, but external failure costs peaked during the first half of the year and now appear to be leveling off. The next step is to find appropriate measures of business activity (bases) to which to relate the data. The quality manager selects a sales base—net sales billed; a cost base—cost of units shipped; and a labor base—factory hours.

Transmotor Division–Total Quality Costs

Elements	Jan.	Feb.	Mar.	Apr.	May
Prevention					
Quality planning	500	550	400	300	350
Data analysis and preventive action	500	500	600	700	650
Planning by other functions	600	400	700	750	700
Development of measurement and control equipment	0	50	0	0	0
Training	0	0	0	0	0
Quality system audits	0	0	0	0	0
Other prevention expenses	200	250	250	200	375
Total prevention costs	1,800	1,750	1,950	1,950	2,075
Appraisal					
Inspection and test—purchased material	5,200	5,000	5,950	4,920	5,900
Laboratory acceptance testing	925	925	925	925	925
Maint. and calibration of equipment	3,840	3,840	3,840	3,840	3,840
Depreciation of capital equipment	695	695	695	695	695
Inspection	52,300	53,250	52,275	52,325	51,250
Testing	29,120	30,950	30,050	28,425	29,350
Set-up of inspection and test	(Included in "Inspection" and "Testing")				
Process and product audits	0	0	0	0	0
Checking labor	2,710	2,805	2,740	3,117	3,240
Inspection and test material	475	80	316	940	510
Outside endorsement	0	0	0	0	0
Personnel qualification	0	0	0	30	0
Review of test and inspection data	0	0	0	0	0
Field testing and inspection	0	0	0	0	0
Accumulation of cost data	0	0	0	0	0
Total appraisal costs	95,265	97,545	96,791	95,217	95,710
Internal Failure					
Scrap—division					
Caused	25,170	15,025	19,112	18,997	28,040
Rework—division					
Caused	5,200	6,150	6,210	4,925	9,010
Supplier-caused losses	1,200	1,099	1,248	1,170	1,370
Troubleshooting	2,080	1,975	2,125	2,020	2,115
Retest and reinspection	(not separated from inspection costs)				
Remedial engineering	4,200	4,250	7,125	8,010	7,850
Substandard product costs	0	0	0	0	0
Shop downtime	(not identifiable)				
Extra production operations	(not identifiable)				
Total internal failure costs	37,850	28,499	35,820	35,122	48,385
External Failure					
Product warranty	19,670	22,300	22,960	24,850	22,100
Returned product cost	1,800	1,800	1,800	1,800	1,800
Field service	7,100	7,100	7,100	7,100	7,100
Total external failure costs	28,570	31,200	31,860	33,750	31,000
TOTAL QUALITY COSTS	163,485	158,994	166,421	166,039	177,170
MEASUREMENT BASES					
1. Net sales billed	1,525,000	1,420,500	1,872,500	1,810,200	1,798,400
2. Factory hours	82,650	83,152	82,164	81,245	82,360
3. Costs of units shipped	1,225,000	1,315,500	1,275,250	1,095,650	1,080,975

Figure 5.10. Total quality costs—Transmotor Division.

Transmotor Division–Total Quality Costs

June	July	Aug.	Sept.	Oct.	Nov.	Dec.	Total
250	0	200	250	0	100	100	3,000
750	250	800	750	1,000	900	900	8,300
650	650	650	600	700	700	650	7,750
0	0	0	0	0	0	0	50
0	0	0	250	0	0	0	250
0	0	0	0	0	0	0	
190	750	260	460	225	190	220	3,570
1,840	1,650	1,910	2,310	1,925	1,890	1,870	22,920
6,010	3,900	6,410	7,125	6,500	6,400	7,450	70,765
925	925	925	925	925	925	925	11,100
3,840	3,840	3,840	3,840	3,840	3,840	3,840	46,080
695	695	695	695	695	695	695	8,340
53,200	48,875	51,450	52,050	52,725	51,400	50,575	621,675
31,940	30,125	35,830	35,750	38,700	43,525	44,100	407,865
0	0	0	0	0	0	0	
3,120	3,250	3,325	3,390	3,470	3,515	3,570	38,252
425	270	317	430	525	130	100	4,518
0	0	0	0	0	0	0	
0	0	0	0	30	0	0	60
0	0	0	0	0	0	0	
0	0	0	0	0	0	0	
0	0	0	0	0	0	0	
100,155	91,880	102,792	104,205	107,410	110,430	111,255	1,208,655
33,980	9,060	20,050	22,150	18,220	27,110	24,140	261,054
6,020	7,800	10,500	12,250	10,875	12,900	12,040	103,880
2,715	1,110	1,795	1,745	1,890	1,375	2,160	18,877
2,170	2,050	2,265	2,450	2,645	2,725	2,945	27,565
9,100	10,460	13,610	12,990	13,060	11,550	13,510	115,715
0	0	0	0	0	0	0	
53,985	30,480	48,220	51,585	46,690	55,660	54,795	527,091
20,990	20,500	19,550	18,850	20,110	18,900	19,750	250,530
1,800	1,800	1,800	1,800	1,800	1,800	1,800	21,600
7,100	7,100	7,100	7,100	7,100	7,100	7,100	85,200
29,890	29,400	28,450	27,750	29,010	27,800	28,650	357,330
185,870	153,410	181,372	185,850	185,035	195,780	196,570	2,115,996
1,896,750	2,086,550	2,314,640	2,402,500	2,276,550	2,697,540	2,625,400	24,726,530
91,200	83,750	96,750	112,750	115,750	115,700	91,250	1,118,471
1,205,620	1,125,050	1,397,450	1,334,150	1,400,500	1,602,930	1,625,625	15,683,700

Figure 5.10. *(continued)*

These data are collected from accounting and industrial engineering, and costs from each category are expressed as a percent of the bases chosen. Graphs of these percentages are shown as Figures 5.12, 5.13, and 5.14, respectively.

When expressed as a percent of sales, total costs, appraisal, and external failure show a downward trend, while prevention and internal failure are essentially unchanged. These trends, however, are not valid, since sales in this case is not a good measure of the kind of activity producing the costs. Most of product billed originated from warehouse stocks for the first half of the year. Except for a December spike in quality costs as a percent of factory hours, the ratio plots using factory hours exhibit roughly the same trends as those using costs of units shipped (the December rise was due to a dip in factory hours because of the December holiday period). Total costs peaked about midyear and appear to be decreasing. Appraisal and external failure cost ratios display a slightly downward trend. Prevention has not changed. This analysis invites attention to the increasing internal failure cost ratio. It is found that the major contributors to the increase are rework, scrap, and remedial engineering. These three elements were responsible for 91 percent of the internal failure costs. The largest dollar contributor is scrap, contributing 50 percent of the internal failure costs. Graphs of internal failure costs, as percentages of costs of units shipped, are shown in Figure 5.15.

This leads to the question "Where are these costs being generated?". The quality manager requests a breakdown of the source of the three largest dollar contributors to the internal failure costs: scrap, rework, and remedial engineering. It is found that three sections of the shop (Winding, Feeder 1, and Feeder 5) generated 82 percent of the scrap during the previous year. Two sections (Winding and Assembly) contributed 73 percent of the rework charges, and one model (Model T) accounted for 60 percent of the remedial engineering. Figure 5.16 shows Pareto graphs of these cost breakdowns.

The quality manager now has enough information to begin to develop a corrective action program. To be effective, it must involve both the manufacturing manager and the engineering manager, since the elements which are the largest contributors to internal failure costs are the responsibility of these functional managers. The quality manager must also examine costs which are his own responsibility–prevention and appraisal. Reductions in overall costs will require a program of cooperative effort.

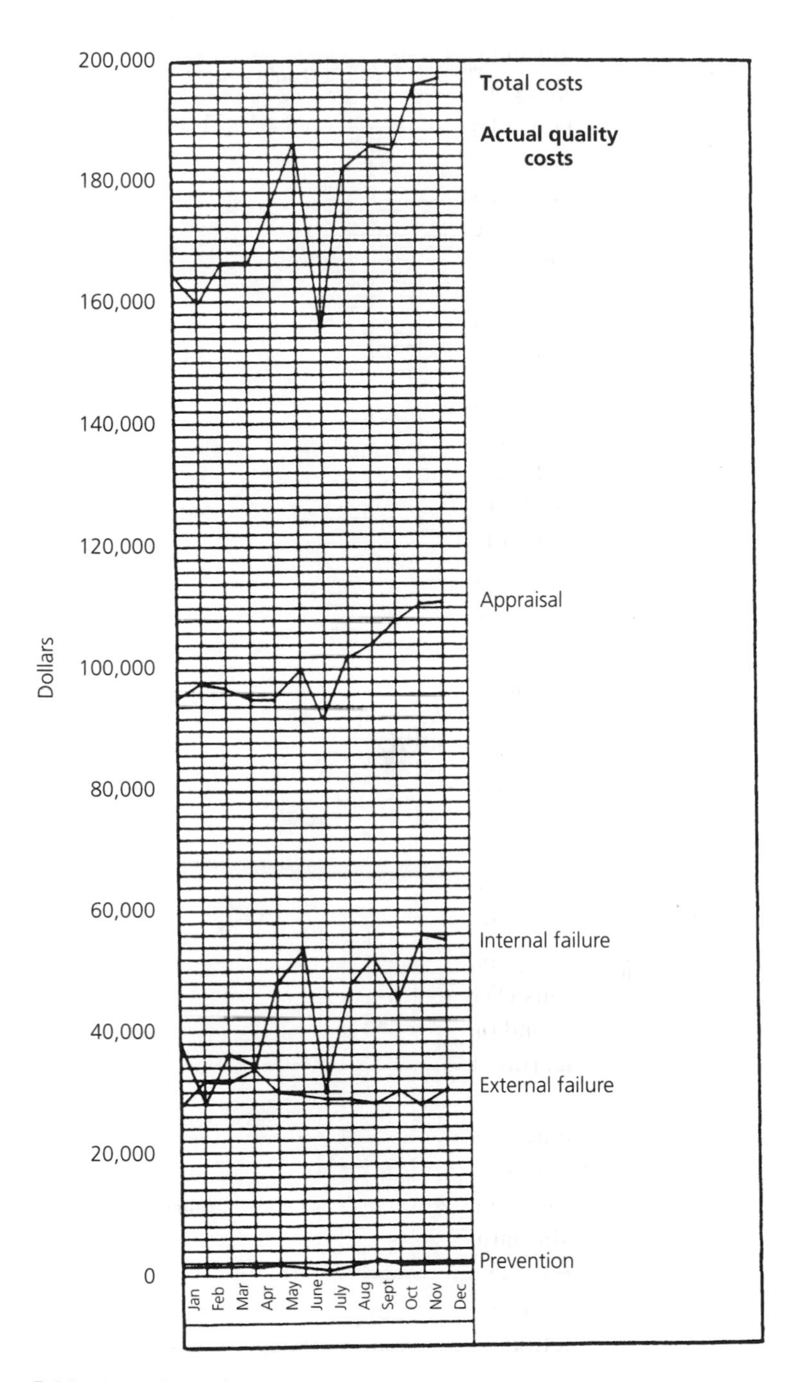

Figure 5.11. Actual quality costs.

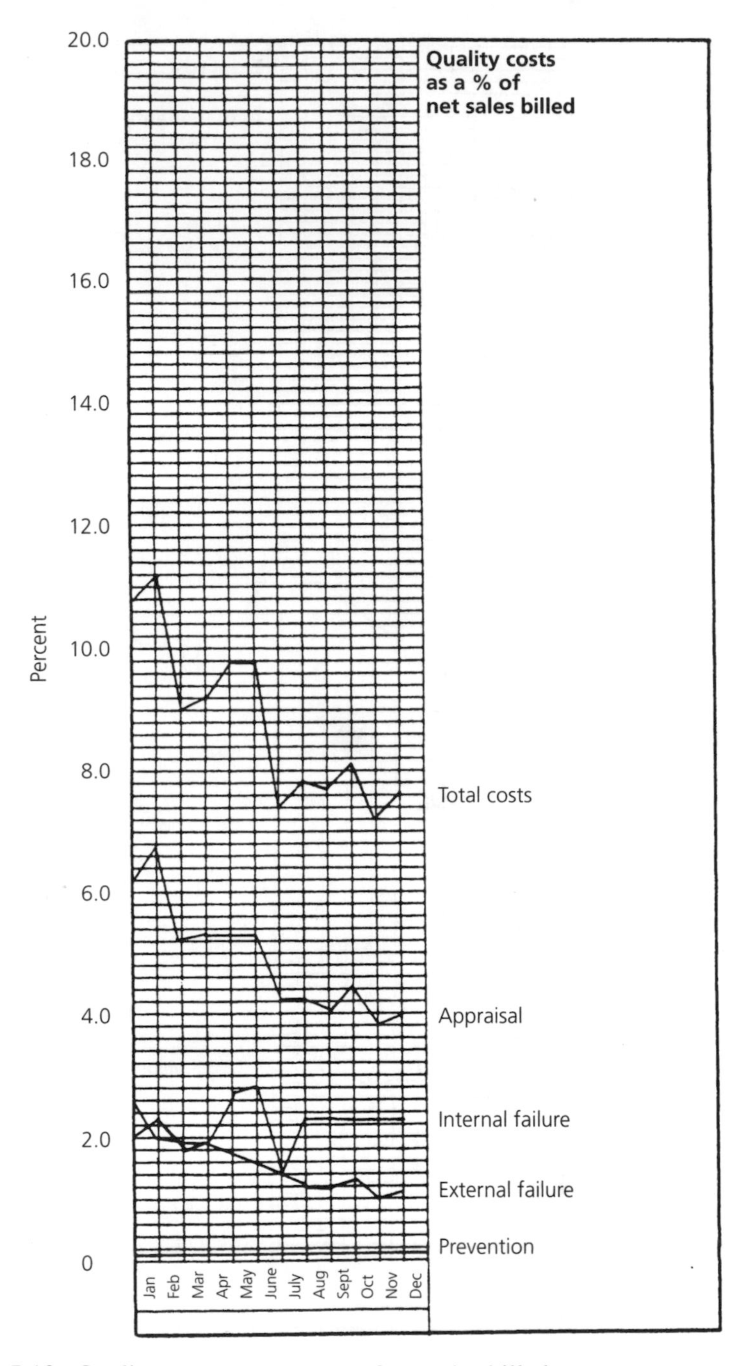

Figure 5.12. Quality costs as a percent of net sales billed.

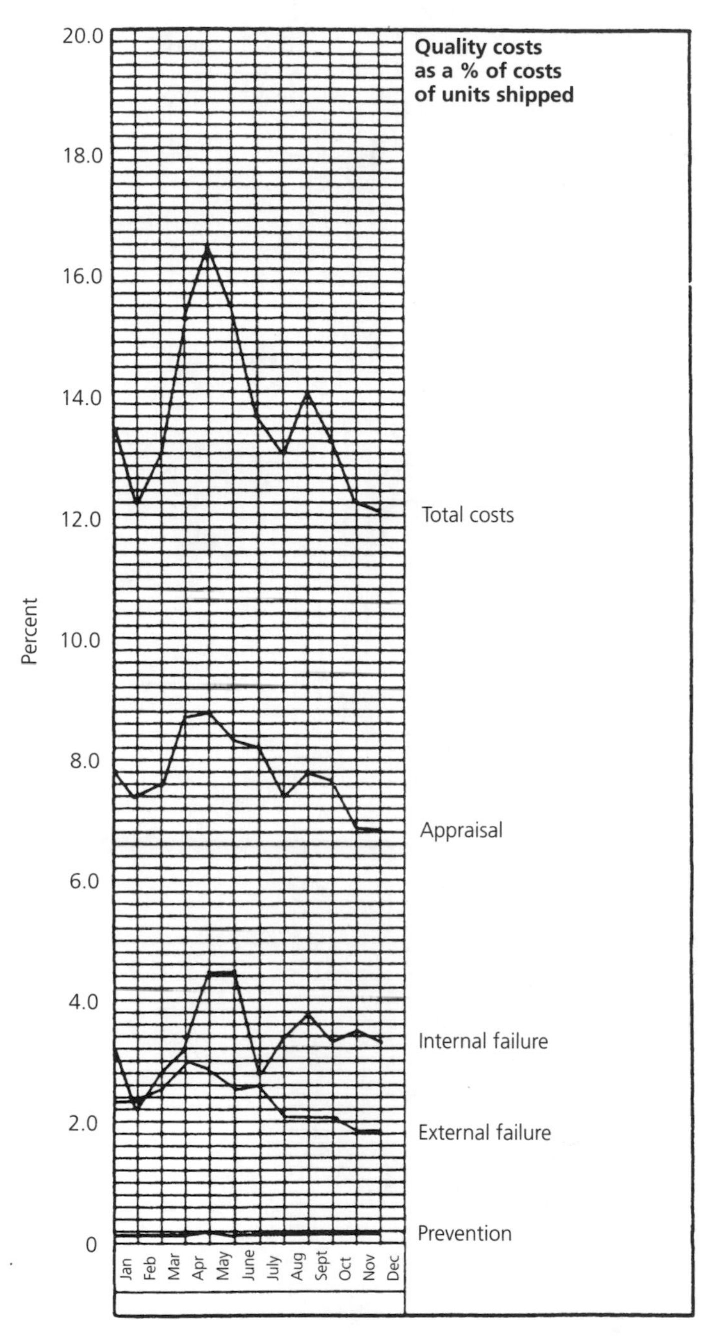

Figure 5.13. Quality costs as a percent of costs of units shipped.

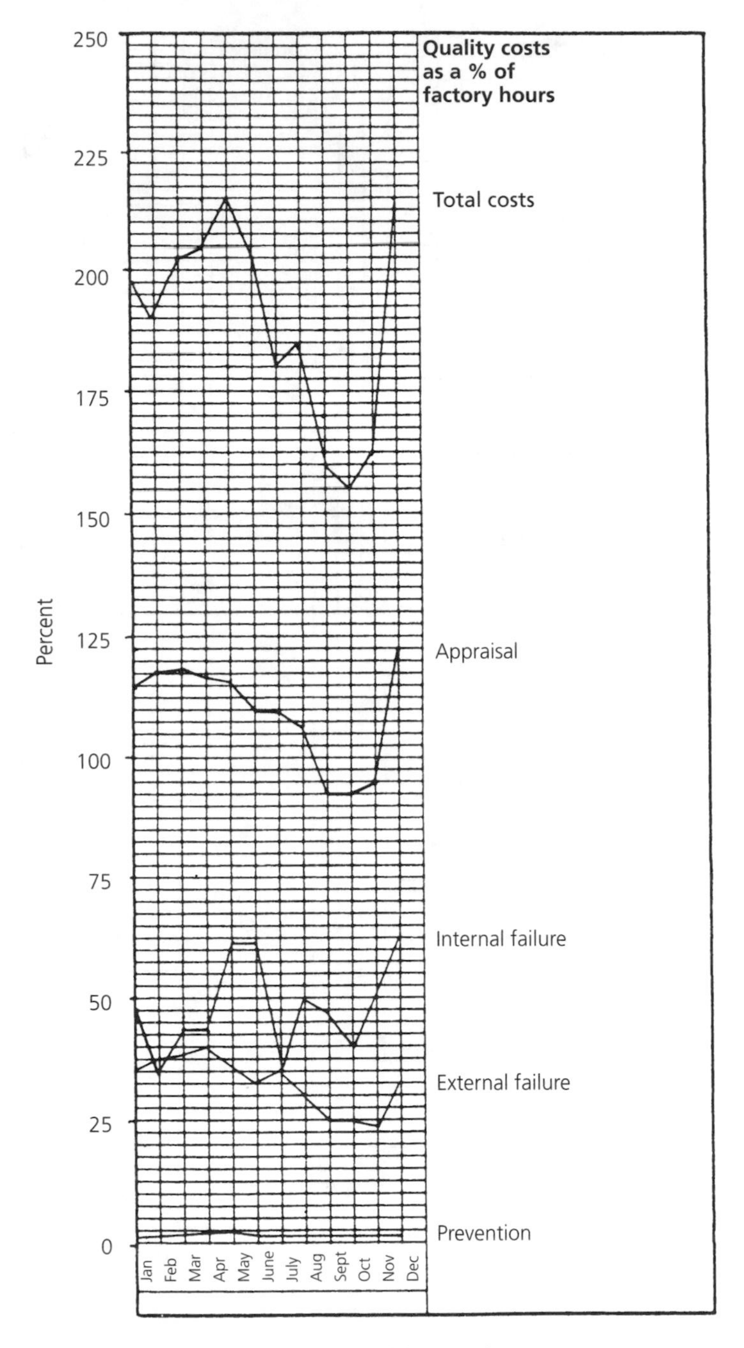

Figure 5.14. Quality costs as a percent of factory hours.

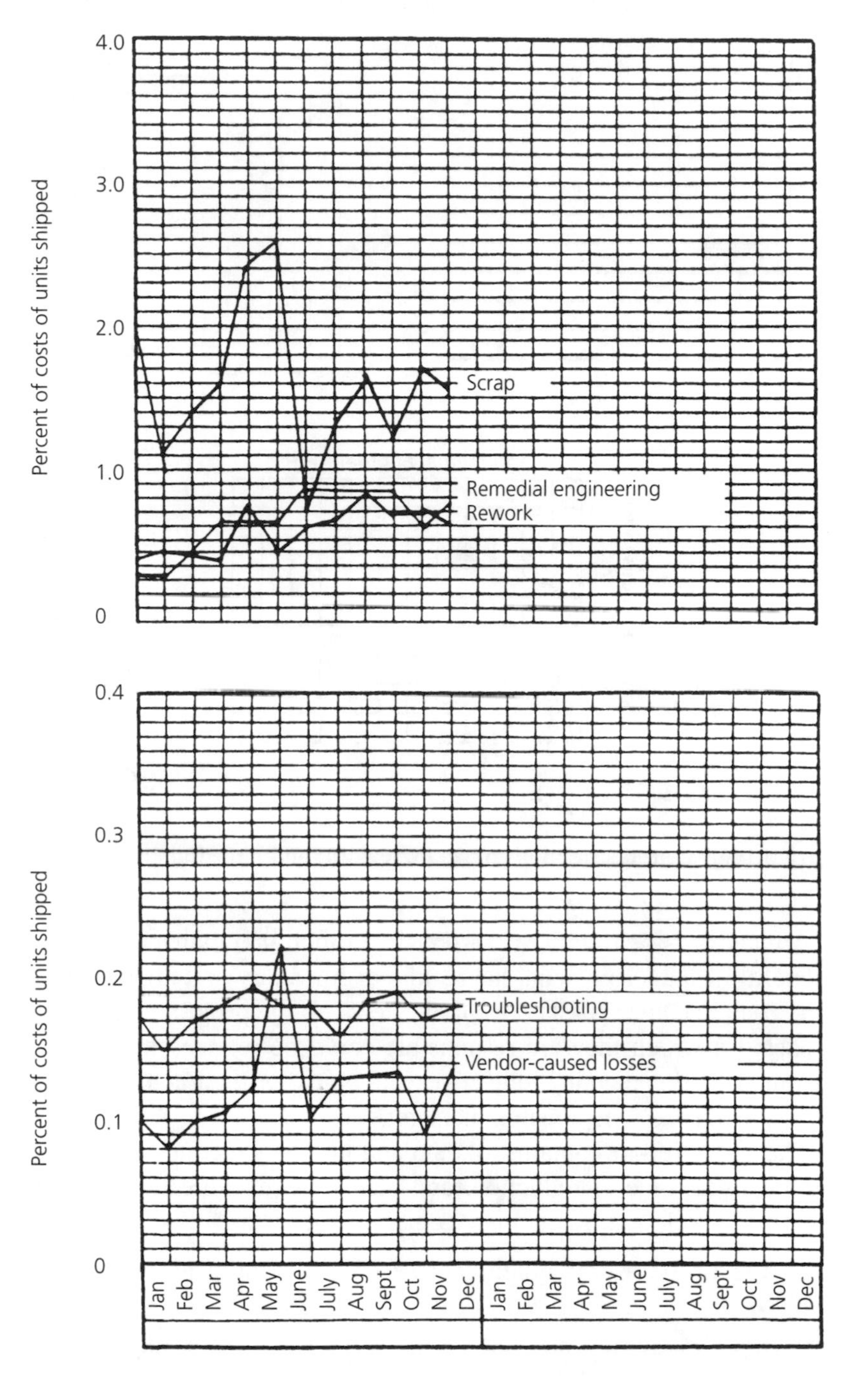

Figure 5.15. Internal failure costs.

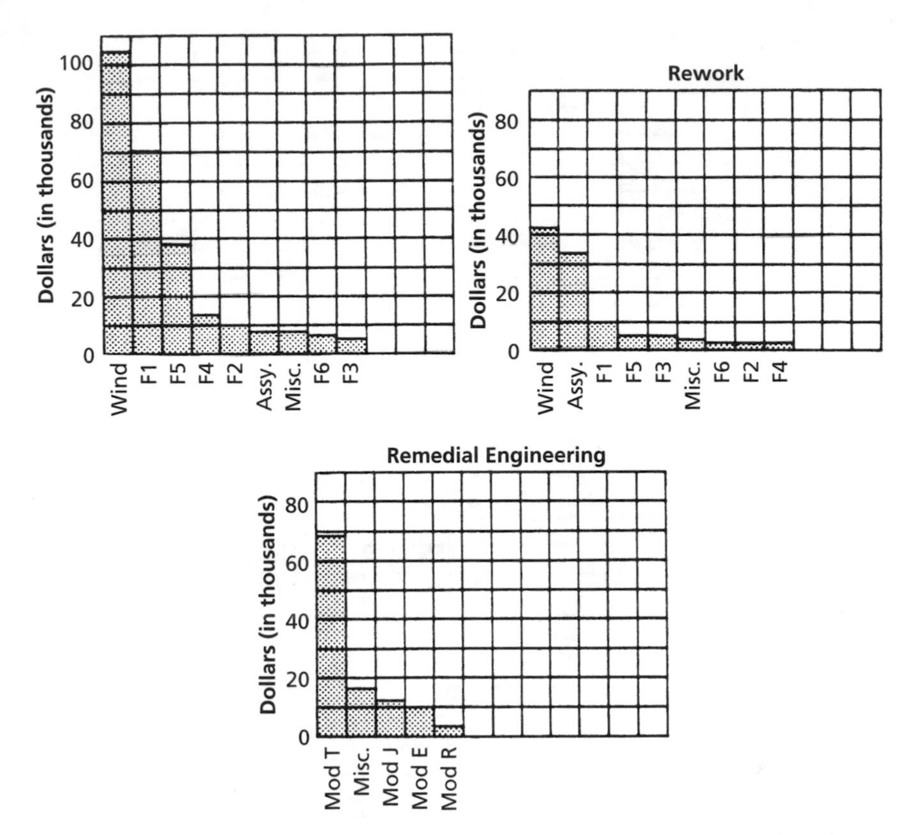

Figure 5.16. Pareto distributions of scrap, rework, and remedial engineering.

A meeting is held with the responsible functional managers, at which the quality manager presents the results of his study and analysis to this point. Each manager is asked for their views on the program and whether the costs for which they are responsible could be reduced and, if so, by how much. At this meeting, objectives and plans for their achievement are solicited from each responsible manager.

The initial report contains all data and graphs generated in the study, the objectives for cost reduction, and plans for reaching the objectives. Objectives developed by the management team are as follows:

1. Reduce the overall quality costs to 6.7 percent of net sales billed within one year
2. Reduce appraisal costs to 3.3 percent of net sales billed within two years, and to 3.6 percent within one year

3. Reduce internal failure costs to 1.8 percent of sales within one year
4. Maintain external failure costs at no more than 1.1 percent of sales

Action programs for attainment of these objectives are as follows:

1. Hire an additional quality engineer charged with the responsibility for identification of the causes of high cost problems and coordination of corrective action
2. Reassign the present quality engineer to the task of finding less costly ways of inspection and test, and ways of eliminating 100 percent inspection
3. Set up teams consisting of representatives of manufacturing, engineering, and quality in the sections of the shop having high scrap and rework costs
4. Set up a task force to determine the cause of the excessive remedial engineering costs on the Model T unit; set an objective for reduction of the costs, and report progress regularly
5. Determine the causes of the highest cost field problem. If shop-caused, assign to the shop teams for action. If caused by design or application, assign to the task force for attention. Set objectives and require reporting
6. Issue a quality cost report each quarter, showing performance against objectives and discussing major problem areas and plans for reduction of costs

At this point, we leave the Transmotor quality manager with the knowledge that he is well on his way to eliminating many of his headaches and making the quality function a profit contributor for the division.

THE TEAM APPROACH

Once a problem has been identified and reported and the involved personnel are committed to action, the job is started but far from complete. The efforts of the people involved must be planned, coordinated, scheduled, implemented, and followed up. Normally, problems can be thought of as one of two types: those which one individual or department can correct with little or no outside help and those requiring coordinated action from several activities in the organization. Examples of the first type of problem include operator-controllable defects, design errors, and inspection errors. Examples of the second type include product performance problems for which a cause is not known, defects caused by a combination of factors not under one department's control, and field failures of unknown cause.

An elaborate system is not required to attack and solve problems of the first type. Most can and should be resolved at the working level with the foreman, engineer, or other responsible parties. Usually, the working personnel of these departments have sufficient authority (employee empowerment) to enact corrective action, within defined limits, without specific approval of their superiors.

Unfortunately, problems of the second type are normally the most costly and are not as easily solved. Causes of such problems can be numerous and unknown. Solutions may require action from several sources. The investigation of the problem and the planning of its solution must be coordinated and scheduled to assure that effective action is taken. One of the best devices for doing this is the quality improvement team. Working with the data and problem analysis reports and headed by an individual who is interested in solving the problems, this team develops the plan and then coordinates and schedules the investigation and action. It has been found that an interested individual with line responsibility (such as a general foreman) makes the best chairperson for such a group. Each project should be docketed and action scheduled. Meetings should be held regularly and minutes published.

Case Study 1—Profit Improvement

A major electrical firm initiated a corporate program to identify, analyze, and reduce quality costs. It was called the Product Integrity Improvement (PII) program. A formal management commitment to improvement of quality and an organized approach to obtaining this improvement have led to profit improvement at several divisions. This example describes the approach used and the results obtained in one location.

In most industrial environments, the highest segments of total quality costs are found in internal and external failure costs. Therefore, most organized efforts to reduce costs and improve profits are concentrated in this area. It should be stated, however, that by placing greater emphasis in the prevention activity, a significant improvement in quality costs will be realized. The PII program was intended to focus attention on all phases of quality costs and thereby improve the quality, safety, reliability, and environmental effects of products, while reducing total quality costs.

Establishing and Implementing the Division PII Program. It was decided to implement the PII program in the example division to place greater emphasis on the total quality costs. The primary events that occurred to establish and implement this program were as follows:

1. Received top management commitment, support, and involvement
2. Organized the PII program in the division
   a. Assigned responsibility for the PII program to a member of the division manager's immediate staff
   b. Established a PII council to assist the PII program manager in determining the overall approach, developing division strategy, and implementing the program; the council members included the division engineering manager, manufacturing manager, controller, and quality manager
   c. Conducted a PII seminar with headquarters quality assurance assistance to introduce the concept to responsible management personnel
3. Identified the quality cost elements and selected account sources
4. Collected all the quality costs for the division for the previous twelve months to establish the total quality cost baseline
5. Analyzed the division quality cost data and identified the most significant quality cost expenditures. Analysis of the data indicated that internal failure costs were requiring a disproportionate expenditure and should receive the highest priority for action. As a result of this analysis, quality costs were found to be

	Percent of Sales
Prevention	0.1
Appraisal	1.5
Internal failure	2.3
External failure	1.5
Total	5.4

Internal failure costs were analyzed to find the high cost contributors, with the following results:

	Approximate Percent of Total Internal Failure Cost
Cores	5
Wire	20
Coil winding—assembly	35
Final assembly/test	15
Other	25

The coil winding—assembly area was selected since collectively it accounted for the largest portion of the total internal failure cost.

6. Determined basic problems and underlying causes of the problems and assigned responsibility for corrective action

   a. Identified three underlying causes:

      (1) operator winding errors
      (2) damage to coils in handling
      (3) design problems

   b. Established a quality improvement team made up of

      Manufacturing manager—chairperson
      Quality manager
      Manufacturing engineering—equipment problems
      Engineering—design problems
      General foreman—operator problems

7. Established quality cost improvement objectives as an integral part of the division's profit plan

8. Created reporting systems to provide accurate cost visibility and to measure improvement performance

9. Met weekly to review progress, establish plans, and assign new tasks to be completed

10. Reviewed monthly total quality costs against the objectives and initiated corrective action where needed

11. Educated, trained, and emphasized the importance of everyone doing the job right the first time. Employee involvement was most important in attempts to achieve improvement. This was accomplished in a number of ways:
    a. General foreman, quality supervisor, section foreman meetings, at which they
        (1) identified key projects to be worked on
        (2) planned programs for improvement
        (3) reviewed progress
    b. Defect charts for each manufacturing section, showing objectives and actual costs
    c. Workplace meetings to establish a quality conscious attitude
    d. Training programs for certain critical skill, high cost areas
12. Recognized individuals and/or groups that made significant contributions toward improvement

Results obtained from this program were significant.

Costs as a Percent of Sales

	Previous Year Actual	Current Year Objectives	Current Year Actual
Prevention	0.1	0.1	0.1
Appraisal	1.5	1.3	1.2
Internal failure	2.3	2.0	2.1
External failure	1.5	1.1	1.2
Total	5.4	4.5	4.6

Summary. The success of a PII program depends on

1. Top management involvement and support
2. Visible total quality cost data
3. Setting division objectives for improvement and monthly reporting of performance against objectives
4. Organizing for improvement

5. Establishing a quality improvement team
6. Employee involvement and recognition

The benefits to be gained from a properly implemented PII program include

1. Reduced total quality costs, with a corresponding increase in profits
2. Improved product performance, product integrity, and adherence to schedule
3. Increased customer acceptance of products and services
4. Increased repeat sales and new sales from improved product reputation

Case Study 2—Failure Cost Improvement

A major connector manufacturer elected to enter the connector market with a new connector design to MIL-SPEC requirements. The following discussion illustrates how in four years the product assembly failure cost was reduced from $180,000 per year to $20,000 per year.

History. During the program's early phases, typical start-up problems associated with new manufacturing techniques, planning, and training were faced. These items were resolved one-by-one until assembly failure costs decreased to approximately $180,000, an amount that is still considered above normal for a new connector program.

Three years later, a failure costs plateau of $150,000 per year had been reached, a figure that still was comparatively high. It was not known that a considerable portion of failure dollars originated in the assembly departments. Using the financial data available, failure costs by specific cost center in the assembly departments were identified (each cost center is responsible for the assembly of a specific connector type).

It was observed that two specific cost centers contributed to over 75 percent of the assembly departments' total failure costs through that period. One major cost center was where bonded assemblies for other connectors were manufactured. This area was also the target for major cost improvements.

From the table on page 131, it can be seen that, using the first half of the year as a base and holding sales constant through the second half of the year, another large dollar failure cost year would result in the connector area. The problem needed to be attacked immediately.

Failure Costs by Cost Center

	CC:2441 (Bonding) ($000)	CC:2450 (Connector Assembly) ($000)
First half, year 1	57.6	67.0
Second half, year 1	17.7	34.0
Total, year 1	75.3	101.0
Total, year 2	41.2	22.0
Net Savings	34.1	79.0

Approach. A review of the prior six months' failure history was initiated. All of the discrepancy reports were evaluated, summarized, and categorized, and high scrap and rework cost areas were found (see Figure 5.17).

It was apparent from this summary that nearly 85 percent of all rejections occurred as the result of contaminated parts due to improperly applied or excessively applied adhesives. As a result of the excessive cleaning needed to remove the adhesives, an average of 80 connectors per month were scrapped. This alone amounted to almost $20,000 per year.

Cause. Based on these data, the causes of the problems were found to be

1. Methods used for adhesives application needed updating for this new connector series.
2. Operators required additional training in the application of adhesives.
3. Both operators and inspectors did not understand the complete workmanship standards developed for this program. As a result, the operators were performing unnecessary rework.
4. Some of the operators were causing a larger percentage of rework and scrap than others.

Corrective Measures. Once the causes were identified, a corrective action team composed of a quality engineer, an industrial engineer, and the production supervisor was organized. The production supervisor was appointed to head the team.

This team accomplished the following:

1. The first two months were directed to reviewing manufacturing instructions, revising methods, obtaining new tools, and revising the workmanship standards.

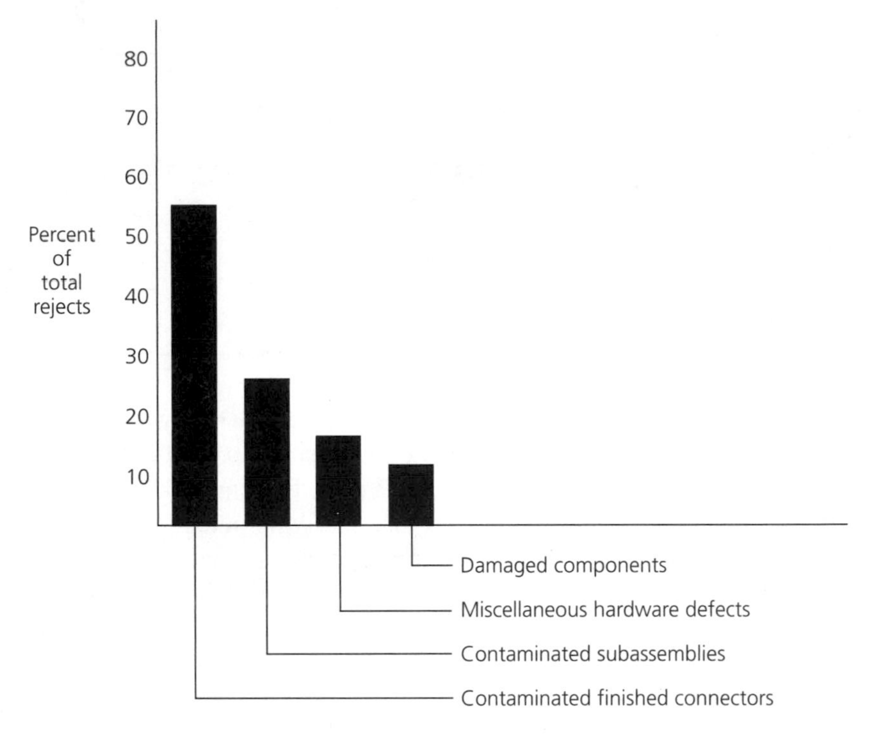

Figure 5.17. Rejection causes.

2. A new method requiring the application of adhesives through the use of a silkscreen technique was introduced.
3. Operators causing a larger percentage of rework and scrap were either retrained or replaced.
4. The inspectors were retrained in the requirements of the modified workmanship standards.

Costs for these changes were approximately $4,000 in tooling and $3,000 in labor.

Results. The table on page 131 compares the results of the first half of year 1 to the second half of year 1. Failure costs in this area decreased dramatically. Note that the failure dollars in the bonded assembly cost center also decreased as a result of application of the same techniques learned in the connector area.

The table also compares the results of year 1 to those of year 2. The results yielded a net savings in failure costs of almost $80,000 for year 2 in the connector area, despite increased sales volume. There was also a $34,000 savings in the bonding area.

Summary. By using the tools available and the team approach, a problem was identified, its cause found, and corrective action initiated to prevent recurrence. This resulted in a net savings equivalent to a sales increase of over $350,000 on these products. This was accomplished by recognizing that small pieces of a larger problem can more easily be digested and resolved one at a time.

TEAM-BASED PROBLEM SOLVING

Quality costs are especially useful for quality improvement teams, as they enable the teams to quantify the financial impact of their projects, both for themselves and for their management. The following example integrates quality costs with team problem solving and, although taken from a service organization, works equally well for manufacturing organizations.

Step 1. Form or Select Cross-Functional Teams

The best way to obtain management support is to show how team-based quality cost techniques can improve the organization's bottom line. By focusing on key business processes, such as order administration, new product development, sales, service or manufacturing, quality cost measurements can be used to show an "as is" vs. a "could be" performance baseline.

Let's take customer complaints as an example of a problem to be solved and form a team to address this issue. A cross-functional team for this problem might include team members from Sales (the team leader), Customer Service, Manufacturing, Engineering, and Quality.

Step 2. Initiate Problem Solving

To be successful with team-based quality cost techniques, team members must understand basic problem-solving techniques. This includes how to write problem statements, develop cause-and-effect diagrams (also known as Ishikawa and "fishbone" diagrams), and be able to brainstorm for potential root causes of problems.

Typically, the quality professional is the key person who will plan for and propose that team-based quality cost techniques be undertaken. Usually, the quality professional is already familiar with the concept of quality

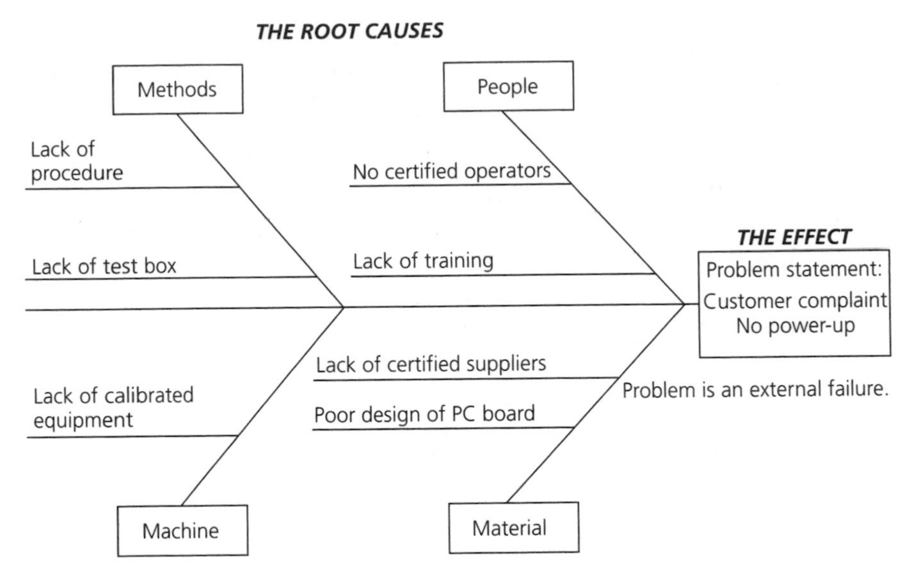

Figure 5.18. Cause-and-Effect diagram.

costs and problem solving. If needed, training should be obtained for the quality costs project leader and/or implementation team on the principles of quality costs. A quality costs refresher course can be most helpful to reopen the thought process and generate new ideas.

In our example of customer complaints, the team decided to look at the types of customer complaints and how often they occurred. This information can usually be obtained from the Customer Service or Quality departments, which are likely to be tracking complaints by type. In our example, it is determined by the team to look at a specific customer complaint—"no power-up"—based on the fact that it occurred frequently and directly impacted the external customer.

As a result of team brainstorming, the cause-and-effect diagram shown in Figure 5.18 resulted.

Step 3. Calculate the Failure Cost of One Occurrence

Once the cause-and-effect diagram(s) have been developed and brainstorming for a root cause has taken place, it's time to calculate the cost of one occurrence for the problem selected. A worksheet can be created like Table 5.1.

Note that when creating a Cost of Quality Worksheet, it should be kept simple. Initially, include only the basic "tasks" that must be performed to

Table 5.1. Cost of quality worksheet.

Tasks	Average Hours per Task	Hourly Rate	Cost of Element	Material Costs	External Failure ($)	Internal Failure ($)	Total Failure Cost
1. Customer Service answers phone and records information.	0.10	$35	$3.50	n/a	$3.50	n/a	$3.50
2. Forwards info to Quality Assurance	0.10	$35	$3.50	n/a	$3.50	n/a	$3.50
3. Q/A investigates the problem.	1.50	$50	$75.00	n/a	$75.00	n/a	$75.00
a. Q/A performs destructive test on another stock part.	0.50	$50	$25.00	n/a	$25.00	n/a	$25.00
b. Cost of part	n/a	n/a	n/a	$43.63	$43.63	n/a	$43.63
4. Fix process in manufacturing.	2.25	$50	$112.50	n/a	$112.50	n/a	$112.50
5. Contact customer with fix and new part.	0.75	$50	$37.50	n/a	$37.50	n/a	$37.50
				$43.63	$43.63	n/a	$43.63
				Total			$344.26

Problem/Nonconformance Description: Customer Complaint—No Power-Up *Problem Code: EF-NP*

find and fix the problem. Be sure to list the time in the "Average Hours per Task" column in decimal hours. Task time can be obtained by using industrial engineering estimates or by simply asking the people involved in the corrective action process. Remember that these are averages and do not have to be exact measurements. Quality cost reporting should be used for management reporting, not for detailed financial reporting; hence, solid estimates are acceptable.

The "Hourly Rate" column is the average "loaded" hourly rate, i.e., including benefits, for the department performing the task. This rate can be obtained from the Finance Department. If such information is not available, simply determine the average hourly rate by dividing the total wages charged to the department by the number of employees in the department. For example, if six people work in the Customer Service Department and the weekly payroll is $8350, the average hourly rate is $8350/40 hours/week, equaling $208.75/hour, which is then divided by six people, to equal $34.80/hour per person. In the example, the average hourly rate of $35/hour is used for the Customer Service Department. If more than one person is involved in the process, multiply the number of employees by the figure in the "Cost of Element" column. A similar approach is taken for other departments involved in the process.

The "Cost of Element" column is the result of the Average Hours per Task multiplied by the Hourly Rate. The "Material Costs" column contains those expenses that are true "out-of-pocket" costs, such as inventory items, part costs, unplanned travel expenses, and other real "receipted" expenses.

When deciding whether the cost of the problem is an External or Internal Failure, simply note where the defect is found. All external failures are found by the customer; hence, all the cost calculations remain in the "External Failure" column. The cost is either all external or all internal failure, not a mixture of both. The costs are then added horizontally across the worksheet and totaled in the "Total Failure Cost" column. The total cost of one occurrence, in this example, is $344.26, which is obtained by adding the final column.

It is helpful to code the problem. In this example, "EF-NP" is used and recorded in the worksheet to abbreviate the problem description of "Customer Complaint—No Power-Up"—External Failure. Such coding is useful when quality cost information is put into a software program to determine trends.

Step 4. Calculate the Total Failure Cost for a Given Period

Now that the cost of one occurrence for the problem has been calculated, the actual number of times this problem occurred needs to be determined. This information can usually be obtained from quality problem or defect reports, such as Customer Service call-in logs and inspection sheets or from audit reports.

In this example, if there were 48 occurrences in one year, the total external failure cost for "Customer Complaints—No Power-Up" would be $16,524.48 annually ($344.26 multiplied by 48 occurrences). A problem that once may have appeared insignificant or tolerable now has renewed attention using quality cost failure dollars.

Step 5. Rank Problems by Failure Dollars Using Pareto Analysis

You can now repeat the costing process for several other problems or defect types. Both the number of occurrences and the cost of quality for both internal and external failures can be viewed.

In the example, the failure cost Pareto analysis worksheet, ranked by annual failure costs would look like Table 5.2. Notice that the most frequently occurring problem or defect does not always have the highest failure cost. Taking corrective action on the "no power-up" problem, selected by the team, will give the most return. Quality cost analysis helps prioritize problem-solving activities. Of course, considerations such as criticality, complexity, and ease and timeliness of solution also come into play. But, before investing much time or money in solutions, it is important to have quality cost data showing significant financial impact.

Table 5.2. Pareto analysis of failure costs.

Problem Description	Failure Type	Annual Failure $	Number of Annual Occurrences
No power-up	EF	$16,524.48	48
Computer downtime	IF	$11,838.11	20
Order shipped late	EF	$9,333.58	36
Paperwork incomplete	IF	$6,423.15	121

IF = Internal Failure EF = External Failure

Table 5.3 Proposed prevention plan & costs.

Root Cause Description	Proposed Tasks to Eliminate	Hours	$ Rate Needed	Total $
Lack of procedure	Write procedure	3.0	$50/hr.	$150
No certified operators and lack of training	Train and certify operators	40.0	$35/hr.	$1400
Lack of calibrated equipment	Calibrate equipment	2.0	$35/hr.	$70
Lack of a test box	Make a test box	4.4	$50/hr.	$220
Lack of certified suppliers	Find ISO registered supplier	2.0	$35/hr.	$70
Poor design of PC board	None	n/a	n/a	n/a
Total prevention investment required				**$1910**

Problem Description: Customer Complaint—No Power-Up (an External Failure)

Step 6. Look at the Cause-and-Effect Diagram and Propose a Prevention Plan

A prevention plan to eliminate the problem's root causes can now be proposed. This is done by looking at the fishbone diagram and developing a plan for the application of prevention resources.

Using our example of customer complaints—no power-up, which had an external failure cost of $16,524.48 annually, and the associated fishbone diagram (Step 2), the proposed prevention costs can be calculated as in Table 5.3.

Step 7. Set Team Goal for Reducing Frequency of Occurrence

The next step is for the problem-solving team to estimate the level of occurrence reduction they believe is possible, if the proposed prevention resources are made available. Depending on the complexity of the problem and the associated fishbone diagram, some teams may commit to a 100 percent reduction (goal of zero defects), while others may commit to something less. Be careful not to overcommit. Should something outside the control of the team occur, an aggressive goal can be discouraging to the team and commitment can diminish.

In the example, the team selected a 50 percent reduction goal—that is, reducing the number of occurrences from forty-eight to twenty-four per

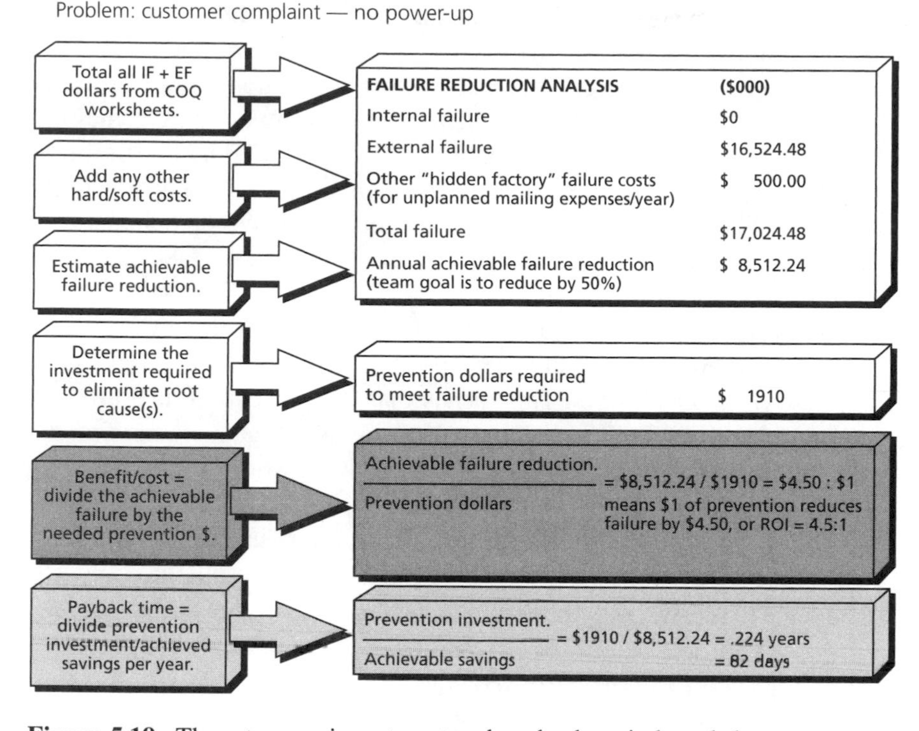

Figure 5.19. The return on investment and payback period worksheet.

year, for the problem of customer complaints—no power-up with an annual external failure cost of $16,524.48.

Step 8. Calculate the Return on Investment (ROI) and Payback Period

Once the reduction goal is set and the prevention plan developed, you can calculate the return on investment (benefit/cost) and payback period (the time it takes to break even on the investment spent on prevention). This is done for each problem selected and can be calculated using a worksheet like the one shown in Figure 5.19.

The example shows the external failure cost of forty-eight occurrences for the problem of "customer complaints—no power-up, which totals $16,524.48 annually. An additional $500 was added for unplanned premium freight charges, which was obtained from Finance, giving a total external failure cost of $17,024.48. Recall that the team assigned to this problem committed to reducing the number of occurrences to twenty-four, a 50 percent reduction—that is, reducing failure costs by $8,512.24. This is shown in the figure as the "Annual Achievable Failure Reduction."

Recall from the prevention plan, that the prevention dollars proposed is $1910. The benefit/cost ratio is then calculated by dividing achievable failure reduction dollars by prevention dollars ($8512.24/$1910), a ratio of 4.5:1. This means a return on investment of $4.50 for every dollar invested. When compared with other costed problems, or perhaps even those assigned to other teams, this problem could be selected as one worthwhile to pursue.

The payback period is calculated simply by taking the inverse of the benefit/cost ratio. In the example, $1910/$8512.24 equals a payback period of 0.224 years, or 82 days. This means that the prevention investment of $1950 will pay for itself in less than three months. Again, comparing this calculation to other costed problems could prove it worthwhile to pursue.

Both the return on investment and the payback period calculations can be used to select the problem with the highest return and shortest payback period, helping teams show the results of effective problem solving to management.

Step 9. Make Presentation to Management

Using the return on investment and payback period worksheet, the team can now make a presentation to management, requesting that the prevention funds be authorized. This format is particularly useful when other problems are costed or when other teams are seeking the same prevention funds. Prevention funds are limited, and usually the funding of all improvement projects at the same time is not feasible. By using this worksheet, management can now evaluate and select which problems teams should pursue, based on which problems have the highest return on investment with the shortest payback period.

Step 10. Track Progress and Repeat Process on Another Problem

As with any quality improvement project, progress must be measured and tracked. The technique presented offers a simple approach—counting the number of occurrences. By counting the decrease of occurrences, the cost of quality will also show a decrease. Numbers can easily be summarized by week, month, or other selected reporting periods. After the plan has been implemented and progress has been made, the team can repeat this quality cost problem-solving process to make further improvements in the company.

Implementation Guidelines

Four guidelines should be considered when implementing team-based cost of quality problem-solving techniques:

1. The team-based quality cost problem-solving technique is centered around the identification of a problem and tasks that result each time a problem occurs. These tasks are then assessed under the traditional quality cost definitions of external and internal failure. The total cost of the problem on a per occurrence basis results.
2. Team-based quality cost problem-solving techniques should be used with existing teams or teams that are planned. Don't re-invent the wheel or call this a "new and improved quality program." Make Quality Costs part of the team's weekly or monthly reporting process.
3. Finance should review and approve calculation worksheets and any assumptions. Don't create a new accounting system. Team-based quality cost problem-solving techniques are not intended to modify or replace the existing accounting system. It's calculations are estimates but are determined with logic and rationale. Existing "appraisal" systems can be used to capture the frequency of occurrence and are likely to be readily available.
4. Provide training. Some users experience difficulty with team-based problem-solving techniques when first introduced to the technique.

Conclusion

The methodology presented is intended to provide a roadmap of how quality costs can be calculated by problem-solving teams. It provides a focus to process improvement teams, managers, and others who are involved in quality improvement.

WORKING WITH SUPPLIERS TO REDUCE SUPPLIER QUALITY COSTS

Supplier quality costs can be reduced by working with suppliers. Some companies debit suppliers for the scrap and rework occurring in the buyer's plant to place the responsibility for failures where it hurts most—in the pocketbook. In the long run, however, this may be counterproductive, as some suppliers may ask for a price increase to cover this situation. Another method often used is to reduce the amount of business given to the offender, rewarding the good performer with a greater share of the "order pie".

A far more positive approach is to use supplier quality costs to identify needed supplier quality improvements. The buying company can then initiate projects jointly with suppliers to resolve the problems that are the source of high quality costs. Perhaps the problems can be solved through buying company actions. Maybe the specifications are incorrect, or the seller really doesn't know the application of their component in the total product. Ensuring specifications are correct helps to assure the procurement of good parts, and also helps to assure that good parts are not wrongly rejected.

In other cases, it may be that the seller's manufacturing process needs upgrading through better tooling. Through joint projects using supplier costs as facts, these problems can be solved, resulting in better products and lower costs to both parties.

As was discussed in chapter 4 (page 74), a company should use quality costs in its supplier relationships. Through this tool, the buying company can determine the costs and suppliers on which to focus. After making this determination, the buying company can suggest to these suppliers that they adopt a quality cost program, if appropriate, or perform special quality studies to obtain improvements in the quality of their products. However, discretion must be used. Small companies may not be able to support this effort, and there can be special circumstances in other companies that would prohibit a successful application. Supplier quality costs can also be used by the buying company as a basis for starting joint quality improvement projects with its suppliers.

Most important of all is that any quality costs program is incomplete without an effective corrective action program. The mere act of collecting quality costs will do nothing for your company but add costs. Only through pinpointing and permanently solving problems can a company progress in improving quality and productivity while reducing costs.

GAINING JUSTIFICATION FROM CUSTOMER SATISFACTION*

Quality cost techniques can be supplemented to justify changes for improving customer satisfaction. The monetary gain to a company by having more satisfied customers can be quantified. A more satisfied customer has a much greater willingness to repurchase from a company. The payoff is a gain in repeat sales and an accompanying increase in cash flow in the future.[1]

*Material for this section was extracted from "Driving Buyer Satisfaction by Quality Cost" by William O. Winchell, published in the Transactions of the 50th ASQC Annual Quality Congress, ASQ Milwaukee, 1996.[1]

Background

Some of the values and beliefs of a company necessary for an effective continuous improvement effort include

1. Focus is on buyers and their needs.
2. The judgment on the quality of products is recognized as being in the eyes of the buyer.
3. Prevention of problems must be of primary importance.

In a continuous improvement environment, quality cost techniques must provide a focus on the buyer. The approach that follows supports continuous improvement efforts. It recognizes that buyer perceptions form the benchmark of quality. It also provides justification for changes that can prevent problems that affect the buyer.

Buyer Satisfaction

In a sense, quality is like beauty. Like beauty, quality is in the eyes of the beholder and, with quality, the buyer is the beholder. This perception of a buyer is of great importance to a company. A more satisfied customer will have a greater willingness to repurchase from a company in the future. This relationship is shown in Figure 5.20.

Figure 5.20. Buyer perception of quality.

Based on data from marketing study (Juran and Gryna, 1993 page 87)[2]

Payoff

The potential monetary gain, or payoff, to a company by having more satisfied customers is often quite large. A more satisfied customer has a much greater willingness to repurchase from a company. However, this payoff is not immediate but sometime in the future. This requires a long-range outlook by a company.

In contrast, the penalties for lack of buyer satisfaction are severe. An unhappy buyer could tell as many as thirty-five other persons about the problem. This secondary effect may have a severe impact on future sales.

The payoff, or monetary gain, to a company in seeking better customer satisfaction is defined as follows:

> *Gain in Contribution Margin:* Cash flow from the incremental gain in revenue minus incremental increase in cost due to additional repeat sales from more satisfied customers

The following steps are suggested to calculate the gain in contribution margin resulting from a projected increase in buyer satisfaction:

1. *Find the relationship between buyers' perceptions of quality and repurchase intentions.* This requires a marketing study involving the current buyer base. The buyers chosen for the survey are those likely to be repurchasing soon. Buyers are asked to rate how they feel about the quality of the product. Then they are asked if they are willing to repurchase a similar product, from the same company. Figure 5.20 shows the results of such a study.

2. *Determine when repurchases are likely to be made.* For most companies, repurchases are made near the end of the life cycle of the product. This is usually well beyond the warranty period. For some companies, sales records may contain this information, but, for other companies, a marketing study of the current customer base may be required. Buyers would be asked when they expect to repurchase a similar product. Figure 5.21 is a profile of buyers' repurchase intentions for a product. All buyers initially purchased the product at time "0." It is noted that each company and each product within a company may have a different profile.

3. *Assess the current perceptions of buyers regarding the quality of the product.* Finding the current perceptions of buyers also requires a

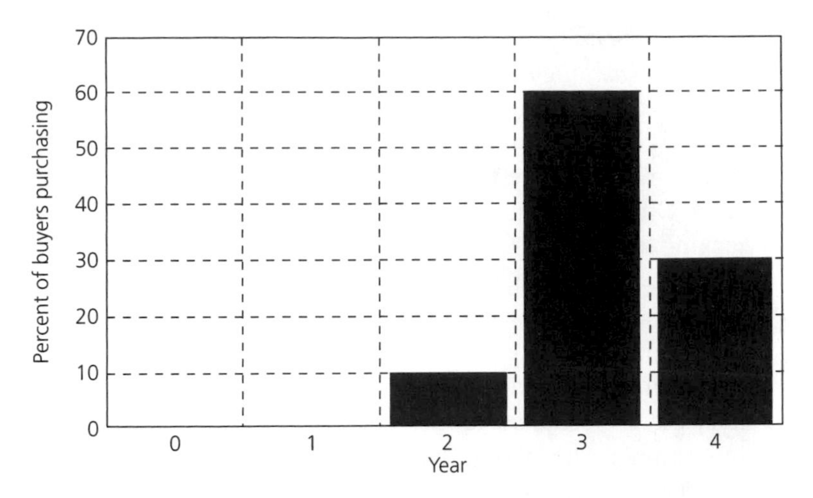

Figure 5.21. Profile of when buyers in year 0 will repurchase.

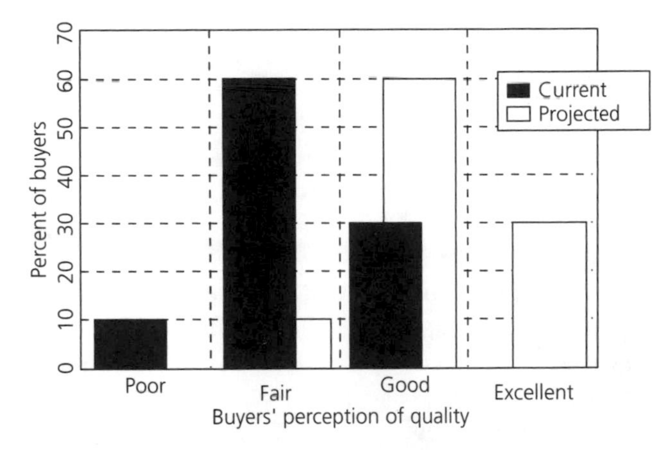

Figure 5.22. Buyers' current and projected perceptions of quality after proposed increase in customer satisfaction.

marketing study of the customer base. To reduce the effort, the marketing studies suggested in Steps 1 and 2 and this step may be combined into one survey. For this step, buyers are asked to rate how they feel about the product that they use. Figure 5.22 contains the results of such a study. Note that only 30 percent of the customers rated the product good or better. Many would feel that this leaves a lot of room for a significant improvement in customer satisfaction.

4. *Project the change in perceptions of quality about the product to be sought by making improvements.* Much judgement is required as to what level of satisfaction should be sought. The payoff for a company is contingent on the size of the increase projected. For example, a larger increase will result in more monetary gain from repeat sales. On the other hand, a larger increase will be much more challenging to obtain. Aiding in this judgement is knowledge of the current level of customer satisfaction found in Step 3. Benchmarking of how buyers feel who own competitive products may also be useful. A marketing study is necessary to provide benchmarks as to how competitors are satisfying customers. Figure 5.22 also contains the projected perceptions of quality after a proposed increase in customer satisfaction. Note that customer perceptions are projected to be one notch up after improvements are made.

5. *Calculate the percent of buyers willing to repurchase under current levels of customer satisfaction.* The calculation of current levels of customer satisfaction, in terms of "composite percentage willing to repurchase," is shown in Table 5.4. Sources of data in this table are:

Column	Label	Source of Data
1	Buyers' Perception	Figure 5.20
2	% Willing to Repurchase	Figure 5.20
3	% of Buyers	Figure 5.22

The product of columns 2 and 3 is entered in the fourth column ("Adjusted % Willing to Repurchase") after converting from necessary percentages to decimals. The total of the entries in the fourth column comprises the "composite percentage willing to repurchase." This measure of the current level of customer satisfaction is a weighted average of the data for the various perceptions. Table 5.4 shows that only 29.4 percent of the buyers are currently willing to repurchase.

6. *Calculate the percent of buyers willing to repurchase under the projected levels of customer satisfaction.* A similar calculation can be made for the projected levels of customer satisfaction and is shown in Table 5.5. The sources of data and the calculations are identical to that described in Step 5. The measure of the projected level of customer satisfaction (composite percentage willing to repurchase) shows that 66.6 percent are now likely to repurchase.

Table 5.4. Calculation of buyers willing to repurchase with current levels of customer satisfaction.

Buyers' Perception	% Willing to Repurchase	% of Buyers	Adjusted % Willing to Repurchase
Poor	0	10	0.0
Fair	18	60	10.8
Good	62	30	18.6
Excellent	92	0	0.0
Composite % willing to repurchase		100	29.4

Table 5.5. Calculation of buyers willing to repurchase with proposed improvement in customer satisfaction.

Buyers' Perception	% Willing to Repurchase	% of Buyers	Adjusted % Willing to Repurchase
Poor	0	0	0.0
Fair	18	10	1.8
Good	62	60	37.2
Excellent	92	30	27.6
Composite % willing to repurchase		100	66.6

7. *Calculate the gain in percent of buyers willing to repurchase if projected levels of customer satisfaction are obtained.* The gain in buyers willing to repurchase is the difference in composite percentage willing to repurchase found in Step 6 (66.6 percent) minus that found in Step 5 (29.4 percent), or 37.2 percent. In other words, repeat sales from the projected increase in buyer satisfaction more than doubled.

8. *Calculate the gain in contribution margin for each year that repurchases are made if projected levels of customer satisfaction are obtained.* Table 5.6 illustrates the calculation made for the gain in contribution margin if projected levels of customer satisfaction are obtained.

Table 5.6. Calculation of gain in contribution margin due to gain in repeat sales through proposed improvement in customer satisfaction.

Year	% Buyers Repur-chasing	Gain in % Willing to Repurchase	Volume Bought Year 0	Contribution Margin $/Unit	Gain Total Contribution Margin
0	0				0
1	0				0
2	10	37.2	200,000	4.75	35,340
3	60	37.2	200,000	4.75	212,040
4	30	37.2	200,000	4.75	106,020

The sources of data for the columns in this table are

Column	Label	Source of Data
1	Year	Figure 5.21
2	% of Buyers	Figure 5.21
3	Gain in % Willing To Repurchase	Step 7
4	Volume Bought Year 0	Sales records
5	Contribution Margin $/Unit	Cost accounting

The product of columns 2 through 5 for each row is entered in the sixth column ("Gain Total Contribution Margin"). Note that this calculation requires converting necessary percentages to decimals. The payoff for the company or gain in total contribution margin is shown for years 2 through 4. This is when buyers will make repurchases. However, investment resulting in better buyer satisfaction would mostly be made in year 0—the year the product is built and sold. For this example, the payoff in more repeat sales, and added cash flow, will be realized from two to four years after the product is built and sold. This requires a long-range outlook on justification of investments for improved customer satisfaction.

9. *Find the present worth in year 0 of gain in contribution margin for future years.* Investments to improve customer satisfaction must mostly be made in year 0 of the product life prior to shipping. Therefore, the present worth in year 0 of the benefits listed in Table 5.6 for years 2–4 must be calculated. This will allow an "apples to

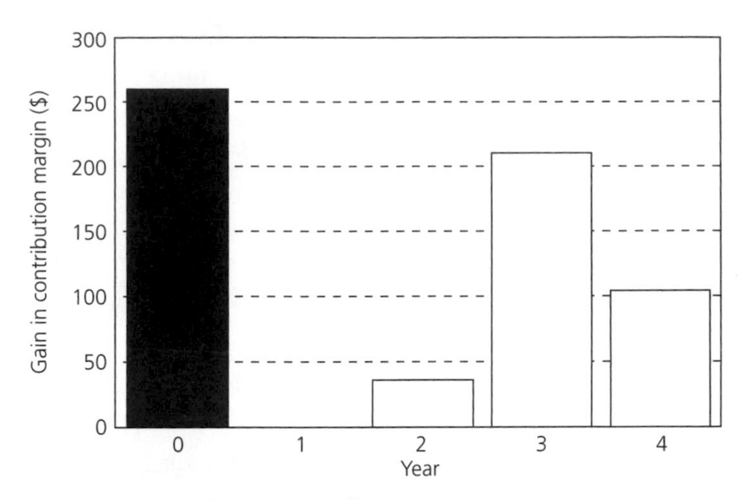

Figure 5.23. Gain in contribution margin. Shows present worth in year 0 of gain in contribution margin through more repeat sales in years 2–4. Additional repeat sales projected by proposed increase in customer satisfaction. A compound interest factor of 10 percent was assumed. (Donald G. Newnan, *Engineering Economic Analysis,* 4th ed. (San Jose: Engineering Press, 1991).

apples" comparison of the benefits to the cost of making the necessary changes required in year 0. Figure 5.23, shows this relationship. Engineering economic principles[3] can be used to make this calculation. For the example, assuming a 10 percent compound interest factor, the calculation is

Present Worth = Sum (Future Amount × Compound Amount Factor)

(Year 2) = $35,340 × .8264 = $29,205
(Year 3) = $212,040 × .7513 = $159,306
(Year 4) = $106,020 × .6830 = $72,412

(Year 0) = $260,923

Justification

Over $260,000 has been identified by the new approach for justification of changes leading to improvement of customer satisfaction. This is in addition to the funds that may be identified by traditional quality cost techniques.

Traditional quality cost techniques may identify other funds supporting changes leading to improved customer satisfaction through reductions concerning

- *Warranty claims.* The total cost of claims paid to the buyer or user, after acceptance, to cover expenses, including repair costs, such as removing defective hardware from a system, or cleaning costs due to a food or chemical service accident. Where a price reduction is negotiated in lieu of warranty, the value of the reduction should be counted.
- *Liability costs.* Company-paid costs due to liability claims, including the cost of product or service liability insurance
- *Penalties.* The cost of any penalties incurred because of less than full product or service performance achieved (as required by contracts with buyers or by government rules and regulations)
- *Buyer/user goodwill.* Costs incurred, over and above normal selling costs, to buyers or users who are not completely satisfied with the quality of a delivered product or service, such as costs incurred because buyers' quality expectations are greater than what they receive

Investment

The ASQ Quality Costs Committee in 1986 broadened the focus of the definitions of quality costs clearly beyond manufacturing. The definitions of cost correspond to the activities in the quality system for producing a product or service. This starts in marketing and extends through the other functions relating to product development and production. In view of this, quality cost definitions are used to show where possible investments can be made to upgrade customer satisfaction.

About 80 percent of the perception of buyer satisfaction depends on whether a product meets the true needs of the buyer. The funds identified could justify important improvements in assessing buyer needs and then validating that these needs are met. Improvements may be in the following quality activities:

- *Marketing/buyer/user.* Costs incurred in the accumulation and continued evaluation of buyer and user quality needs and perceptions (including feedback on reliability and performance) affecting their satisfaction with the company's product or service. This includes marketing research, buyer/user perception surveys/clinics, and contract/document review.

- *Product/service design development.* Costs incurred to translate buyer and user needs into reliable quality standards and requirements and manage the quality of new product or service developments prior to the release of authorized documentation for initial production. This includes design quality progress reviews, design support activities, product design–qualification test, and service design–qualification field trials.
- *Special product evaluations.* This includes life testing and environmental and reliability tests performed on production units.

The remaining 20 percent of the perception of buyer satisfaction depends on how a company handles complaints and solves problems. The funds identified could also justify desirable changes for these activities. This may include

- *Evaluation of field stock and spare parts.* Includes cost of evaluation testing or inspection of field stock resulting from engineering changes, storage time (excessive shelf life), or other suspected problems
- *Complaint investigations/buyer or user service.* Total cost of investigating, resolving, and responding to individual buyer or user complaints or inquiries, including necessary field service
- *Retrofit costs.* Costs to modify or update products or field service facilities to a new design change level, based on major redesign due to design deficiencies.

Although not a quality cost, improvement of customer satisfaction may also require an investment in upgrading the product or processes involved in making the product.

Conclusions

Relative to the suggested approach that supplements traditional quality cost techniques, the following is concluded:

1. Quantifying the monetary gain to a company by having more satisfied customers provides significant justification for making improvements affecting customer satisfaction.
2. Companies using this approach must have a long-range outlook. The monetary gain is in the future when repurchases are made by buyers.
3. Future monetary gain must be equated to the present to match when investments for improvements will be made. This can be done using engineering economics principles. By doing this, an "apples to apples" comparison can be made between investment costs and expected benefits or monetary gain.
4. The suggested approach expands traditional cost techniques by providing an analysis that is customer-focused. This type of analysis is more "in-tune" with continuous improvement efforts taking place in many companies.

Chapter 6

Service/Software Case Studies

Although most examples and case studies provided throughout this text apply equally well to both manufacturing and service industry organizations, they were obtained primarily from manufacturing concerns. To even the score for service and software readers, additional case studies obtained from actual service and software development operations are included in this chapter.

BANKING

Eleven business units of Banc One Corporation participated in a study of quality costs, customer satisfaction, and quality deficiencies/defects. The relationship between these three measurable components of quality was explored. Correlation analysis was performed using these three metrics. Interesting relationships emerged that can help predict what you will find and improve in an organization if each one of the metrics is measured over time.

Attacking high cost of quality opportunities reduces cost, defects, and errors and significantly increases customer satisfaction—and delight. A cost of quality analysis helps prioritize the opportunities for improvement. This prioritization process assures that those opportunities which will have the biggest impact on the bottom line will be selected. The quality improvement team processes used to attack cost of quality opportunities will be discussed (see Figure 6.1). Banc One uses this process on an ongoing basis to allocate resources, and to motivate or assign quality improvement teams to improve opportunities. In recent years, they have enhanced net income by $20 million annually through the application of these processes.

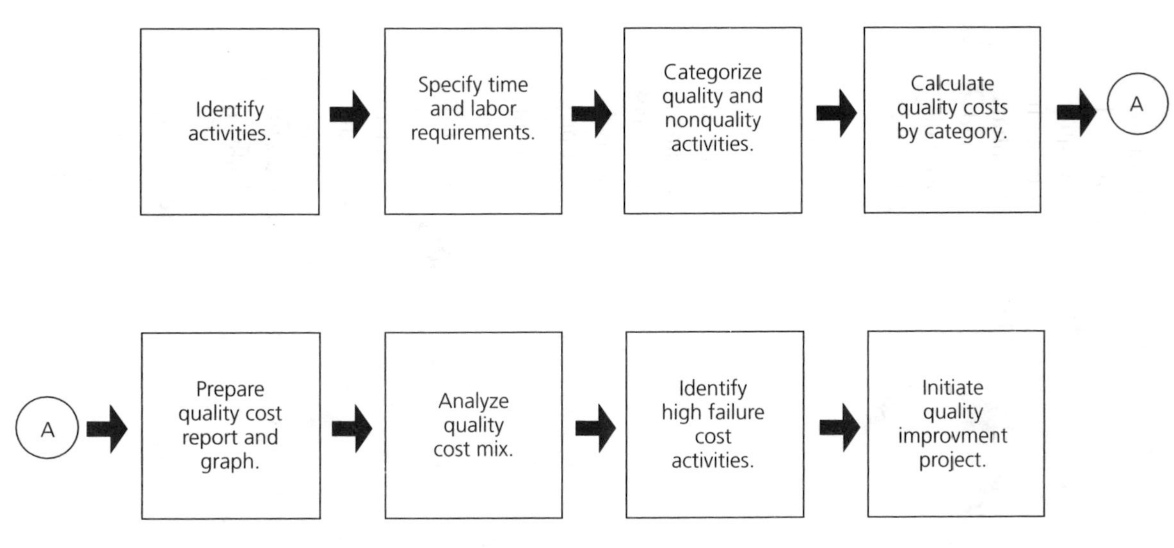

Figure 6.1. The Banc One quality improvement process.

Introduction

Within the service industry, as within manufacturing concerns, there are costs associated with providing and ensuring a high-quality product and/or service, and these costs are designated as quality costs. In order to understand the economic impact that quality costs have on the financial position of a bank and how they can be used to enhance that position, it is crucial that quality costs be defined, measured, and analyzed and action be taken to manage them. The four quality cost categories of prevention, appraisal, internal failure, and external failure as they relate to the *banking industry* are defined as follows:

- *Prevention*–Prevention costs are proactive activities that are accomplished before or during processing or service delivery. Prevention costs are those costs associated with operations or activities that keep failure from happening and keep appraisal costs to a minimum. Examples of prevention activities are new product review, quality planning, quality improvement team meetings, training programs, written policies and procedures, analysis of quality information, and quality information/improvement projects.
- *Appraisal*–Appraisal costs are those costs incurred to project or predict quality levels and to ascertain the condition of a product or service in order to determine its degree of conformance to quality standards or specifications. Examples of appraisal activities are inspection of incoming work, supplies and material, periodic inspection of work in process, checking, balancing, verifying, final inspection, shopper surveys, customer surveys, focus groups, and analysis of customer correspondence/complaints.
- *Internal failure*–Internal failure costs are those costs that are incurred as a result of correcting the service or products produced that do not conform to standards or specifications *prior to* delivery to the customer. Examples of internal failure are machine downtime, scrap and waste due to improperly processed forms or reports, and rework of incorrectly processed work.
- *External failure*–External failure costs are those costs that are incurred as a result of correcting the service or products produced that do not conform to standards or specifications *after* delivery to the customer or correcting a product or service that customers perceive

do not conform to their specified standard. Examples of external failure costs are investigation time, payment of interest penalties, reprocessing of an item, scrap due to improperly processed or incorrect forms or reports, time spent with disgruntled customers, and lost or never acquired business due to providing poor service or having a poor quality reputation.

Most appraisal and all failure costs were considered the "cost of poor quality." These costs would disappear if the product or service was defect free or if it conformed to standards and specifications during or at the time of completion or delivery.

If all four categories of quality costs are added together, they are called total quality costs for a product, function, or service. In aggregate, these costs range from 10 percent to 30 percent of sales or 25 percent to 40 percent of operating expense. The latter is the way quality costs are measured in banks, as they do not have sales. This range has been verified in banking time and time again. It represents a tremendous opportunity to reduce cost and increase customer satisfaction.

Objective

The objective of a quality cost measurement is to aid a company in determining by function, by product, or by product line where the highest costs of quality are, so that improvement efforts can be targeted there. The goal should be to improve quality and productivity and, hence, profitability by reducing quality costs. Revenue can also be increased by increasing customer satisfaction, resulting in increased loyalty and repurchase.

The quantitative data from quality cost measurement supplies management with necessary information so that they can optimize quality improvement resource allocation. High appraisal and failure costs alert management to problems that may have been previously overlooked. As a result, improvement projects can be undertaken which reduce cost, improve quality, and therefore increase productivity and profitability. A companywide program alerts the employees as to the emphasis being placed on quality and their responsibility to meet the company's quality objectives. The companywide commitment to quality increases productivity, since work that is done right the first time does not need to be redone. Further, increased productivity and higher profitability and customer satisfaction should give the company a better position in the competitive marketplace.

Getting Started

The company's specific objective will determine how the process is to be implemented. However, there are basic guidelines that should be followed when implementing quality cost measurement. Start small. Do not attempt to quality cost every product, service, or function within the company. Start with activities that you suspect may have high failure or appraisal costs. Once you have decided the area to be measured, begin data collection.

First, a complete list of all operations or activities or jobs is developed in order to estimate costs based on actual operating activity and expense. The list details each task or operation performed in the area and the time spent performing each task. Prevention activities and time spent performing them are also included on this list, since they are part of total quality costs. A flowchart should be developed to assure all activities are captured and to balance labor activities and costs. Time can be allocated as a percentage of total available labor time or directly as total hours spent. The latter is recommended. Total hours spent performing all tasks should equal total labor hours available in the area. In either case, the total number of labor hours available in an area must be ascertained and specified. The average salary level of the employees in the area must also be determined. Each activity is then categorized as a quality (into one of the four categories) or nonquality (production) activity. Once quality activities, salary level, and time spent performing the activities have been specified, quality costs can be calculated by multiplying the labor time for each activity by the average salary level.

The expense statement is analyzed to determine if any other direct expenses are quality cost items. If so, they are assigned to a specific quality cost category.

Examples of other direct expenses are internal or external training expenses charged (an example of prevention), the purchase/maintenance of test equipment (an example of appraisal), the destruction of forms (an example of internal failure), and the payment of interest penalties or customer income lost due to poor quality (an example of external failure).

The activities and their related costs, by category, are listed on the quality cost report and are totaled (see Figure 6.2). Only those activities that fall into the four categories are listed. The largest single opportunities of appraisal as well as failure are identified. High appraisal costs are also signs of possible improvement opportunities that can be reduced with proper prevention. If all cannot start immediately, a Pareto diagram can be developed with this data to determine which project to undertake first (see Figures 6.3 and 6.4).

Operation	Prevention	Appraisal	Internal Failure	External Failure	Total
Making a Loan					
2. Run a credit check	0	0	26.13	0	$26.13
8. Prepare and put thru GL tickets and I/L input sheets	0	0	248.19	0	$248.19
9. Review documents	0	3,013.78	7.84	0	$3,021.62
10. Make document corrections, gather additional documents or information	0	0	1,013.65	0	$1,013.65
11. Prepare tickler file, review and follow up on titles, insurance, 2nd mtgs., and UCC's	0	156.75	0	0	$156.75
12. Review all output	0	2,244.14	0	0	$2,244.14
13. Correct rejects and incorrect output	0	0	425.84	0	$425.84
15. Work associated with the incomplete collateral report	0	0	0	78.38	$78.38
16. Work associated with dealer calls dealing with any problems and the time to research and communicate	0	0	0	2,481.88	$2,481.88
17. I/L system downtime	0	0	519.89	0	$519.89
18. Time spent training or being trained on I/L	1,366.34	0	0	0	$1,366.34
Loan Payment					
1. Receive and process payments from all sources	0	261.25	783.75	0	$1,045.00
2. Respond to inquiries when no coupon is presented with payments	0	0	783.75	0	$783.75
Loan Payoff					
2. Receive and process payoff and release document	0	0	13.06	0	$13.06
4. Research payoff problems	0	0	13.06	0	$13.06
Total Cost of Quality	$1,366.34	$5,675.92	$3,835.15	$2,560.25	$13,437.66
Cost of Quality as a % of Total Quality Cost	10.17%	42.24%	28.54%	19.05%	100.00%
Cost of Quality as a % of Reported Salary Expense	2.60%	10.79%	7.29%	4.87%	25.54%

Figure 6.2. Quality cost report—installment loans.

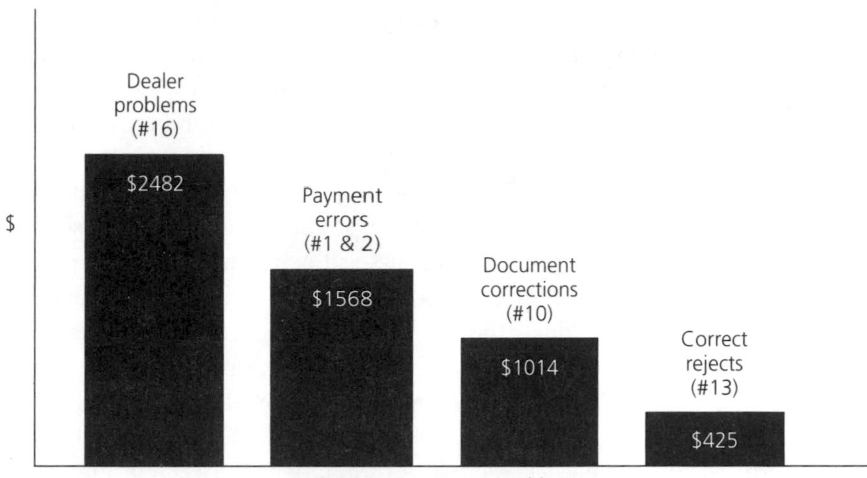

Figure 6.3. Pareto diagram—failures.

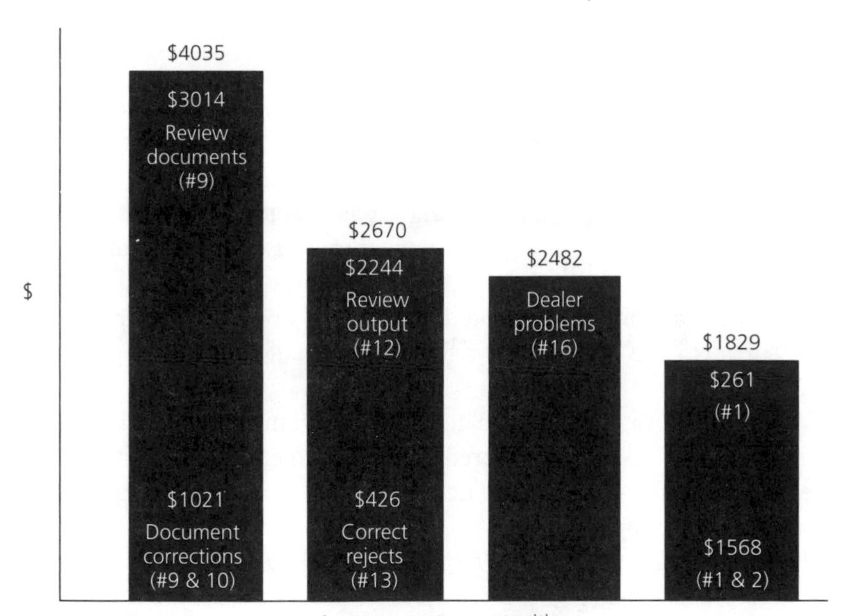

Figure 6.4. Pareto diagram—failure and appraisal.

The success of a quality improvement project depends on accurately diagnosing and applying cause-and-effect analysis to the problem. The quality costs data specify the symptom or effect, but, until the causes are known, identified, and tested, no action should be taken to correct the problem. To attempt to solve a problem without knowing the cause could increase quality costs and negate the purpose of the quality cost measurement. Having properly identified the cause or causes of the problem, the team can use the improvement project to set goals and a course of action to correct the problem. Potential savings based on the proposed course of action can then be estimated. The team can evaluate the success of the improvement project and the quality cost program by measuring the actual shift or reduction in quality costs, while also measuring the internal quality level and external customer perceptions. Typical improvement activities yielded a range of 5 to 10:1 return on investment. These eleven quality improvement projects yielded an 8:1 average return. Besides the team monitoring the quality cost changes effective at the conclusion of the project, continuous measurement should be done to assure the gain has been held.

Relationship of Cost of Poor Quality to Defects and Customer Satisfaction

The results of the eleven quality cost measurement studies included the percentage of quality costs to total expense, the overall defect rate from quality standards, the largest individual quality improvement opportunity identified, and the overall measure of customer satisfaction for each department or service. When these measurements were correlated, some interesting relationships occurred. A low percent of poor quality costs as a percent of total quality costs predicts a small opportunity for improvement. Conversely, a high percentage usually predicts a large opportunity of improvement.

When defect rates are correlated to improvement opportunities, neither high nor low defect rates predict improvement opportunities of the same relative size. In fact, a low defect rate can often hide large individual improvement opportunities.

The data indicate that where large individual quality cost opportunities exist there is a less then acceptable customer perception of the service level provided. Therefore, defect rates are not very useful in identifying or predicting the level of quality cost improvement opportunities, but customer satisfaction levels can be more accurate in identifying opportunities.

Customer survey results may be a better indicator as to which areas may benefit from quality cost measurement and improvement team efforts. Once the problem has been identified and improved, not only will the cost savings be realized, but there may be a more direct and positive impact on customer satisfaction and retention. Satisfaction increases lead to greater loyalty and repurchases, which lead to greater revenue along with lower costs, which together significantly increase profitability.

EDUCATION

Using Cost of Quality in a University Environment

In 1992 the University of Western Ontario formed a Quality Center to drive quality and productivity improvement within the university. Their early efforts with process improvement teams were not as successful as management had hoped. One of the major areas that had not been addressed was an effective means of measuring the opportunity for the teams and of measuring the savings to be realized by the improvements recommended.

Cost of quality (CoQ) had been used very effectively by manufacturing organizations for many years to identify opportunities and track improvements. With the service sector's increased interest in quality improvement, CoQ has also been used as a measurement tool for their projects. It was felt that CoQ had excellent potential in a university environment as well.

The Manager of Financial Systems in the Department of Finance was convinced of the value of CoQ as an effective quality improvement measurement tool. He volunteered his department and identified two pilot projects: (1) Major Equipment Replacement and (2) Telephone System Review. A project facilitator/trainer was assigned.

The major concern was to ensure that the application of CoQ would be viewed as a "management tool," rather than a "financial tool". As a management tool, CoQ would enable the process improvement teams to manage their improvement efforts, while as a financial tool it could be seen as just another method to monitor the employees.

For the pilot projects to be successful, it was necessary that the approach and methodology be seen as equally important as the CoQ measurement tool (see Figure 6.5). Team members were given extensive training. The training consisted of a disciplined approach to process improvement. An integrated process improvement and potential problem-solving model was used, supported by appropriate quality tools. In addition to cost

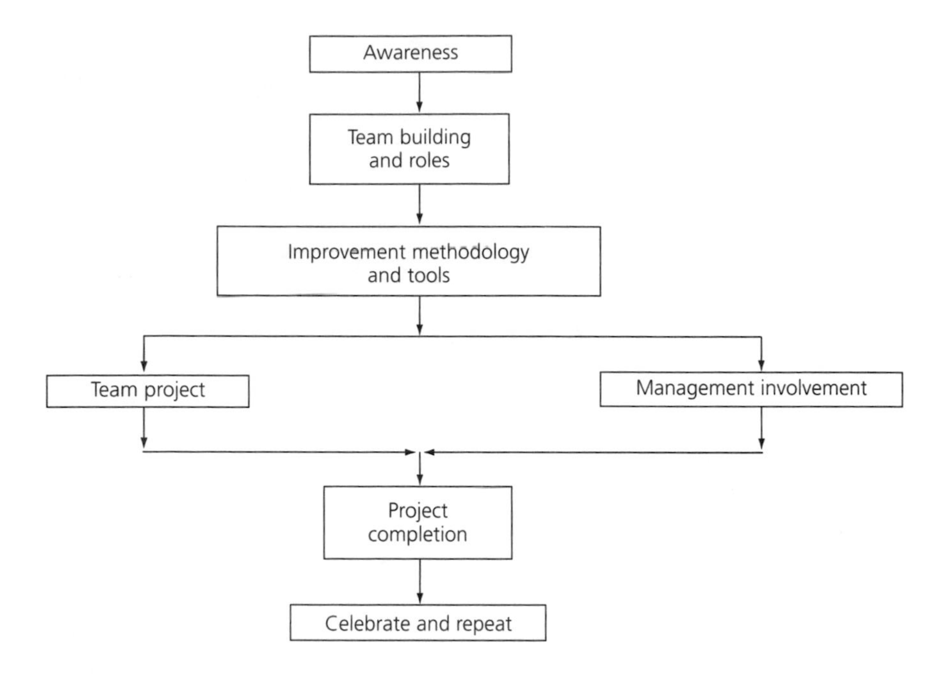

Figure 6.5. Process improvement team methodology.

of quality, these included brainstorming, process mapping, and the seven basic quality tools: Pareto diagram, checksheet, cause-and-effect diagram, scatter diagram, histogram, control chart, and run chart.

Another key factor in the success of the pilot projects was management's role in the support and guidance of the improvement teams. One of the most significant challenges faced by the management team was to free up time for the improvement team members to work on their projects. The team members spent 25 percent of their time on their projects. This meant that part of their daily work had to be off loaded or delayed. Some areas were more successful than others in reassigning work. It was essential that the teams see quality improvement as part of their job and not something else to be added to their duties. The key role of the management team was to monitor the progress of the team by focusing on the activities or steps of the team's process and not the results of the team efforts. By ensuring the team followed all the appropriate steps, the results would follow.

1. Major Equipment Replacement Project

The purpose of this first project was to develop a process within the Finance Department for equipment replacement. Equipment included personal computers, copiers, facsimile, microfiche, and microfilm. The project would need to address individual needs assessment, training, and communication. The team consisted of six members from the Financial Department.

The team initially documented and flowcharted the current equipment replacement process. They found that the decision to replace equipment was being made by one individual, using a very informal process based on the best assessment of the need. The team then conducted customer focus group meetings to gather information on perceptions of the current process. What was found was that there was a lack of communication with staff members on the current equipment replacement process, and the existing procedure did not provide feedback to the individuals if their request for equipment was not approved. The perception was that the current method was not objective. In many cases, input from the individuals requesting the equipment was not used.

The team then surveyed a sample of members of the Department of Finance to determine the level of equipment and training satisfaction. Using the information collected, the team was able to estimate the cost of quality for the existing process. The results of this data are shown in Figure 6.6. The team based an estimate of loss in productivity on the level of dissatisfaction expressed by those surveyed. They determined the number of individuals using that type of equipment. As a result, it was possible to calculate the annual CoQ by multiplying the number of individuals, times hours per year, times an average hourly salary rate of $28. The annual CoQ for equipment was approximately $210,000. They also calculated the CoQ for computer training to be approximately $145,000, bringing the total annual CoQ to almost $355,000.

The team then developed an equipment replacement process using a team approach. This included annual budget preparation, repairs, reserve appropriations, and computer training to be centralized within the Department of Finance. They then presented management with a list of seven recommendations complete with implementation costs (see Figure 6.7).

Result. The recommendations had a one-time cost of approximately $2200 and an annual cost of approximately $12,500. The savings represented a payback period of less than one month.

Description	Total Replies[a]	Weighted Average of Satisfaction Level (10=max)[a]	Weighted Average Level of Dissatisfaction[b]	Estimated Productivity Loss[b]	Finance Total Staff[c]	Estimated % of Staff Involved[d]	Weekly Average Hours Used[e]	Weeks per Year	Average Hourly Salary[f]	Estimated Annual Cost of Quality
Personal computer	17	7.3	2.7	27% ×	45 ×	89% ×	10 ×	46 ×	$28 =	$140,324
Copier	19	7.1	2.9	29% ×	45 ×	100% ×	2 ×	46 ×	$28 =	$ 34,166
Fax	17	5.4	4.6	46% ×	45 ×	89% ×	1 ×	46 ×	$28 =	$ 23,661
Microfiche	10	5.8	4.2	42% ×	45 ×	53% ×	0.3 ×	46 ×	$28 =	$ 3,644
Microfilm	10	4.0	6.0	60% ×	45 ×	53% ×	0.4 ×	46 ×	$28 =	$ 7,321
Estimated cost of quality for equipment										$209,316
Computer training[g]	19	7.5	2.5	25% ×	45 ×	100% ×	10 ×	46 ×	$28 =	$144,900
Estimated cost of quality for equipment and training										$354,216

[a]These schedules are based on the survey of nineteen members in the department.

[b]A satisfaction level of 10 (100 percent) indicated full productivity. A satisfaction level of 7 indicated a 70 percent level of productivity and, accordingly, a 30 percent loss in productivity.

[c]Approximate number of nonmanagerial staff in the Department of Finance.

[d]Estimated percentage of staff involved is the number of responses divided by the sample size (19) (e.g., 17/19 = 89%).

[e]Average weekly hours that equipment is used was determined by the survey.

[f]Average hourly salary for nonmanagerial staff is estimated at $28 per hour.

[g]When we asked people in the survey if they were adequately trained to use their computer, only two people felt that they were adequately trained to perform computer-related functions. On a weighted average basis, staff in the survey felt that they were 75 percent trained to use their computers. Accordingly, lack of training is estimated to reduce productivity of personal computer usage by 25 percent.

Figure 6.6. Costs of quality—Department of Finance, Equipment and Training.

Start up costs:		
Initial assessment of inventory and training	50 hours @ $28 =	$1,400
Database design	14 hours @ $33 =	462
Database approval	4 people @ 2 hours @ $44 =	352
		$2,214
Annual costs:		
Annual time for team meetings	12 meetings @ 3 hours for 3 people @ $33 =	$3,564
Ongoing support time for team meetings	12 meetings @ 3 hours for 3 people @ $33 =	3,564
Maintenance of inventory	1 hour per month @ $33 =	396
Communications time	7 hours per month for 1 person @ $33 =	2,772
Estimated annual costs		$10,296
Total estimated costs for implementation:		$12,510

Average hourly salaries:
Nonmanagerial $28/hr
PMA $33/hr
Managerial $44/hr

Figure 6.7. Estimated implementation costs.

2. Telephone System Review Project

The purpose of this second project was to review the existing telephone system and make recommendations for improvement to maximize customer satisfaction in a cost-effective manner. Six members of the Department of Finance volunteered to participate on this project.

The team developed a telephone system review checklist to better understand the magnitude and types of calls being made to the Department of Finance. Next the team conducted a customer focus group to determine the problems that were being experienced by individuals contacting the Department of Finance. The most frequent problems identified were

1. Calls transferred to the wrong area
2. Incomplete messages received
3. a. Picking same phone

   b. Picking same phone with disconnect

4. Not telling someone when leaving their office
5. Expert not available when immediate help needed
6. Inexperienced or temporary help answering calls
7. General calls go to Director of Finance
8. Not using available options
9. Secretary clearing phone mail box

The team then summarized the cost of quality for the current process (see Figure 6.8). They first determined the time it would take to correct the problem for each of the first seven problem types. For example, the time wasted when a call had been transferred to the wrong area was 6.5 minutes. For the last two problems—paying for options not used and clearing phone mail, they calculated the cost of each. Clearing phone mail varied from department to department, depending on who was involved and the number of messages. Based on the information collected through the checklist, they then calculated the CoQ for each type of problem. Again, these varied in cost from area to area, depending on frequency of errors. The total CoQ for the Telephone Systems Review project was approximately $65,500 per year.

The team then developed an employee telephone survey to solicit input from the users on suggestions for improvement. Using input from their customers, the team developed recommendations in eleven areas. The cost of quality was recalculated, based on these recommendations (see Figure 6.9).

Result. The CoQ after implementation of the recommendations would be about $18,900 per year. Part of the new CoQ included approximately $1600 for training. This project resulted in an annual savings of about $46,600.

Conclusion

These two pilot projects clearly demonstrated that cost of quality is an excellent management tool. It was shown that CoQ can be used effectively to identify opportunities and track improvements, not only in manufacturing and service sectors, but also in the university community.

	FABA[a]	Gen. Acct.	Audit	Fees	Research	General	Total
1. Transfer call to wrong area 6.5 min.		7/day 4447.63	1/week 190.61	10/day 6353.75			10,991.99
2. Message not complete 6.5 min.						1/day 635.38	635.38
3. a. Picking same phone 6.5 min.		3/day 1906.13	5/day 4765.31	6/day 3812.25			10,483.69
b. Picking same phone with disconnect 8 min.		4/day 3128.00		2/day 1564.00			4,692.00
4. Not telling someone when leave office 6.5 min.	8/day 7624.50						7,624.50
10 min.		3/day 2932.50		2/day 1955.00	3/day 2932.50		7,820.00
13 min.					1/day 1270.75		1,270.75
5. Person needs immediate help—expert not there (e.g., student awards, systems problem) 15 min.	1/day 2199.38	1/day 1466.25	6/week 2639.25	2/day 2932.50			9,237.38
6. Inexperienced or temp. help 5 min.						160 days 1st month 1/person (8) 306.67	306.67
7. General calls going to director 10 min.						4/week 1564.00	1,564.00
8. Having options not used Paying for options not activated						660.24	660.24
9. Clearing the phone mail box	6524.81	1466.25	2199.38				10,190.44
						TOTAL	**65,477.02**

5 days, 51 weeks, 0.383333 Staff ($23/hr), 0.575 PMA ($34.5/hr), 0.766666 Sen. PMA ($46/hr)
[a]*FABA = Financial Analysis and Budget Administration*

Figure 6.8. Cost of quality—*before* telephone system review.

	FABA[a]	Gen. Acct.	Audit	Fees	Research	General	Total
1. Transfer call to wrong area 0 min.		7/day 0.00	1/week 0.00	10/day 0.00			0.00
2. Message not complete 0.5 min.						1/day 48.88	48.88
3. a. Picking same phone 0 min.		3/day 0.00	5/day 0.00	6/day 0.00			0.00
b. Picking same phone with disconnect 0 min.		4/day 0.00		2/day 0.00			0.00
4. Not telling someone when leave office 2.5 min.	8/day 2932.50						2,932.50
2.5 min.		3/day 733.13		2/day 488.75	3/day 733.13		1,955.00
2.5 min.					1/day 244.38		244.38
5. Person needs immediate help–expert not there (e.g., student awards, systems problem) 2.5 min.	1/day 366.56	1/day 244.38	6/week 439.88	2/day 488.75			1,539.56
6. Inexperienced or temp. help 0 min.	160 days 1st month 1 call /person (8 new people) 0.00						0.00
7. General calls going to director 0 min.						4/week 0.00	0.00
8. Having options not used Paying for options not activated						0.00	0.00
9. Clearing the phone mail box	4985.25	1466.25	2639.25				10,557.00
10. Training 1 hour						25 @$23 21 @$34.50 6 @$46	1,575.50
						TOTAL	**18,852.81**

[a] *FABA = Financial Analysis and Budget Administration*

Figure 6.9. Cost of quality—*after* telephone system review.

SOFTWARE DEVELOPMENT

Cost of Software Quality (CoSQ) at Raytheon's Electronic Systems (RES) Group

Introduction

The intent of this case study is to provide visibility into a benchmark software development organization that currently uses CoSQ to document the results of its improvement program, and to observe how CoSQ concepts relate to the consistent production of high-quality software. The Raytheon Electronic Systems (RES) organization was chosen as a case study subject because, using a CoSQ approach, it was able to show specific, measured benefits from its software improvement efforts. Moreover, the group collected data and lessons learned about its CoSQ implementation activities. See the discussion of RES CoSQ activities in Chapter 4's section on Software Quality Costs.

Although RES is in the contract systems business, it are similar in many ways to the commercial software supplier who wants to achieve a successful and profitable business by satisfying customers with a high-quality software (or system) product delivered on time and within budget. Although there are many reasons to use CoQ in an organization, RES used it to measure and demonstrate the effects of its ongoing software improvement program. Specifically, CoSQ was used to show the costs and benefits of its investments over the chronology of its improvement program. This is a good example of the way in which a few leading organizations are using CoSQ today

RES and Its Improvement Program

Raytheon Electronic Systems (previously the Raytheon Equipment Division) builds real-time, mission-critical, embedded software systems under contract to defense and commercial customers. It builds these systems in the domains of air traffic control, vessel traffic management, digital communications, ground and shipboard radar, satellite communications, undersea warfare, military command and control, and combat training. The systems it builds are large and typically range in size from 70–500 KDSI (thousand delivered source instructions).

Since 1988 RES has been engaged in a software improvement initiative which was driven by the need to overcome overrunning schedules and budgets, and the crisis-driven environment that resulted. Subsequently, once budgets and schedules came under some control, it turned its attention to the goal of reducing rework.

The RES improvement initiative covered roughly 350–600 professionals. The investment for the initiative has been steady at about $1 million per year. The SEI CMM (Software Engineering Institute—Capability Maturity Model)–based approach was later adopted and used to help focus its improvements. Following this approach, it was self-assessed at CMM Level 1 in 1988, Level 2 in 1990, and Level 3 in 1992, and as of 1995 it operated all new projects starting at Level 4. (For a description of the SEI CMM levels, see Table 4.3 in the Software Quality Costs section of Chapter 4.) In 1995, RES won the coveted IEEE Computer Society's Software Process Achievement Award.

RES's improvement program strategy included a dual focus on product and process. The product focal point areas included system definition, requirements definition, inspections and integration, and qualification testing. The process focal point areas included development planning and management controls, training, and pathfinding.[1]

Cost of Software Quality

CoSQ was chosen as one of four measures to track, because it provided a framework to determine rework levels, as well as the overall return on investment (ROI) of RES's improvement program. The other measures chosen were software productivity, cost performance index, and overall product quality.

The following describes how RES used CoSQ as a method for tracking rework and calculating ROI in their software improvement program. It is adapted from previously published sources[2, 3, 4, 5]

RES's CoSQ Model. Cost of software quality was considered the sum of two components: the cost of nonconformance (rework costs) and the cost of conformance (prevention and appraisal costs). RES determined that they needed to track these quality cost categories. The model shown in Figure 6.10 was used to accumulate them.

In this model, CoSQ is the sum of the costs of appraisal, prevention, and rework. The focus on rework is important, because it represents the major component of waste and scrap of software development. One of the most costly activities in software development today is reworking or redoing what has already been done. There are many underlying reasons why this happens, but mostly because of flawed requirements, changing conditions, and unexpected problems. For some reason, software professionals have

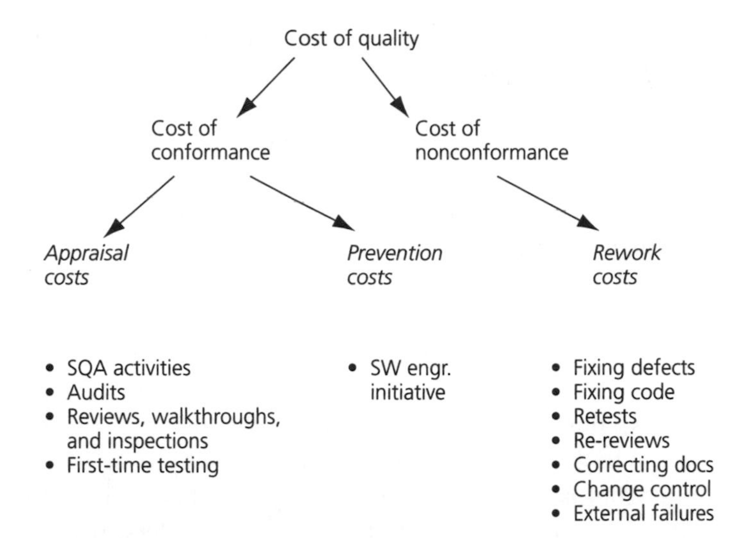

Figure 6.10. RES's CoSQ model.

come to accept mountains of rework as part of their everyday activities—in some cases, they do not think of it as rework. For example, precious schedule time is spent on fixes for code defects when software doesn't perform as expected, or on redesign of a user interface because the customer expects something different from what is provided. Many software engineers think of this as the way things are supposed to happen.

The definitions of each subcategory (within the CoSQ categories of appraisal, prevention, and rework) which were rather brief for reasons of simplicity, were subject to misinterpretation. This was addressed by refining the definitions as experience was gained in using them. This required five iterations of the initial data-gathering exercise before a satisfactory level of consistency of definition was obtained.

Breaking these basic quality cost categories (rework, appraisal, and prevention) into subcategories, defining the subcategories, and assigning project activities and costs to them proved to be a difficult task for RES. This was because the existing work breakdown structure used on the software projects did not correspond well to the CoSQ categories.

CoSQ Data Gathering. Project costs were collected using the conventional work breakdown structure, and project leaders periodically manually reassigned all costs to the cost of quality subcategories. The projects'

CoSQ data were then combined. The improvement initiative costs were factored in as a separate prevention project. These were then used to produce the organizational CoSQ average and trend data.

Long-term, plans were to develop a common work breakdown structure to provide as close a mapping to the cost of quality as possible. This would also entail a revision of the cost accounting system and possibly the time card reporting system as well.

Experiences and Lessons Learned

CoSQ Model Usage Lessons. RES encountered a number of experiences using the CoQ model. Many questions arose about how to allocate costs to subcategories. There was quite a variation in the methods used to break down the actual costs to the defined cost bin. This was resolved by refining the subcategory definitions and by analyzing and comparing the suballocation algorithms used by the six target project leaders. It was necessary to have the project leader, rather than an administrator, generate the data because the project leader possessed the firsthand knowledge of project particulars, as well as good engineering judgment.

Using the CoSQ Data to Understand the Impact of Improvement. Table 6.1 shows the RES distribution of total project costs into CoSQ categories, to track the impact of its improvement program over the years. Starting at CMM Level 1 in 1988, RES introduced its software process improvement (SPI) program. Using the results of tracking fifteen projects, it achieved CMM Level 3 practices in a little over three years. As seen in Figure 6.11, at the Level 1 stage, RES's CoSQ fluctuated between 55 percent and 67 percent of total project costs and, by the time of reaching Level 3 process maturity in 1991, its CoSQ had dropped to approximately 40 percent of total project cost. In 1990, when RES was approaching CMM Level 3, RES's total CoSQ was about 45 percent of total project costs, and its ratio of conformance to nonconformance costs was approximately 1.5. In 1994, when RES was adopting a goal of CMM Level 4, RES's total CoSQ was about 24 percent of total project costs, and its ratio of conformance to nonconformance costs was approximately 3.0.

Rework Cost Savings. Figure 6.11 also shows the trend in the average cost of rework from the start of the improvement initiative. In the two years prior to the initiative, the rework costs had averaged about 41 per-

Table 6.1. CoSQ tracking at specific points in time.

	Other Project Costs	Rework (Nonconformance)	Appraisal		Prevention
			(Conformance)		
1988	34%	44%	15%		7%
1990	55%	18%	15%		12%
1992	66%	11%	———	23%	———
1994	76%	6%	———	18%	———

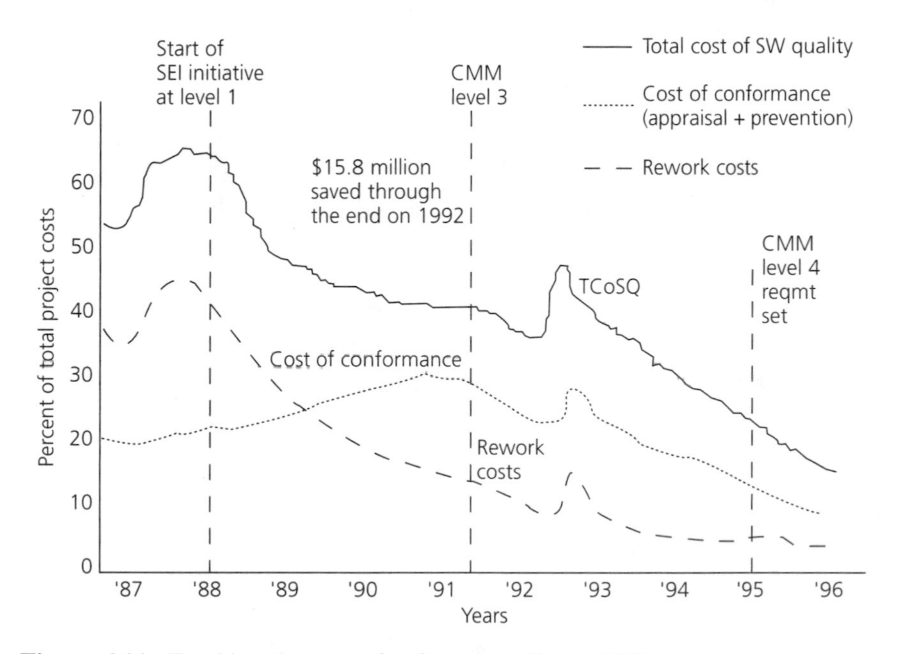

Figure 6.11. Tracking the cost of software quality at RES.

cent of total project costs. In the two years following, that value had dropped to about 20 percent, and the trend was continuing downward. In 1995, TCoSQ was approximately 25 percent of total project costs, and the rework due to both internal and external failures had been reduced to around 6 percent of total project costs.

Rework savings were achieved at the expense of a small increase in conformance costs. For example, appraisal costs rose when informal reviews were replaced by formal inspections, and prevention costs rose when inspection training was instituted. Also, rework costs associated with fixing defects found during design rose from about 0.75 percent to about 2 percent of project cost, and those associated with fixing defects found during coding rose from about 2.5 percent to about 4 percent of project cost.

The major reduction in rework costs was that associated with fixing source code problems found during integration, which dropped to about 20 percent of its original value. The second largest contributor to the rework reduction was the cost of retesting, which decreased to about half its initial value. This clearly indicates that the additional costs of performing formal inspections and the training that must precede it are justified on the basis of finding problems earlier in the process, resulting in more efficiency.

Software Quality. The ultimate measure of quality is the contribution that software has made to RES's success with software-intensive systems. Improvements made have enabled success on several major software-intensive programs and has allowed RES to tackle larger software projects. This was concretely demonstrated on several complex system projects by removing software from the critical path, and even delivering early, thus earning incentives. The primary quantitative measure that RES uses to assess overall product quality is the defect density in the final software products. This density factor is measured as the number of software trouble reports (STRs) per thousand lines of delivered source instructions (KDSI) on each project. The project densities are combined to compute a monthly weighted average to yield a time plot (trend chart) of the Software Quality Level (STRs/KDSI). As shown in Figure 6.12, the average level of quality improved from about 17.2 STRs/KDSI to about 4 STRs/KDSI, about a four times improvement.

Productivity. Data were collected from individual projects on their productivity in terms of equivalent delivered source instructions (EDSI) per man-month of development effort. The data was combined from all projects using a weighting function, and the results showed the average productivity was, in fact, increasing as a function of time—meaning that jobs were costing less. Overall, RES achieved a 170 percent increase in software productivity, as measured on twenty-four projects over seven years.

Predictability. Management needed to be reassured that the improved productivity figures were being used to bid new jobs. This issue was addressed by collecting CPI (Cost Performance Index) data on the project's budgeted (predicted) cost and actual cost at completion (CAC). This

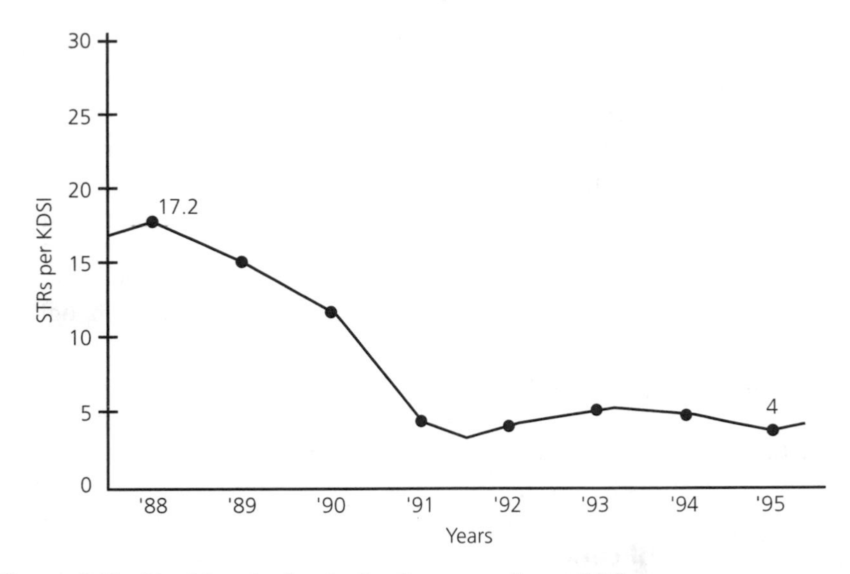

Figure 6.12. Tracking the level of software quality at RES.

CPI ratio (CAC/Budget) for each project was then used to compute the monthly weighted average (using the same approach as the cost of quality) to yield a plot of this time-variant measure. The results were encouraging, showing that the cost performance index was improved dramatically from about the 20 percent overrun range prior to the start of the initiative to the 1 percent to 2 percent range by early 1993. Overall, the Cost Performance Index (CAC/budget) went from about 1.43 to 1.00 in the first three years and has been steady at about 1.00 since.

Other ROI Results. RES has won additional business based on its process maturity results (no amount reported). Software personnel work less overtime than before, and this has led to lower turnover rates. The overall payoff of its improvement program is reported to be 7.5 times (not including a $9.6 million schedule incentive award in 1991)—for example, in 1990, it spent $1.1 million on improvements and determined that the cost of nonconformance was reduced by $8.2 million in that year. Other leading organizations have realized similar bottom-line benefits.[6]

CoSQ Costs and Benefits. CoSQ analysis cost RES about $25,000 of overhead for the first-time exercise. It repeated the CoSQ analysis exercise about a year later and added the analysis process to the normal senior management process reviews on a semi-annual basis.

The CoSQ analysis used by RES was determined to be a viable mechanism for them to measure the overall effect of software process improvement. It can be used to isolate software waste/scrap and to try to drive it to zero. The information learned in applying the approach benefited the projects involved in the analysis by providing early feedback. The improvement of the organization's standard process was also facilitated.

Institutionalization of CoSQ Tracking. By 1993, after three years, the data-gathering exercise for CoSQ had become more routine. Although the full analysis was being made semi-annually, some department managers were requiring their project leaders to provide the CoSQ data along with their normal monthly tracking data. In retrospect, more emphasis could have been placed on transitioning to a common work breakdown structure geared to the collection of CoSQ.

Case Study Implications

RES's use of the CoSQ approach was pioneering and, as such, they learned many lessons that others do not have to learn the hard way. CoSQ was primarily used as an after-the-fact measure of its SPI program's cost and benefits, rather than as a tool to guide its SPI program (which was the CMM). It is expected that other organizations using the CMM approach to SPI will want to do likewise. Therefore, a detailed analysis of the CMM vs. CoSQ will be needed, so that investment opportunities can be better focused on high-impact areas. This analysis should be focused on the impact of prevention activities in the eighteen CMM key process areas on internal and externally induced rework.

RES encountered specific difficulties in the following areas:

- When and how the CoSQ data was gathered, analyzed, reported, and used
- How the model clashed with other models that were already in use
- The lack of an existing Work Breakdown Structure, (WBS) with well-defined categories that correspond easily to CoSQ
- How the model was defined at the detailed levels
- How the model was implemented in the organization
- How CoSQ was used for root cause analysis
- How the model was used to stimulate SPI and quality improvements

These difficulties can be overcome with appropriate training and coaching.

RES's use of CoSQ occurred within the context of its contract-oriented systems business; therefore, the CoSQ approach was adapted to the specifics of that situation. A more general approach will likely need to be modified for use in other situations, with different business success parameters. These situations include

- Standard product-oriented businesses
- Service delivery situations
- Technology-based start-ups

Appendix A
Basic Financial Concepts

To understand the relationship of quality costs to company cost accounting systems, it is best to start with a traditional cost structure (see Figure A.1). An explanation of this normal distribution of costs follows.

PRIME COSTS

Prime costs are the basic or standard costs of product manufacture or service operations, and they consist of two parts:

1. *Direct materials.* Raw materials, semifinished product, and finished product. They are to be distinguished from supplies, such as typewriter ribbons, coolants, and cutting tools, which are committed in the operation of the business but not directly in the end-product.
2. *Direct labor.* Labor applied to convert direct materials or other input into the finished product. Direct labor costs are those which can be specifically identified with basic product manufacturing or service operations. The wages and related costs of workers who assemble inputs into finished goods, who operate equipment integral to the production process, or who deal directly with customers in delivering a service are considered as direct labor costs.

OVERHEAD COSTS

Overhead costs are all costs incurred in direct support of prime costs—that is, in direct support of product manufacturing or service operations. Overhead consists of three parts:

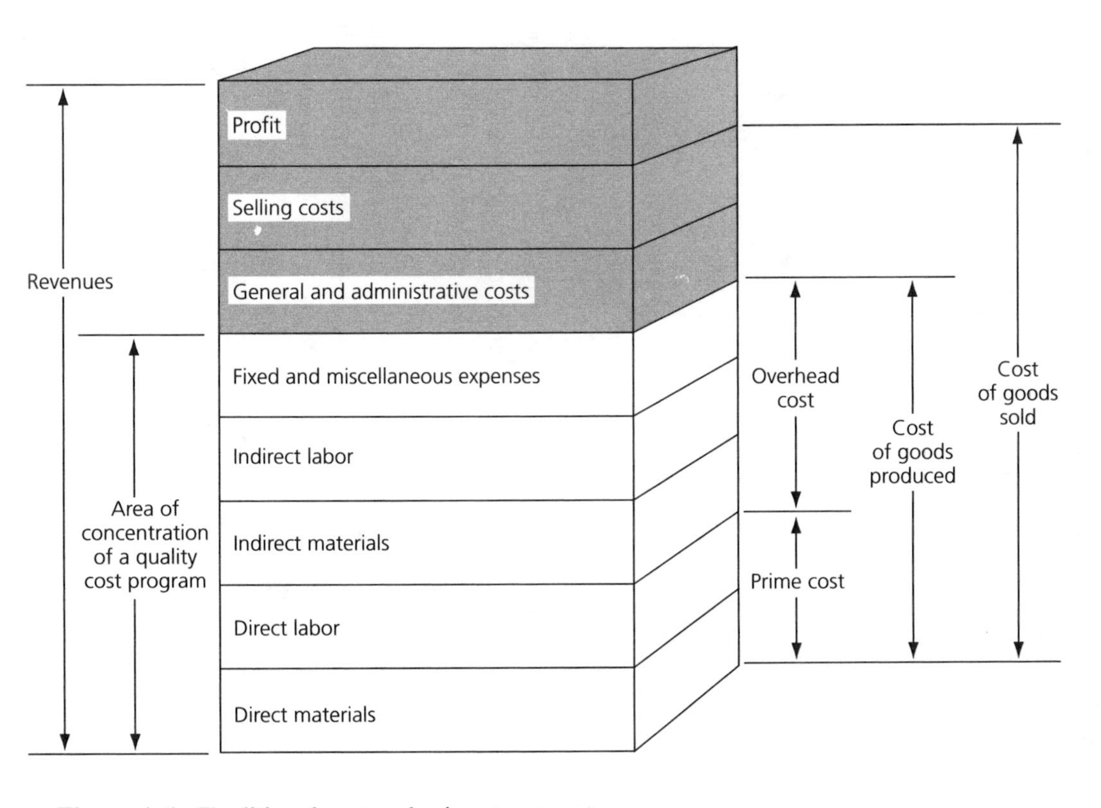

Figure A.1. Traditional cost and price structure.

1. *Indirect materials.* Supplies consumed in operations but not directly a part of the end-product. Included in this category of overhead costs are items such as protective boxes for material handling, packaging supplies, perishable tools, clerical supplies, and communication costs.
2. *Indirect labor.* Wages and salaries earned by employees who do not work directly on the end-product or service but whose services are directly related to the production process or service provided. Included in this category are supervisors, operations support engineers and technicians, material handlers, storeroom personnel, and janitors.
3. *Fixed and miscellaneous expenses.* Depreciation, taxes, rent, warranties, and insurance on the assets used in operations are included in this category of expenses.

COST OF GOODS PRODUCED

The cost of goods produced, the basic or standard cost of product manufacturing or service operations, is the total of prime costs and overhead costs.

COST OF GOODS SOLD

To arrive at the total cost to a company of the delivery of products or services to customers, two additional areas of cost must be added to the cost of goods produced:

1. *Selling costs.* Those costs incurred in an effort to achieve sales and in transferring the completed product or service to the customer. In addition to direct sales costs, categories of costs include marketing, advertising, warehousing, billing, and transportation costs.
2. *General and Administrative (G&A) costs.* A catchall classification for all other business-incurred costs. Categories generally include financial, personnel, legal, public relations, and information systems.

REVENUES AND PROFIT

The last rung in the traditional cost structure is pretax profit, which is simply the difference between revenues and cost of goods sold.

We can now look at the traditional cost structure in relation to a quality cost program. A significant portion of the costs defined in the quality cost system will appear in the cost of goods produced. It should be clear that any reduction in the cost of quality has a positive effect on profit. The full significance of quality cost reductions can be appreciated when it is realized that some high quality cost problems affect costs in all five categories of the cost of goods produced.

MECHANICS OF QUALITY COST COLLECTION

The method of accumulating costs in a going concern requires some basic segregation within the traditional cost structure. The chart of accounts defines in greater detail the costs incurred in the total operation. The number of accounts in the chart of accounts, as well as account descriptions, vary from company to company. All are developed, however, to suit the needs of that particular concern. A significant portion of the costs in a quality cost program are already identified as a result of previous requirements for other purposes. Some details can be found in the chart of accounts. Generally, job orders, work orders, or other similar systems are used to further define costs within accounts.

A quality cost program identifies a portion of the financial structure in a slightly different manner than do traditional financial methods. It concentrates in areas where expenses are necessary because the organization is not able to operate at 100 percent performance to standard. It is advisable to use the same nomenclature that present financial documents carry whenever possible. Use account descriptions from the chart of accounts, unit or department names, product line nomenclature, and any other source of terminology that will lend itself to the understanding of quality performance throughout the company.

The accounting cycle and costing procedure begins with the recording of original business transactions and proceeds to the final preparation and summarizing of Balance Sheets and Profit and Loss (P&L) Statements. As daily business transactions occur, they are recorded in a journal. For the typical business, many types of journals abound, including cash, sales, purchase, and general journals. The ledger is the next step. *Posting* is the term usually applied to this process. Periodically, the financial condition of the concern is stated on the Balance Sheet and the results of operation on the P&L Statement. These are prepared from ledger accounts. The Balance Sheet shows the financial health of the business at a particular date, while the P&L Statement is a record of the financial gain or loss during a period of time.

GENERAL ACCOUNTING PRACTICES

The rules and conventions of accounting are commonly referred to as "principles." The term *principle* is used here to mean "a general law or rule adopted as a guide to action; a settled ground rule or basis of conduct or practice." This definition describes a principle as a general law or rule to be used as a guide to action; accounting principles do not prescribe exactly how each event occurring in a business should be recorded. Consequently, there are a great many activities in the accounting practice that differ from one company to another. Differences reflect the fact that the accountant has considerable latitude within the "generally accepted accounting principles" in which to express their own ideas as to the best way of recording and reporting a specific event.

Accounting principles are man-made. Unlike the principles of mathematics, physics, chemistry, and the other natural sciences, accounting principles were not deduced from basic axioms, nor is their validity verifiable by observation and experiment. Instead, they have evolved by the following process: (1) a problem is recognized; (2) someone works out a good solution to this problem; (3) if other people agree that this is a good solution to this problem, its use is gradually accepted; and (4) it then becomes an accounting principle. Moreover, some previously accepted principles fall from favor with the passage of time. This evolutionary process is continuous.

THE BALANCE SHEET

Resources owned by a business are called assets. The claims of various parties against these assets are called equities. There are two types of equities: (1) liabilities, which are the claims of creditors—that is, everyone other than the owners of the business; and (2) owner's equity, which is the claim of the owners on the business. Since all assets of a business are claimed by someone (either by owners or by some outside party), and since the total of these claims cannot exceed the amount of assets to be claimed, it follows that assets equal liabilities. Accounting systems are set up in such a way that a record is made of two aspects of each event that affects these records—changes in assets and changes in equities.

Let's assume a man starts a business by depositing $20,000 of his funds in a bank account. The dual aspect of this action is that the business now has an asset in the form of $20,000 in cash, and the owner has a claim against this asset also of $20,000.

Assets (cash) $20,000 = Equities (owner's) $20,000

If the business then borrows $10,000 from a bank, the financial records would indicate an increase in cash, making the amount $30,000 and a claim against this cash by the bank in the amount of $10,000. The financial records (Balance Sheet) would show the following:

Cash	$30,000	Owed to bank	$10,000
		Owner's equity	$20,000
Total assets	$30,000	Total equities	$30,000

Every event affects both sides of the Balance Sheet, thus the term *double entry* system.

The practice of listing assets on the lefthand side and equities on the righthand side of the Balance Sheet is common in the United States. The righthand side of the Balance Sheet may be viewed as a description of the sources of capital with which it operates, and the lefthand side as a description of the form in which that capital is invested on a specified date.

Assets are valuable resources owned by a business which were acquired at a measurable money cost. Liabilities are the claims of outsiders against the business, and the owner's equity section of the Balance Sheet shows the claims of the owners. The owner's equity increases through earnings (the results of profitable operations) and decreases when earnings are paid out in the form of dividends.

Useful information may be obtained from the analysis of succeeding Balance Sheets. Comparative Balance Sheet analysis is the study of the trend of the same items, groups of items, or computed items in two or more Balance Sheets of the same business enterprise on different dates. Comparative analysis portrays the trends of particular features of a business enterprise, such as liquidity and debt/equity ratios.

THE PROFIT AND LOSS STATEMENT

The accounting report that summarizes revenue items, expense items, and the difference between them for an accounting period is called the Profit and Loss (P&L) Statement, or sometimes the Income and Expense Statement. The information on the P&L Statement is usually more important than information on the Balance Sheet, because it reports the results of current operations.

Like any accounting report, the P&L Statement should be prepared in the form most useful to those who use it, and to whatever level of detail is required. No specific format is used, but the following basic categories of cost are found on most P&L Statements:

1. *Sales.* The total invoice price of goods delivered to customers plus cash sales made during the period equals gross sales. The sales value of goods rejected by customers and credit given because goods were not as specified are identified separately and netted out of gross sales to provide actual (net) sales.
2. *Cost of Goods Sold.* This item is described as part of the traditional cost structure. It includes the cost of goods produced, selling costs, and G&A costs.
3. *Gross Profit.* The difference between net sales and cost of goods sold
4. *Selling Expenses.* The cost of selling the goods produced
5. *Net Profit.* The difference between gross profit and selling expenses, sometimes called operating profit
6. *Provisions for Income Tax.* Estimated liability for federal income tax
7. *Net Income.* Net gain or loss, which is determined by subtracting provisions for income tax from profit before income tax

The traditional cost structure, previously discussed, relates well to the P&L Statement. The area of concentration of a quality cost program focuses on the cost of goods produced. Quality cost reductions can increase profits or permit a reduction in price while maintaining a constant profit. The P&L Statement will always reflect reduced costs of goods sold with a corresponding increase in gross profit—the essence of quality cost program objectives.

Appendix B
Detailed Description of Quality Cost Elements

For future reference and use, detailed quality cost elements are identified in numerical sequence (see Figure B.1 for summary). Not every element is applicable to all businesses. It is up to the reader to determine applicability in each case. This list is not meant to contain every element of quality cost applicable to every business. It is intended to give the reader a general idea of what type of elements are contained within each cost category to help in deciding individual classifications for actual use. If a significant cost exists that fits any part of the general description of the quality cost element, it should be used. In many cases, activities involve personnel from one or more departments. No attempt is made to define appropriate departments, since each company is organized differently.

1.0 PREVENTION COSTS

The costs of all activities specifically designed to prevent poor quality in products or services.

1.1 Marketing/Customer/User

Costs incurred in the accumulation and continued evaluation of customer and user quality needs and perceptions (including feedback on reliability and performance) affecting their satisfaction with the company's product or service.

1.1.1 Marketing Research

The cost of that portion of marketing research devoted to the determination of customer and user quality needs—attributes of the product or service that provide a high degree of satisfaction.

1.0 **PREVENTION COSTS**
1.1 Marketing/Customer/User
1.1.1 Marketing Research
1.1.2 Customer/User Perception Surveys/Clinics
1.1.3 Contract/Document Review
1.2 Product/Service/Design Development
1.2.1 Design Quality Progress Reviews
1.2.2 Design Support Activities
1.2.3 Product Design Qualification Test
1.2.4 Service Design—Qualification
1.2.5 Field Trials
1.3 Purchasing Prevention Costs
1.3.1 Supplier Reviews
1.3.2 Supplier Rating
1.3.3 Purchase Order Tech Data Reviews
1.3.4 Supplier Quality Planning
1.4 Operations (Manufacturing or Service) Prevention Costs
1.4.1 Operations Process Validation
1.4.2 Operations Quality Planning
1.4.2.1 Design and Development of Quality Measurement and Control Equipment
1.4.3 Operations Support Quality Planning
1.4.4 Operator Quality Education
1.4.5 Operator SPC/Process Control
1.5 Quality Administration
1.5.1 Administrative Salaries
1.5.2 Administrative Expenses
1.5.3 Quality Program Planning
1.5.4 Quality Performance Reporting
1.5.5 Quality Education
1.5.6 Quality Improvement
1.5.7 Quality System Audits
1.6 Other Prevention Costs

2.0 **APPRAISAL COSTS**
2.1 Purchasing Appraisal Costs
2.1.1 Receiving or Incoming Inspections and Tests
2.1.2 Measurement Equipment
2.1.3 Qualification of Supplier Product
2.1.4 Source Inspection and Control Programs
2.2 Operations (Manufacturing or Service) Appraisal Costs
2.2.1 Planned Operations Inspections, Tests, Audits
2.2.1.1 Checking Labor
2.2.1.2 Product or Service Quality Audits
2.2.1.3 Inspection and Test Materials
2.2.2 Set-Up Inspections and Tests
2.2.3 Special Tests (Manufacturing)
2.2.4 Process Control Measurements
2.2.5 Laboratory Support
2.2.6 Measurement (Inspection and Test) Equipment
2.2.6.1 Depreciation Allowances
2.2.6.2 Measurement Equipment Expenses
2.2.6.3 Maintenance and Calibration Labor
2.2.7 Outside Endorsements and Certifications
2.3 External Appraisal Costs
2.3.1 Field Performance Evaluation
2.3.2 Special Product Evaluations
2.3.3 Evaluation of Field Stock and Spare Parts
2.4 Review of Test and Inspection Data
2.5 Miscellaneous Quality Evaluations

Figure B.1. Detailed quality cost element summary.

3.0 **INTERNAL FAILURE COSTS**
3.1 Product/Service Design Failure Costs (Internal)
3.1.1 Design Corrective Action
3.1.2 Rework Due to Design Changes
3.1.3 Scrap Due to Design Changes
3.1.4 Production Liaison Costs
3.2 Purchasing Failure Costs
3.2.1 Purchased Material Reject Disposition Costs
3.2.2 Purchased Material Replacement Costs
3.2.3 Supplier Corrective Action
3.2.4 Rework of Supplier Rejects
3.2.5 Uncontrolled Material Losses
3.3 Operations (Product or Service) Failure Costs
3.3.1 Material Review and Corrective Action Costs
3.3.1.1 Disposition Costs
3.3.1.2 Troubleshooting or Failure Analysis Costs (Operations)
3.3.1.3 Investigation Support Costs
3.3.1.4 Operations Corrective Action
3.3.2 Operations Rework and Repair Costs
3.3.2.1 Rework
3.3.2.2 Repair
3.3.3 Reinspection/Retest Costs
3.3.4 Extra Operations
3.3.5 Scrap Costs (Operations)
3.3.6 Downgraded End-Product or Service
3.3.7 Internal Failure Labor Losses
3.4 Other Internal Failure Costs

4.0 **EXTERNAL FAILURE COSTS**
4.1 Complaint Investigations/Customer or User Service
4.2 Returned Goods
4.3 Retrofit Costs
4.3.1 Recall Costs
4.4 Warranty Claims
4.5 Liability Costs
4.6 Penalties
4.7 Customer/User Goodwill
4.8 Lost Sales
4.9 Other External Failure Costs

Figure B.1. *(continued).*

1.1.2 Customer/User Perception Surveys/Clinics

The cost of programs designed to communicate with customers/users for the expressed purpose of determining their perception of product or service quality as delivered and used, from the viewpoint of their expectations and needs relative to competitive offerings.

1.1.3 Contract/Document Review

Costs incurred in the review and evaluation of customer contracts or other documents affecting actual product or service requirements (such as applicable industry standards, government regulations, or customer internal specifications) to determine the company's capability to meet the stated requirements, prior to acceptance of the customer's terms.

1.2 Product/Service/Design Development

Costs incurred to translate customer and user needs into reliable quality standards and requirements and to manage the quality of new product or service developments prior to the release of authorized documentation for initial production. These costs are normally planned and budgeted and are applied to major design changes as well.

1.2.1 Design Quality Progress Reviews

The total cost, including planning, of interim and final design progress reviews, conducted to maximize conformance of product or service design to customer or user needs with regard to function, configuration, reliability, safety, produceability, unit cost, and, as applicable, serviceability, interchangeability, and maintainability. These formal reviews will occur prior to release of design documents for fabrication of prototype units or start of trial production.

1.2.2 Design Support Activities

The total cost of all activities specifically required to provide tangible quality support inputs to the product or service development effort. As applicable, design support activities include design document checking to assure conformance to internal design standards; selection and design qualification of components and/or materials required as an integral part of the end-product or service;

risk analyses for the safe use of end-product or service; produceability studies to assure economic production capability; maintainability or serviceability analyses; reliability assurance activities, such as failure mode and effects analysis and reliability apportionment; analysis of customer misuse and abuse potential; and preparation of an overall quality management plan.

1.2.3 Product Design Qualification Test

Costs incurred in the planning and conduct of the qualification testing of new products and major changes to existing products. Includes costs for the inspection and test of a sufficient quantity of qualification units under ambient conditions and the extremes of environmental parameters (worst case conditions). Qualification inspections and tests are conducted to verify that all product design requirements have been met or, when failures occur, to clearly identify where redesign efforts are required. Qualification testing is performed on prototype units, pilot runs, or a sample of the initial production run of new products. (Some sources consider this an appraisal cost.)

1.2.4 Service Design—Qualification

Costs incurred in the qualification or overall process proving of new service offerings and major changes to existing offerings. Involves planning for and performing a pilot or trial run using prototype or first production supplies as required. Includes detailed measurements or observations of each aspect of the service offering under normal and worst case conditions, for a sufficient quantity of units or time as applicable, to verify consistent conformance to requirements, or to identify where redesign efforts are required. (Some sources consider this an appraisal cost.)

1.2.5 Field Trials

The costs of planned observations and evaluation of end-product performance in trial situations—usually done with the cooperation of loyal customers but also includes sales into test markets. At this stage of product or service life, a company needs to know much more than “Did it work?” or “Did it sell?” (Some sources consider this an appraisal cost.)

1.3 **Purchasing Prevention Costs**

Costs incurred to assure conformance to requirements of supplier parts, materials, or processes and to minimize the impact of supplier nonconformances on the quality of delivered products or services. Involves activities prior to and after finalization of purchase order commitments.

1.3.1 **Supplier Reviews**

The total cost of surveys to review and evaluate individual suppliers' capabilities to meet company quality requirements. Usually conducted by a team of qualified company representatives from affected departments. Can be conducted periodically for long-term associations.

1.3.2 **Supplier Rating**

The cost of developing and maintaining, as applicable, a system to ascertain each supplier's continued acceptability for future business. This rating system is based on actual supplier performance to established requirements, is periodically analyzed, and is given a quantitative or qualitative rating.

1.3.3 **Purchase Order Tech Data Reviews**

The cost for reviews of purchase order technical data (usually by other than purchasing personnel) to assure its ability to clearly and completely communicate accurate technical and quality requirements to suppliers.

1.3.4 **Supplier Quality Planning**

The total cost of planning for the incoming and source inspections and tests necessary to determine acceptance of supplier products. Includes the preparation of necessary documents and development costs for newly required inspection and test equipment.

1.4 **Operations (Manufacturing or Service) Prevention Costs**

Costs incurred in assuring the capability and readiness of operations to meet quality standards and requirements; quality control planning for all production activities; and the quality education of operating personnel.

1.4.1 **Operations Process Validation**

The cost of activities established for the purpose of assuring the capability of new production methods, processes, equipment, machinery, and tools to initially and consistently perform within required limits.

1.4.2 Operations Quality Planning

The total cost for development of necessary product or service inspection, test, and audit procedures; appraisal documentation system; and workmanship or appearance standards to assure the continued achievement of acceptable quality results. Also includes total design and development costs for new or special measurement and control techniques, gages, and equipment.

1.4.2.1 Design and Development of Quality Measurement and Control Equipment

The cost of test equipment engineers, planners, and designers; gage engineers; and inspection equipment engineers, planners, and designers.

1.4.3 Operations Support Quality Planning

The total cost of quality control planning for all activities required to provide tangible quality support to the production process. As applicable, these production support activities include, but are not limited to, preparation of specifications and the construction or purchase of new production equipment; preparation of operator instructions; scheduling and control plans for production supplies; laboratory analysis support; data processing support; and clerical support.

1.4.4 Operator Quality Education

Costs incurred in the development and conduct of formal operator training programs for the expressed purpose of preventing errors—programs that emphasize the value of quality and the role that each operator plays in its achievement. This includes operator training programs in such subjects as statistical quality control, process control, quality circles, and problem-solving techniques. This item is not intended to include any portion of basic apprentice or skill training necessary to be qualified for an individual assignment within a company.

1.4.5 Operator SPC/Process Control

Costs incurred for education to implement program.

1.5 Quality Administration

Costs incurred in the overall administration of the quality management function.

1.5.1 Administrative Salaries

Compensation costs for all quality function personnel (such as managers and directors, supervisors, and clerical) whose duties are 100 percent administrative.

1.5.2 Administrative Expenses

All other costs and expenses charged to or allocated to the quality management function not specifically covered elsewhere in this system (such as heat, light, and telephone).

1.5.3 Quality Program Planning

The cost of quality (procedure) manual development and maintenance, inputs to proposals, quality recordkeeping, strategic planning, and budget control.

1.5.4 Quality Performance Reporting

Costs incurred in quality performance data collection, compilation, analysis, and issuance in report forms designed to promote the continued improvement of quality performance. Quality cost reporting would be included in this category.

1.5.5 Quality Education

Costs incurred in the initial (new employee indoctrination) and continued quality education of all company functions that can affect the quality of product or service as delivered to customers. Quality education programs emphasize the value of quality performance and the role that each function plays in its achievement.

1.5.6 Quality Improvement

Costs incurred in the development and conduct of companywide quality improvement programs, designed to promote awareness of improvement opportunities and to provide unique individual opportunities for participation and contributions.

1.5.7 Quality System Audits

The cost of audits performed to observe and evaluate the overall effectiveness of the quality management system and procedures. Often accomplished by a team of management personnel. Auditing of product is an appraisal cost. (See 2.2.1.)

1.6 Other Prevention Costs

Represents all other expenses of the quality system, not previously covered, specifically designed to prevent poor quality of product or service.

2.0 APPRAISAL COSTS

The costs associated with measuring, evaluating, or auditing products or services to assure conformance to quality standards and performance requirements.

2.1 Purchasing Appraisal Costs

Purchasing appraisal costs generally can be considered as the costs incurred for the inspection and/or test of purchased supplies or services to determine acceptability for use. These activities can be performed as part of a receiving inspection function or as a source inspection at the supplier's facility.

2.1.1 Receiving or Incoming Inspections and Tests

Total costs for all normal or routine inspection and/or test of purchased materials, products, and services. These costs represent the baseline costs of purchased goods appraisal as a continuing part of a normal receiving inspection function.

2.1.2 Measurement Equipment

The cost of acquisition (depreciation or expense costs), calibration, and maintenance of measurement equipment, instruments, and gages used for appraisal of purchased supplies.

2.1.3 Qualification of Supplier Product

The cost of additional inspections or tests (including environmental tests) periodically required to qualify the use of production quantities of purchased goods. These costs are usually one-time costs, but they may be repeated during multiyear production situations. The following are typical applications:

a. First article inspection (detailed inspection and worst case tests) on a sample of the first production buy of new components, materials, or services
b. First article inspection for second and third sources of previously qualified end-product key components
c. First article inspection of the initial supply of customer-furnished parts or materials
d. First article inspection of the initial purchased quantity of goods for resale

2.1.4 Source Inspection and Control Programs

All company-incurred costs (including travel) for the conduct of any of the activities described in 2.1.1 and 2.1.3 at the supplier's plant or at an independent test laboratory. This item will normally include all appraisal costs associated with direct shipments from supplier to the customer, sales office, or installation site.

2.2 Operations (Manufacturing or Service) Appraisal Costs

Operations appraisal costs generally can be considered as the costs incurred for the inspections, tests, or audits required to determine and assure the acceptability of a product or service to continue into each discrete step in the operations plan from start of production to delivery. In each case where material losses are an integral part of the appraisal operation, such as machine setup pieces or destructive testing, the cost of the losses is to be included.

2.2.1 Planned Operations, Inspections, Tests, Audits

The cost of all planned inspections, tests, and audits conducted on a product or service at selected points or work areas throughout the overall operations process, including the point of final product or service acceptance. Also includes the total cost of any destructive test samples required. This is the baseline operations appraisal cost. It does not include the cost of troubleshooting, rework, repair, or the sorting of rejected lots, all of which are defined as failure costs.

2.2.1.1 Checking Labor

Work performed by individuals other than inspectors as in-process evaluation. Typically, part of a production operator's job.

2.2.1.2 Product or Service Quality Audits

Personnel expense as a result of performing quality audits on in-process or finished products or services.

2.2.1.3 Inspection and Test Materials

Materials consumed or destroyed in control of quality, such as by tear-down inspections, over-voltage stressing, drop testing, or life testing.

2.2.2 Set-Up Inspections and Tests

The cost of all set-up or first piece inspections and tests used to assure that each combination of machine and tool is properly adjusted to produce acceptable products before the start of each production lot, or that service processing equipment (including acceptance and test devices) is acceptable for the start of a new day, shift, or other time period.

2.2.3 Special Tests (Manufacturing)

The cost of all nonroutine inspections and tests conducted on manufactured product as a part of the appraisal plan. These costs normally include annual or semi-annual sampling of sensitive product for more detailed and extensive evaluations to assure continued conformance to critical environmental requirements.

2.2.4 Process Control Measurements

The cost of all planned measurements conducted on in-line product or service processing equipment and/or materials (such as oven temperature or material density) to assure conformance to preestablished standards. Includes adjustments made to maintain continued acceptable results.

2.2.5 Laboratory Support

The total cost of any laboratory tests required in support of product or service appraisal plans.

2.2.6 Measurement (Inspection and Test) Equipment

Since any measurement or process control equipment required is an integral part of appraisal operations, its acquisition (depreciation or expense), calibration, and maintenance costs are all included. Control of this equipment assures the integrity of results, without which the effectiveness of the appraisal program would be in jeopardy.

2.2.6.1 Depreciation Allowances

Total depreciation allowances for all capitalized appraisal equipment.

2.2.6.2 Measurement Equipment Expenses

The procurement or build cost of all appraisal equipment and gages that are not capitalized.

2.2.6.3 Maintenance and Calibration Labor

The cost of all inspections, calibration, maintenance, and control of appraisal equipment, instruments, and gages used for the evaluation of support processes, products, or services for conformance to requirements.

2.2.7 Outside Endorsements and Certifications

The total cost of required outside endorsements or certifications, such as Underwriter's Laboratory, ASTM, or an agency of the U.S. government. Includes the cost of sample preparation, submittal, and any liaison necessary to its final achievement. Includes cost of liaison with customers.

2.3 External Appraisal Costs

External appraisal costs will be incurred any time there is need for field set-up or installation and checkout prior to official acceptance by the customer. These costs are also incurred when there is need for field trials of new products or services.

2.3.1 Field Performance Evaluation

The total cost of all appraisal efforts (inspections, tests, audits, and appraisal support activities) planned and conducted at the site for installation and/or delivery of large, complex products or the conduct of merchandised services (such as repairs or leasing set-ups).

2.3.2 Special Product Evaluations

Includes life testing, as well as environmental and reliability tests performed on production units.

2.3.3 Evaluation of Field Stock and Spare Parts

Includes cost of evaluation testing or inspection of field stock, resulting from engineering changes, storage time (excessive shelf life), or other suspected problems.

2.4 Review of Test and Inspection Data

Costs incurred for regularly reviewing inspection and test data prior to release of the product for shipment, such as determining whether product requirements have been met.

2.5 Miscellaneous Quality Evaluations

The cost of all support area quality evaluations (audits) to assure continued ability to supply acceptable support to the production process. Examples of areas included are stores, packaging, and shipping.

3.0 INTERNAL FAILURE COSTS

Costs resulting from products or services not conforming to requirements or customer/user needs. Internal failure costs occur prior to delivery or shipment of the product, or the furnishing of a service, to the customer.

3.1 Product/Service Design Failure Costs (Internal)

Design failure costs can generally be considered as the unplanned costs that are incurred because of inherent design inadequacies in released documentation for production operations. *They do not include billable costs associated with customer-directed changes (product improvements) or major redesign efforts (product upgrading) that are part of a company-sponsored marketing plan.*

3.1.1 Design Corrective Action

After initial release of design for production, the total cost of all problem investigation and redesign efforts (including requalification as necessary) required to completely resolve product or service problems inherent in the design. (Some sources consider this a prevention cost.)

3.1.2 Rework Due to Design Changes

The cost of all rework (materials, labor, and applicable burden) specifically required as part of design problem resolutions and implementation plans (effectivity) for required design changes.

3.1.3 Scrap Due to Design Changes

The cost of all scrap (materials, labor, and applicable burden) required as part of design problem resolutions and implementation plans (effectivity) for design changes.

3.14 Production Liaison Costs

The cost of unplanned production support efforts required because of inadequate or incomplete design description and documentation by the design organization.

3.2 Purchasing Failure Costs

Costs incurred due to purchased item rejects.

3.2.1 Purchased Material Reject Disposition Costs

The cost to dispose of, or sort, incoming inspection rejects. Includes the cost of reject documentation, review and evaluation, disposition orders, handling, and transportation (except as charged to the supplier).

3.2.2 Purchased Material Replacement Costs

The added cost of replacement for all items rejected and returned to supplier. Includes additional transportation and expediting costs (when not paid for by the supplier).

3.2.3 Supplier Corrective Action

The cost of company-sponsored failure analyses and investigations into the cause of supplier rejects to determine necessary corrective actions. Includes the cost of visits to supplier plants for this purpose and the cost to provide necessary added inspection protection while the problem is being resolved. (Some sources consider this a prevention cost.)

3.24 Rework of Supplier Rejects

The total cost of necessary supplier item repairs incurred by the company and not billable to the supplier—usually due to production expediencies.

3.2.5 Uncontrolled Material Losses

The cost of material or parts shortages due to damage, theft, or other (unknown) reasons. A measure of these costs may be obtained from reviews of inventory adjustments.

3.3 Operations (Product or Service) Failure Costs

Operations failure costs almost always represent a significant portion of overall quality costs and can generally be viewed as the costs associated with defective product or service discovered during the operations process. They are categorized into three distinct areas: material review and corrective action, rework/repair costs, and scrap costs.

3.3.1 Material Review and Corrective Action Costs

Costs incurred in the review and disposition of nonconforming product or service and the corrective actions necessary to prevent recurrence.

3.3.1.1 Disposition Costs

All costs incurred in the review and disposition of nonconforming product or service, in the analysis of quality data to determine significant areas for corrective action, and in the investigation of these areas to determine the root causes of the defective product or service.

3.3.1.2 Troubleshooting or Failure Analysis Costs (Operations)
The cost of failure analysis (physical, chemical, etc.) conducted by, or obtained from, outside laboratories in support of defect cause identification. (Some sources consider this a prevention cost.)

3.3.1.3 Investigation Support Costs
The additional cost of special runs of product or controlled lots of material (designed experiments) conducted specifically to obtain information useful to the determination of the root cause of a particular problem. (Some sources consider this a prevention cost.)

3.3.1.4 Operations Corrective Action
The actual cost of corrective actions taken to remove or eliminate the root causes of nonconformances identified for correction. This item can include such activities as rewriting operator instructions, redevelopment of specific processes or flow procedures, redesign or modification of equipment or tooling, and development and implementation of specific training needs. Does not include design (3.1.1) or supplier (3.2.3) corrective action costs. (Some sources consider this a prevention cost.)

3.3.2 Operations Rework and Repair Costs
The total cost (labor, material, and overhead) of reworking or repairing a defective product or service discovered within the operations process.

3.3.2.1 Rework
The total cost (material, labor, and burden) of all work done to bring nonconforming product or service up to an acceptable (conforming) condition, as authorized by a specific work order, blueprint, personal assignment, or planned part of the standard operating process. Does not include rework due to design change (3.1.2).

3.3.2.2 Repair
The total cost (material, labor, and burden) of all work done to bring nonconforming product up to an acceptable or equivalent, but still nonconforming, condition; normally accomplished by subjecting the product to an approved process that will reduce but not completely eliminate the nonconformance.

3.3.3 Reinspection/Retest Costs

That portion of inspection, test, and audit labor that is incurred because of rejects (includes documentation of rejects, reinspection or test after rework/repair, and sorting of defective lots).

3.3.4 Extra Operations

The total cost of extra operations, such as touch-up or trimming, added because the basic operation is not able to achieve conformance to requirements. These costs are often hidden in the accepted (standard) cost of operations.

3.3.5 Operations Scrap Costs

The total cost (material, labor, and overhead) of defective product or service that is wasted or disposed of because it cannot be reworked to conform to requirements. *The unavoidable losses of material (such as the turnings from machining work or the residue in a food mixing pot) are generally known as waste (check company cost accounting definitions) and are not to be included in the cost of quality.* Also, in the definition of quality costs, the amount received from the sale of scrap and waste material (salvage value) is not to be deducted from gross scrap failure costs.

3.3.6 Downgraded End-Product or Service

Price differential between normal selling price and reduced selling price due to nonconforming or off-grade end-products or services because of quality reasons. Also includes any costs incurred to bring up to saleable condition.

3.3.7 Internal Failure Labor Losses

When labor is lost because of nonconforming work, there may be no concurrent material losses, and it is not reflected on scrap or rework reports. Accounting for the cost of labor for such losses is the intent of this item. Typical losses occur because of equipment shutdowns and reset-up or line stoppages for quality reasons and may be efficiency losses or even allocated for by "labor allowances."

3.4 Other Internal Failure Costs

4.0 EXTERNAL FAILURE COSTS

Costs resulting from products or services not conforming to requirements or customer/user needs. External failure costs occur after delivery or shipment of the product, and during or after furnishing of a service, to the customer.

4.1 **Complaint Investigations/Customer or User Service**

The total cost of investigating, resolving, and responding to individual customer or user complaints or inquiries, including necessary field service.

4.2 **Returned Goods**

The total cost of evaluating and repairing or replacing goods not meeting acceptance by the customer or user due to quality problems. It does not include repairs accomplished as part of a maintenance or modification contract.

4.3 **Retrofit Costs**

Costs to modify or update products or field service facilities to a new design change level, based on major redesign due to design deficiencies. Includes only that portion of retrofits that are due to quality problems.

4.3.1 **Recall Costs**

Includes costs of recall activity due to quality problems.

4.4 **Warranty Claims**

The total cost of claims paid to the customer or user, after acceptance, to cover expenses, including repair costs such as removing defective hardware from a system or cleaning costs due to a food or chemical service accident. In cases where a price reduction is negotiated in lieu of warranty, the value of this reduction should be counted.

4.5 **Liability Costs**

Company-paid costs due to liability claims, including the cost of product of service liability insurance.

4.6 **Penalties**

Cost of any penalties incurred because of less than full product or service performance achieved (as required by contracts with customers or by government rules and regulations).

4.7 Customer/User Goodwill

Costs incurred, over and above normal selling costs, to customers or users who are not completely satisfied with the quality of a delivered product or service, such as costs incurred because customers' quality expectations are greater than what they receive.

4.8 Lost Sales

Includes value of contribution margin lost due to sales reduction because of quality problems.

4.9 Other External Failure Costs

Appendix C
Bibliography of Publications and Papers Relating to Quality Costs

This third edition of *Principles of Quality Costs* has significantly reduced the number of papers, articles, and other publications included in this bibliography. This was necessitated by the many fine publications on the subject since the second edition and because technology has now enabled the search for quality costs material on the Internet and/or through ASQ's Quality Information Center (QIC). Attempting to list a complete bibliography here would be redundant. The papers and publications included here are those that, in the opinion of the ASQ Quality Costs Committee, have significantly contributed to the field of quality costs. In addition, most papers on the subject (written through 1987) can be found in *Quality Costs—Ideas and Applications, Volumes 1 and 2.* Milwaukee: ASQC Quality Press, 1987 and 1989, respectively.

ASQC Quality Costs Committee, *Guide for Managing Supplier Quality Costs.* Edited by W. O. Winchell. Milwaukee: ASQC Quality Press, 1986.

ASQC Quality Costs Committee. *Guide for Reducing Quality Costs.* Milwaukee: ASQC Quality Press, 1986.

ASQC Quality Costs Committee. *Quality Costs What and How.* Milwaukee: ASQC, 1974.

ASQC Quality Costs Committee. *Quality Costs Ideas and Applications, Volume 1 and 2.* Edited by Jack Campanella and Andrew F. Grimm. Milwaukee: ASQC Quality Press, 1987, 1989.

Atkinson, John Hawley, Jr.; Gregory Hohner; Barry Mundt; Richard B. Troxel; and William Winchell. *Current Trends in Cost of Quality: Linking the Cost of Quality* and *Continuous Improvement.* Montvale, NJ: National Association of Accountants, 1991.

Atkinson, Hawley; John Hamburg; and Christopher Ittner. *Linking Quality to Profits*. Milwaukee: ASQC Quality Press and Montvale, NJ: Institute of Management Accountants, 1994.

Campanella, Jack, and Frank J. Corcoran. "Principles of Quality Costs." In *Annual Quality Congress Transactions*. Milwaukee: American Society for Quality Control, 1982.

Campanella, Jack, and Frank J. Corcoran. "Principles of Quality Costs." *Quality Progress* 16, No. 4 (1983): 16–22.

Corcoran, Frank J. "Quality Costs Principles—a Preview." In *Annual Technical Conferences Transactions*. Milwaukee: American Society for Quality Control, 1980.

Crosby, P. "Quality Is Free." New York: McGraw-Hill Book Company, 1979.

Feigenbaum, Armand V. *Total Quality Control*. 3d ed., Chapter 7. New York: McGraw-Hill Book Company, 1983.

Freeman, H. L. "How to Put Quality Costs to Work." Paper presented at 12th Metropolitan Section All Day Conference, 1960.

Harrington, H. J. *Poor Quality Costs*. Milwaukee: ASQC Quality Press, 1986.

Juran, J. M., and Frank M. Gryna. *Juran's Quality Control Handbook,* 4th ed., Chapter 4. New York: McGraw-Hill Book Company, 1988.

Juran, J. M., and Frank M. Gryna. *Quality Planning and Analysis,* 3d ed., New York: McGraw-Hill Book Company, 1993.

Masser, W. J. "The Quality Manager and Quality Costs." *Industrial Quality Control* 14 (1957): 5–8.

Morse, Wayne J.; Kay M. Poston; and Harold P. Roth. *Measuring and Controlling Quality Costs*. Montvale, NJ: National Association of Accountants, 1987.

Williams, R. J. "Guide for Reducing Quality Costs." In *Annual Quality Congress Transactions*. Milwaukee: American Society for Quality Control, 1982.

Winchell, William O. "Guide for Managing Vendor Quality Costs." In *Annual Quality Congress Transactions*. Milwaukee: American Society for Quality Control, 1981.

References

Chapter 1

1. “The National Conference for Quality, *Quality Progress* 15, no. 5 (May 1952): 14–17.
2. H. J. Harrington, *Poor-Quality Cost* (Milwaukee: ASQC Quality Press, 1987).
3. J. M. Juran and Frank M. Gryna, “Section 4, Quality Costs” in *Juran's Quality Control Handbook,* 4th ed. (New York: McGraw-Hill Book Company, 1988).
4. MIL-Q-9858A, *Quality Program Requirements* (Department of Defense, 1963).
5. F. X. Brown and R. W. Kane, “Quality Costs and Profit Performance” in *Annual Technical Conference Transactions* (Milwaukee: American Society for Quality Control, 1975).
6. Edgar W. Dawes, “Quality Costs—New Concepts and Methods.” in *Annual Quality Congress Transactions* (Milwaukee: American Society for Quality Control, 1987).
7. Diane M. Byrne and Nancy E. Ryan, eds., *Taguchi Methods and QFD*. (Dearborn, MI: ASI Press, 1988).
8. William E. Eureka and Nancy E. Ryan, eds., *The Customer-Driven Company* (Dearborn, MI: ASI Press, 1988).
9. Lance A. Ealey, *Quality by Design*. (Dearborn, MI: ASI Press, 1988).
10. ANSI/ASQC Q9004-1-1994, *Quality Management and Quality System Elements—Guidelines* (Milwaukee: ASQC Quality Press, 1994): 7–8.

11. ANSI/ASQC ISO/DIS10014, *Guidelines for Managing the Economics of Quality-Draft International Standard,* 1996.
12. QS-9000, *Quality System Requirements,* 3d ed., March 1998.

Chapter 2

1. Jack Campanella and Frank Corcoran, "Principles of Quality Costs" in *Annual Quality Congress Transactions* (Milwaukee: American Society for Quality Control, 1982).

Chapter 3

1. J. D. Krause and Frank M. Gryna, *Activity Based Costing and Cost of Poor Quality—a Partnership,* University of Tampa Report No. 109, 1995.
2. J. H. Atkinson, G. Hohner, B. Mundt, R. B. Troxel, and W. Winchell, *Current Trends in Cost of Quality* (Montvale, NJ, National Association of Accountants Publication No. 91259, 1991).
3. D. W. Webster, *Achieving Value Through Activity-Based Costing,* Proceedings of ASQC 49th Annual Quality Congress, Cincinnati, OH, 1995.

Chapter 4

1. Nat R. Briscoe and Frank M. Gryna, *Assessing the Cost of Poor Quality in a Small Business,* The University of Tampa College of Business—Report No. 902, May 1996. Also published in Qimpro Quarterly, India, 1998.
2. J. M. Juran and Frank M. Gryna, *Quality Planning and Analysis,* 3d ed. (New York: McGraw-Hill Book Company, 1993).
3. J. M. Juran and Frank M. Gryna, "Section 22, Quality Improvement" in *Juran's Quality Control Handbook,* 4th ed. (New York: McGraw-Hill Book Company, 1988).
4. S. T. Knox, "Modeling the Cost of Software Quality," *Digital Technical Journal* 5(4) (Fall 1993): 9–16.
5. R. Dion, "Process Improvement and the Corporate Balance Sheet," *IEEE Software* 10(4) (July 1993): 28–35.
6. T. J. Haley, "Software Process Improvement at Raytheon," *IEEE Software* 13(November 1996): 33–41.

7. Mark C. Paulk, Bill Curtis, Mary Beth Chrissis, and Charles V. Weber, *Capability Maturity Model for Software, Version 1.1 (CMU/SEI-93-TR-25)* (Pittsburgh: Software Engineering Institute, Carnegie Mellon University, 1993).
8. *Software Quality Standards: The Costs and Benefits.* A review for the Department of Trade and Industry, Price Waterhouse Management Consultants.

Chapter 5

1. William Winchell, "Driving Buyer Satisfaction by Quality Cost" 50th Annual Quality Congress Transactions. (Milwaukee: American Society for Quality Control, 1996).
2. J. M. Juran and Frank M. Gryna, *Quality Planning and Analysis: From Product Development Through Use,* 3d ed. (New York: McGraw-Hill, Inc., 1993).
3. Donald G. Newnan, *Engineering Economic Analysis,* 4th ed. (San Jose: Engineering Press, 1991).

Chapter 6

1. T. Haley, "Software Process Improvement at Raytheon," *IEEE Software* 13(6) (November, 1996): 33–41.
2. R. Dion, *Quantifying the Benefit of Software Process Improvement,* Proceedings of the SEI/AIAA Software Process Improvement Workshop, November 8, 1990, Chantilly, VA.
3. R. Dion, *Cost of Quality as a Measure of Process Improvement,* Proceedings of the SEI Software Engineering Symposium, September 17, 1992.
4. R. Dion, "Process Improvement and the Corporate Balance Sheet," *IEEE Software* 10(4) (July 1993): 28–35.
5. T. Haley, B. Ireland, E. Wojtaszek, D. Nash, and R. Dion, *Raytheon Electronic Systems Experience in Software Process Improvement,* Technical Report CMU/SEI-95-TR-017, November 1995.
6. H. Krasner, *Accumulating the Body of Evidence for the Payoff of SPI—1997,* see www.utexas.edu/coe/sqi/archive.

INDEX

B

C

D

E

F

K

L

M

N

O

P

R

S

T

U

V

W